THE DISTANCE BETWEEN

AMERICAN LIVES | Series editor: *Tobias Wolff*

THE
DISTANCE
BETWEEN

A MEMOIR

TIMOTHY J. HILLEGONDS

UNIVERSITY OF NEBRASKA PRESS | LINCOLN

Library of Congress Cataloging-in-Publication Data
Names: Hillegonds, Timothy J., author.
Title: The distance between: a memoir
/ Timothy J. Hillegonds.
Description: Lincoln: University of Nebraska
Press, 2019. | Series: American lives
Identifiers: LCCN 2019005284
ISBN 9781496216687 (pbk.: alk. paper)
ISBN 9781496217974 (epub)
ISBN 9781496217981 (mobi)
ISBN 9781496217998 (pdf)
Subjects: LCSH: Hillegonds, Timothy J. |
Alcoholics—United States—Biography. |
Alcoholics—Rehabilitation—United States—
Biography. | Addicts—Rehabilitation—United
States—Biography. | Addicts—Family
relationships—United States—Biography.
Classification: LCC HV5293.H55 A3
2019 | DDC 362.292092 [B]—dc23
LC record available at
https://lccn.loc.gov/2019005284

Set in Questa by E. Cuddy.
Designed by N. Putens.

For Erin, Haley Jade, and Ma

I didn't go to the moon, I went much further—for time is the longest distance between two places.

TENNESSEE WILLIAMS, *The Glass Menagerie*

Contents

Preface

I began writing this book in January of 2014, when I was thirty-six years old and finishing up the last of my writing workshops at DePaul University in Chicago. I had spent the previous two years in the midst of an education—an education that pushed me far beyond the craft of writing and led me, through the books and essays I read, and the conversations I had, to a place where I began to understand some of the hard truths about systematic inequalities in my own life and circumstances, hard truths that many women, people of color, and members of the LGBTQIA+ community simply don't have the option of not knowing.

I was writing about my life, and as I continued to read and examine all I was learning, it became clear to me that the story I wanted to tell, or the way that I understood the story I wanted to tell, had changed. The bare facts were still the same, and so were the people, but I now knew that if I had been born anything other than a white, heterosexual man, my life today—since I hadn't lost it to police violence during one of my countless arrests, or been given a harsher sentence because of the color of my skin, or suffered any other inequity from an inexhaustible list of American justice system discriminations—would be immeasurably different. I now understood my past, and the fact that I caught some truly unexplainable breaks along the way and emerged from it in one piece, as an indisputable example of white male privilege at work. That has been both essential and difficult to know.

It has also been essential and difficult to know and confront the damage I caused to others and myself as a young rage-filled man in the throes of addiction. As you'll read in these pages, I have been violent, and violent toward a woman. I am deeply ashamed, and sorry, and full of regret, and I've written this book, in part, to both interrogate and understand the person I was then, when I was young and angry and addicted, when I was unfamiliar with the realities of privilege and patriarchy, when I knew nothing of my own increasingly toxic masculinity.

Joan Didion wrote, "We are well advised to keep on nodding terms with the people we used to be, whether we find them attractive company or not. Otherwise they turn up unannounced and surprise us, come hammering on the mind's door at 4 a.m. of a bad night and demand to know who deserted them, who betrayed them, who is going to make amends." This book is my attempt at staying in touch with who I was, even though I would often rather forget him. Though I may not be able to make amends, this book is my attempt in that direction, and an attempt to tell my story without flinching.

It's 2019 and we live in a time of reckoning.

This is mine.

Acknowledgments

While my name is the only one on the front of this book, it is because of the generosity and love of these people that it exists:

Thank you to Alicia Christensen for believing in this book and giving it a chance, and to the extraordinary team at the University of Nebraska Press for making it a reality.

To Patrick Madden for his serendipitous introduction to Alicia at AWP 2018.

To Barrie Jean Borich, who once told me, "You learn how to write a book by writing a book," which turned out to be true, but much more difficult than I thought, and for her critical guidance and poignant feedback in the early goings.

Thank you to Elizabeth Kaplan for her early read and revision suggestions, which were so important, and was work she completed out of sheer benevolence.

To Tom Lutz for seeing what this book could become and taking on the project, and for trusting in me to do the work, and for investing an incalculable amount of time during the editing process, and for the many introductions, and for helping me complete it for no reason other than his enviable kindness.

To Ned Stuckey-French for his friendship and limitless knowledge of the essay.

Thank you to my amazing fellow writers at the Iowa Summer Writing Festival for their thoughtful feedback on my early manuscript and an unforgettable two weeks in the summer of 2015: Sue

Ade, Alan Brody, Sarah Conover, Magda Montiel Davis, Ann Green, Ann Garretson Marshall, Terry Marshall, Nancy McGlasson, Dag Scheer, and Amy Turner.

A heartfelt and enormous thank you to the Red Lion Writing Group, whose monthly workshops, discussions, and candor have made me not just a better writer but a better person: Christian Anderson, Libby Kalmbach, Michelle Jensen Keller, Stephanie Klein, Mame Kwayie, and Anastasia Sasewich.

To Hope Edelman for her friendship, keen eye, generous feedback, and sharp instincts.

To the inimitable Michele Morano, for sitting at a table with me in 2012 and telling me I should write creative nonfiction "because that's where the money's at," but more so for her friendship, advice, thoughtfulness, patience, and honesty, and for teaching me how to write, and challenging my thinking, and showing me what to read, and for always pushing me, and for going beyond what could ever be reasonably expected of a mentor, time and time again.

To Joel Hoekstra, my literal and literary cousin, for paving the writer's path before me, and for ceaselessly searching for "truth" in nonfiction.

Thank you to Dan Breems, Rich Dykstra, Kevin Evenhouse, and Tim Kunz for letting me tell part of their stories.

To Nick Bruno for his friendship and poetry.

Thank you to Mike Chalmers for so many things, but certainly for all those conversations about writing we had in Caribou Coffee on Wabash where it all began, and for being someone I look up to and admire, and for all the workout and runs, and the cookies, and for never sitting all the way down on that right hand during the rounds we spent in the boxing ring.

To Dinty W. Moore for publishing my very first essay.

Thank you to Kevin Cunningham for giving me a chance and a job and the life-changing gift of sobriety.

To Maddie, who will always have a piece of my heart.

Thank you to April for the time we spent together, the love we shared, and the memories we made.

Thank you to my family for their continuous love and support throughout this story and all the other ones: Mom and Dad, Heidi and Jon, Aaron and Lauren, and Jillian.

Thank you to Haley Jade for never giving up on us, and for being fierce and fearless and loving and unique, and for being a daughter of whom I couldn't be prouder.

And lastly, thank you to my achingly beautiful wife, Erin, whose strength, discernment, and understanding I couldn't exist without, and whose patience and support are endless, and whose love for the city of Chicago just might rival mine.

CHICAGO

ONE

The sky above Navy Pier was a thick stripe of blue sidewalk chalk, clouds brushed white against the horizon. Around me, Lake Michigan billowed lazily, boats rising and falling in waves. I wiped sweat from my forehead with my shirtsleeve and the breeze picked up, carrying the smell of beer and burgers and churros. I shifted my weight to my left skate as the August sun all but ignited the pavement beneath my wheels. The temperature was pushing a hundred degrees, and Navy Pier was shoulder to shoulder with people. Like a heartbeat, the crowd pulsed.

Next to me, Dan kicked his skate against the ground so his wheels spun. "You ready?" he said, his grin equal parts adrenaline, focus, joy. "Always," I said, laughing. "See you on the flipside," he said, and then he was gone.

I watched as he cut his skates back and forth, hard, digging into the asphalt, propelling himself toward the plywood ramp as fast as his legs would take him. Three hundred people watched, their eyes following him as he closed the distance. Just on the other side of the ramp, standing single file, was the rest of our skate team, plus two volunteers from the audience. Ten people total.

Right before Dan hit the ramp, he bent his knees, and I knew what he felt in that moment, had felt it a thousand times before— that singularity, that brief instant where time somehow folded in on itself, and there was no future, and no past, and the revisions were endless, an entire life rewritten in an instant.

Dan exploded off the ramp, instantly clearing the skate team and volunteers beneath him. He was momentarily pinned to the horizon, a dark shape outlined in cerulean, before landing perfectly and sliding to a stop. The crowd erupted.

To my right, sunlight sliced the tops off the lake's watery ripples and flung flashes of yellow in all directions. The song changed to The Offspring's "Come Out and Play." I turned to the crowd and drank in their energy, felt the American punk rock and heat and excitement fusing together under a thick slab of humidity. I watched as Dan skated up and took his place at the end of the line of people. He looked at me and lifted his head. It was a question. I held up my hand. Spread all my fingers. Signaled the number five. Dan nodded, and I saw him skate up to the crowd. He said something, and five more people stepped forward. Dan placed them in the middle of the line and retook his spot at the end. I looked down at my skates while my heart fired like a Chevy big block.

I took a deep breath and felt invincible. I glanced at the crowd. A guy holding a beer took a half step forward. "You going to jump all those people?" he said.

"Nope," I said, smiling and shaking my head. "I'm going to flip over them."

I dug in, pushed off the ground with my left skate as hard as I could. Every muscle in my body worked to get me to the ramp with as much speed as possible. The crowd faded. The music faded. The world faded.

I hit the launch ramp and entered the atmosphere of my life, flying horizontal, superman position, and felt that I was attached to nothing, not to the earth or the sky or the thick residue my father's absence had left on me, the silt I was just beginning to know. Below me, fifteen people stood erect, their heads tilted skyward. I began to flip forward just as I cleared Dan, the last person in line, and the world disappeared, but I could still feel it, the world, could still feel where I was in relation to it, and then my eyes found the blue they'd been searching for, the horizon, and my body slowly unfolded.

Ten feet past Dan, I landed with such force that my molded plastic wheels exploded, pieces sailing in all directions, bouncing atop the concrete. I slid onto my kneepads. Stopped quickly from the friction. Stood up. Dan looked at me and shook his head. Laughed. And then I was laughing, too, the crowd a frenzy of clapping hands and screaming voices and pumping fists. Dan and I continued to laugh, couldn't stop laughing, because this is what we did, and this thing we did was ours—and because today the world was limitless, and there was nothing, absolutely nothing, we could not do.

* * *

Inline skating, for most people, was nothing more than a blip on the cultural radar of the late '80s and early '90s. It was a passing fad, a temporary movement, a trend that swelled for a brief period of time while skateboarding momentarily faded from public consciousness. But skating never felt temporary or trendy or contrived to me. It felt natural—almost biological—like the expected athletic progression from Neanderthal to Homo sapiens, or from boyhood to adolescence.

From the moment I first tried on inline skates, they seemed an extension of me, a plastic and rubber upgrade to the fleshy hardware I was born with. When I laced them up and ratcheted the buckles tight around my ankles, instantly taller, an entire world opened up, an ecosphere that I could now move through with fluidity and perspective.

And I wasn't alone. A number of my friends—Rich and Joel and Dan—had also put away their childhood skateboards and strapped on their inline skates. But of all of us, it was Dan and I who took to it the fastest, who excelled the quickest, building launch ramps and grind rails, waxing curbs, skating eight miles from my house to his, from his house to mine, from Oak Lawn to Blue Island and back again, almost never tired, fueled by youth and friendship and the knowledge that we were good at this new thing, better than almost anyone else we came across.

In 1992, my friend Joel turned sixteen and got his driver's license, and Dan and I began catching rides to the skate park with him as often as we could. He had a Ford Mustang GT, white with a black ragtop, and he drove it like he had just stolen it wherever we went, slamming the manual transmission into gear, its five-liter V-8 thundering below the hood. It took just over an hour to drive from my parents' house in the southwest Chicago suburb of Oak Lawn to the skate park in Hoffman Estates, and we'd blast the music the entire time, singing and laughing and bragging about every trick we would try once we got there.

During one of our sessions at the skate park, Dan and I were approached by a skater a few years older than us. He had the same enormous kneepads that we did, the same long hair pulled back into a ponytail, the same baggy shorts and beat-up skates, and he told us he'd been watching us the last few times we were there. "I'm putting together a stunt team," he said, taking off his helmet and wiping the sweat off his forehead with the front of his T-shirt. "You guys interested?" Dan and I tried to play it cool, tried to stop the huge grins from appearing on our faces, but we couldn't. "Hell yeah," I said. "Definitely," Dan said. Our smiles were big and toothy.

From that moment forward, we were professionals, and it felt so good to say that to each other, so meaningful, so liberating. On skates, I was able to reimagine the world, see everything differently. I could reframe myself within the Chicago cityscape, within my own life, and at the same time draw myself nearer to the borders, closer to the outer edges of everything we came across. We no longer walked or ran. We glided. Floated. Drifted. Everything I felt—all the anger I was starting to feel for my father leaving, all the trouble I was getting in at school—was packed into the way I skated. I could grind down a handrail in downtown Chicago or latch onto the back of a CTA bus or front flip over a car, and everything else I felt would disappear. At the literal edge of control, one small move away from serious injury, everything felt manageable. In the margin that existed between safety and danger, between assurance and risk, I felt at home.

* * *

Just beginning to climb over the hormonal fence between childhood and adolescence, I found inline skating to be a sort of street therapy, a way to work out the echoes constantly knocking around inside. It was a pressure valve, a release, a way to transform what I didn't yet understand about my emotions into actual, physical movement.

My mother and father divorced when I was two, and even though my father had full visitation rights, he never used them—regardless of the fact that we never lived farther than four miles apart. I was the only child of their marriage, and I stayed with my mother after the divorce, my father fading from our lives almost immediately.

For three years my mother and I lived alone in a small apartment in Crestwood, off a tree-lined street near the Cal-Sag Channel, where the mossy smell of water would drift in through my bedroom window during the summer months. She worked as a teller in a bank off Pulaski Road, her blonde hair permed in tight curls, a hint of blue eye shadow, and I remember the love I felt from her in those days with a pristine clarity.

When I was five years old, my mother remarried, my half-sister Heidi arriving shortly thereafter. Two years after that, Aaron was born, followed eventually by Jillian in 1991, when I was thirteen.

My stepfather, also recently divorced when he married my mother, was kind and patient and loved me—it seemed to me even back then—like I was his own child. He did his level best to fill the role of father for me, to nudge me in a positive direction if he sensed me veering off course, but my biological father's absence became impossible for me to ignore as I grew older. I had begun to wonder why he left; or more specifically, why he never came back, why he never tried to establish a relationship with me.

As a teenager, I started asking about him more frequently.

"What was he like?" I asked my mother once, after a day spent riding my bike through the neighborhood with my friends.

"What do you mean?" she said, walking into the living room with a dustrag in her hand.

"I don't know," I said, following her. "I mean, what did he do for a living?"

She stopped near the windows that looked onto our front yard and Central Avenue. Just past the street, oak trees towered above the power lines, and just past that, just past where we could see, was Oak Lawn Lake, the manmade reservoir where I caught catfish and crawdads as a child.

My mother began to dust an end table, looked at me and smiled, her shoulder-length hair swaying as her arm moved across the furniture. "I told you this already, didn't I?"

It was true that she'd told me on other occasions, but I wanted to hear it again. Because when the words came out of her mouth they were affirmations of a life I didn't know but was somehow still part of. They made me feel like I came from somewhere, that I wasn't just a kid with a mother. There was a father out there, too, a man just as responsible for me as the woman I was now talking with.

She lifted a lamp off the table and dusted beneath it, particles floating into the air, momentarily suspended in the afternoon sunlight. "He was in construction, concrete mostly," she said. "He was a foreman and drove this raggedy pickup truck that was always dirty."

It had been years since I'd seen him, but I felt like I knew what he looked like. In my mind, he wore muddy work boots and Levi's jeans that were speckled with gray concrete. He had brown hair, dark stubble on the sharp point of a chin shaped like mine. I saw him standing on a construction site wearing a flannel shirt and smoking a cigarette with a brown filter.

My mother stopped dusting and looked at me, perhaps sensing that I was thinking about him. "Is everything okay, honey? Where's this coming from?"

Outside the window, a pickup truck rattled down busy Central Avenue, slowing for the train tracks up ahead. I watched its brake lights glow and wondered whether the truck was anything like my father's. My mother studied me. The image of my father on the construction site abruptly shifted to a memory of him watching television from a big fabric chair like the one my mother was standing next to, in the second-floor apartment we had all lived in together. My father had a can of Old Style beer in his hand. I was small and standing near his knee, looking up at him, wishing he would acknowledge me.

"Yeah, Ma, everything's fine," I said, shaking my head to clear the memory. "I was just wondering."

* * *

I also began to question everything I'd been told—about school, about family, about religion. I began to push against all the guardrails that had been set up around me, primarily by acting out in school. My junior high school pranks and disruptive behavior were harmless at first—setting the clocks ahead to shorten class time, making muriatic acid bombs explode during recess—but a few of us had recently upped the ante by unlocking the bathroom window before leaving school one Friday. The junior high I attended wasn't far from my house—just a few blocks south on Central Avenue—and the next day, my friends and I showed up at the school, shimmied through the window, and spent the afternoon running and yelling and high-fiving through the empty hallways, turning on the stereo system in the music room as loud as it would go, jumping from the gym's balcony—arms flailing—onto a forest green crash mat fifteen feet below.

It was fun at first, nothing more than harmless juvenile mischief, but it was thrilling and addicting and we kept at it week after week, eventually emboldened to the point where we were rummaging through teachers' desks and funding our candy habits by stealing the Pop Day money.

Eventually, though, we were caught red-handed by the Oak Lawn Police—a neighbor had noticed us running around the roof—and I felt handcuffs sting my wrists for the first time. My stepfather was so angry when the police called him that he let me sit in the small jail cell for hours before finally picking me up, driving me home in a silence that felt an awful lot like fury.

My mother and stepfather were summoned to the principal's office on numerous occasions—because of the arrest, yes, but also for the endless pranks and commotions that came before—and were forced to beg for the school's forgiveness. "He's just going through a rough time right now," my mother said to the principal during one of her meetings. "I know he's disruptive sometimes, but he's a good kid. We're working with him at home to figure out what's going on."

And to my mother's credit, she was. She walked up to me when I was in the backyard kicking a soccer ball against the fence and practicing footwork drills in the long grass, her blonde hair shining in the afternoon sun, and asked me why I was making the choices I was making. "What's happening with you lately, Tim?" she said while watching me, her voice soft and loving. "You've got to tell me so I can help you." I looked at the soccer ball, rolled it backwards with my foot so that it rode up my laces, and balanced the ball there. "There's nothing to tell, Ma," I said, hopping on one foot to keep the soccer ball from falling. "I just think all the rules are ridiculous. I'm just having fun. It's really not that big of a deal."

She wouldn't let me off the hook that easily, though. She shifted her weight and punctuated the air with her right hand as she spoke. "But it is a big deal, Tim. You can't just do whatever you want whenever you feel like it. The world doesn't work like that." She sighed, watched me drop the ball back to the ground and guide it with my foot over the grass, the blades bending under its weight. "You're so good at so many things, Tim," she said. "And you're smart too. So why all the detentions? Why do I keep getting calls from your principal?"

I didn't know how to say it, but I was simply acting the way I felt— rebellious. The Christian faith I was raised in seemed restrictive and limiting and hypocritical. I went to Sunday school and youth group for the majority of my childhood because I had to, but I began to resent it, began to rebel against it, both in a literal and ideological sense. I became deeply distrustful of church and faith and the belief that there was a God out there who loved me unconditionally.

When I was thirteen, I had stood up in front of the congregation in a white button-down shirt and clip-on tie, professing to know Jesus Christ as my personal Lord and Savior while my parents watched proudly from metal folding chairs in the front row, but I now wondered if I knew what the words I'd professed even meant. I was told to believe in a heavenly father I couldn't see, which seemed difficult to grasp for anyone, let alone a kid who was still searching for the answers of what happened to his earthly one.

Such ideas were not fully formed yet, though, and it would be decades before they would be. So instead of saying anything, I shrugged my shoulders and struck the ball with the top of my right foot, and sent it crashing against the fence.

* * *

One summer afternoon when I was fourteen, after my thoughts and questions about my father had reached a crescendo inside my head, I walked into the kitchen where my mother was doing dishes and demanded she give me his phone number. I'd never asked to call him before, and I could see the concern in her eyes. She grabbed a towel to dry her hands and said, "Are you sure you want to do that, Tim?"

I wasn't sure, but I was determined to call him anyway, to ask him where he'd been and why he had never come around. "Just give me the number, Ma."

She walked over to the Rolodex she kept on the other counter and flipped through it, stopping at the Hs. She pulled a card out and read it silently, her lips pressed together in a tight line. All this time I'd been wondering about him and his number was right there, right in my house, three feet from where I ate my breakfast.

My mother glanced at me tentatively, her hazel eyes locking on my brown ones. "No matter what happens, Tim, I love you," she said, reaching her arm out and handing me the card. I took it, a sudden hesitation in the movement making my arm feel foreign and heavy. I turned around, walked to the portable phone that was hanging on the wall next to a bulletin board that held electric bills and schedules and little reminders my mom would write to herself: *School tuition due Friday; Library books due Wednesday*. I grabbed the receiver, shuffled down the short flight of stairs that led to the side door of our house, and walked outside into the warm summer air. Barefoot, wearing soccer shorts and a T-shirt, I walked around the house to the backyard, the concrete driveway gritty and warm against the soles of my feet. I stopped. Stared at the name on the card—Jim Hillegonds. A one-letter difference between him and me.

His name was written in my mother's handwriting, the same letters she had used on the brown-bag lunches I brought to school, the same handwriting that had written little notes of encouragement I would find inside those lunches and hastily stuff into my pockets before my friends could read them. I clicked the phone on, held it up to my ear to hear the dial tone, and pressed each of the seven digits slowly.

I often wonder what my life would have been like if I hadn't called him that day, if I'd just let his absence fade until I could hardly feel it at all. Would I still have made the same mistakes? Or would the anger that I felt from his abandonment eventually die out, the sting of rejection dulling as the healing power of time slowly mended the wound?

The phone was pressed against my ear, and it was ringing, and my heart was beating faster and faster while the wind rustled through the leaves in the oak trees that lined the edge of our backyard, near the sandbox my stepfather had made for us. I could see my shadow on the ground in front of me, long and lean, and hear the traffic passing on Central Avenue as the cars slowed for the train crossing. A voice answered and said hello.

"Is this Jim?" I asked, my voice shaky and lacking the confidence I'd wanted to have.

"Yeah, who's this?"

"It's Tim. Your son."

There was no pause on the other end, no dramatic deep breath. Just his voice and the words that rolled off his tongue as if he'd said them a thousand times before.

"Timothy James."

Hearing him say my name that day did something to me, sparked a hope inside that blazed like the tip of a welding rod. I'd spent so much time wondering if he'd forgotten about me, thinking that maybe there was a good reason he had stayed away, that I'd never thought about what I'd say if we actually talked. I now wanted to tell him about everything he'd missed in one long breath—all the good things about me that he could be proud of. I wanted to tell him how good an athlete I was and how I could front flip over a parked car on my Rollerblades. I wanted to tell him how fast I could run. How I had taken piano lessons for five years. How I almost never felt fear. I wanted to tell him about all the goals I scored in soccer games and how I had once jumped my BMX bike off a dirt ramp so high that when I landed my handlebars had bent like an M.

But what I wanted even more than all that was to make a deal with him—my forgiveness for his presence. I wanted to tell him that I would excuse every single day he was absent from my life if he'd only promise to be there from now on. The past is the past, I would say, and none of it matters now because we're here and that's what's important.

But instead of saying all that, instead of telling him how I felt, I held my voice and said none of it, and we made small talk that ended with a tentative plan to meet at an upcoming skate show at Navy Pier. Our team had been hired as the entertainment for a McDonald's Corporation event, and we were set to perform our stunt routine at the very tip of the pier, just past the Grand Ballroom. My father agreed to attend the event as my guest, and I imagined he would maybe cheer from the sideline as I landed a trick, and then after, when the show was over and I had pulled off my helmet, that I would skate over to him, slowly, and for the first time since I was three years old, my father and I would meet face to face.

* * *

Even today, I think about that first phone call and what it must have been like for my father to receive it. I wonder where he was standing—was it in the smoke-filled living room of the small apartment I would visit years later, with its stained carpeting that smelled of cat urine and cigarettes, the sounds of traffic from the Tri-State Tollway sifting in through the thin walls? Or was it another apartment, perhaps nicer, some place that I'd never see but always wonder about. What was he wearing that day? The flannel shirt and dusty jeans I always picture him in, or a favorite T-shirt with some long-forgotten beer league softball team logo on it, from when he and my mother played together? What did it feel like for him to have my voice suddenly appear where for so long there was nothing?

* * *

On the night of the show, while Navy Pier's lights lit up the space just outside the Grand Ballroom, the wind blowing gusty off the lake, I thought about what I would say to my father when I saw him. Normally relaxed and loose while I warmed up for shows, I was instead nervous and stiff—and scared, I think now—about what would happen.

As the music played and the show began, my teammates and I launched off ramps high into the nighttime air while cheers from the suit-and-tie-wearing crowd filled the space around us. I constantly scanned the audience after I landed a trick, skating back to the starting point slowly, my baggy T-shirt a flag behind me as I rolled, searching the crowd for a man who might be my father. I didn't know exactly who I was looking for—my mother had burned all her pictures of him some time after the divorce—but I figured I'd know when I saw him. I'd been searching for him for so long, I thought, how could I not? Then, when I was standing on top of a five-foot quarter pipe, the front two wheels of my skate hanging off the edge of the metal coping, I turned my head and it was as if the crowd ceased to move, their cheers somehow silenced by what I saw: an older version of my own face, the features unmistakable. My father's eyes locked with mine and I leaned forward. Dropped in and rode the ramp downward.

After, when the show was over, I kicked off my skates and pulled on my shoes and walked over to him. He was taller than I'd thought he'd be, maybe six feet two, and when we hugged awkwardly, I was surprised by how thick his chest felt when I wrapped my bony arms around him. I'd always thought that in this moment I'd feel confident and assured, that I'd feel proud of myself, but now that it had arrived, I felt self-conscious and skinny in my too-baggy clothes.

After we embraced, he took a step back. "You look good, son," he said.

I smiled and looked at the ground. Suppressed the urge to run. "Thanks, Dad," I said, my face reddening with guilt, aware that I'd just used the same name for him that I had always used for my stepfather.

* * *

I know now that what I truly sought from my father was time—time that would lead to experiences, that would lead to a rekindling, that would lead to the father-son bond I desperately coveted. But I didn't know how to articulate that, and perhaps my father didn't know how to give it, and so one day, a month or two after the show at Navy Pier, we ended up at a greasy spoon off Pulaski Avenue not far from the bank where my mother had worked after he'd left, glancing awkwardly at one another while breaking the yolks of our sunny-side-up eggs with our forks.

"You're pretty good at that whole skating thing, Tim," he said, reaching for his coffee cup. "When I saw you flip over those people at Navy Pier—man, that was cool."

I smiled, leaned forward into the attention. "Yeah, it's pretty crazy, right?" I did the math in my head and remembered that I'd flipped over seven people, less than half of what I'd done in the other Navy Pier show with Dan. "But that's really nothing compared to what we've done at some of the other shows." I glanced up to gauge his reaction, wanting to savor it before I even finished my sentence. "The most I've ever flipped is fifteen."

He took a sip of his coffee and set the cup down. Leaned back against the vinyl and folded his arms across his chest. He smiled. "Wow, Tim. That's really something."

From across the booth I studied my father's features. His brown hair fell unevenly over his ears, and his forehead stretched farther than it should have, from the tops of his eyebrows to just past the curve in his scalp, where his hairline had begun to recede. His brown eyes, the same color as mine, stared back at me through thin, unremarkable eyelids.

"Yeah," I said, looking back down to my plate, wanting to say more, not knowing how. Because, really, what more was there? That I was good and talented and worthy of his love? That he could be proud of me? That I'd done all I could to earn him as my father, and he shouldn't turn away from that?

Maybe. But like so many sentences I had yet to write back then, those words were decades away from forming. Even if I'd had them, I doubt I would have taken the risk. There was simply far too much to lose.

* * *

My father and I didn't meet often, and there was no regularity, but we did find ourselves across from one another occasionally over the next few years. The meetings usually started in a diner like the one off Pulaski Road—either he would pick me up at my house, where Heidi and Aaron would peek out of the blinds in the kitchen window to get a glimpse of him, or my mother would drop me off at a restaurant, leaning over to kiss me before I got out of the car. But each time we met, I got the feeling that we were both faking it, trying to act, stuck in a stage play where neither of us knew the lines. He did not know how to be my father nor I how to be his son.

Or perhaps it's fairer to say that he didn't know how to be the father I wanted him to be—the one I had built up in my mind during the years he was absent. That version of him was embarrassingly proud of me, could barely endure the time between our visits. Instead, our interactions were nothing more than superficial encounters, just forceful enough to leave a ripple or two on the surface of our lives.

Our conversations inevitably stalled, and when they did, my father would say what must have seemed the only thing he could. "What do you think? Is there anything you need? Let's go get you something."

It was nearing a holiday—Christmas, I think, perhaps when I was fifteen—when we walked into a Best Buy store in Crestwood, a few miles from my house in Oak Lawn.

"You want a video camera, right?" my father asked. "So you can film your skating shows?"

"Yeah, but you don't have to do that," I said while scanning for a sign that would point us to the cameras. "They're so expensive."

As we stood there in the aisle together, Sonys and Panasonics and huge Magnavox VHS recorders lined next to each other on a shelf, I took in the prices, wondered what it would cost my father to buy my forgiveness. $549? $799? $999? What pecuniary offering? What monetary sacrifice? What dollar amount could be placed on how sorry he was, how angry I felt?

I picked a Sony Hi-8 8mm camcorder off the shelf near me and switched the power on, flipped open the screen attached to the side. I swept the camera over and aimed it at my father, the upper half of his body framed within the tiny screen. For years I'd been searching for him, and finally here he was, a few feet away. I realized it was far easier to look at the image of him captured in the screen, to stare at the idea of him, than to look at the man who'd made me and left.

"Is that the one you want?" he asked.

"Yeah. I mean, I guess. It's pretty sweet."

He reached down and grabbed a box from the shelf below. "All right then. Let's get it."

"Oh, man. Wow, Dad—thanks." I knew that I had to call him Dad at that moment, knew that's how this transaction worked. "You don't have to buy it, though. Seriously."

"I know, son." We walked to the register together and the cashier scanned the bar code on the package. The total flashed across the screen and my father turned to me. "I want to get this for you because I love you, Tim."

I stiffened, and my father's body was a dark silhouette against the light coming in from the doors behind him. Outside was a parking lot, and beyond that a road that led to an apartment my mother and I moved into after the divorce, once she got her feet back underneath her. We were maybe a mile away. Had my father even known we lived there?

The numbers on the register totaled just over $800, and he counted off nine hundred-dollar bills for the cashier.

I felt the resistance inside me, the truth of what was really happening eating like acid at the lining of my stomach. I knew the transaction wasn't complete, that there was one more thing to do.

I swallowed and smiled. Found his eyes with mine.

"I know, Dad. I love you too."

* * *

We made promises to each other every time we met. He always said, "I'll call you in a few days," and I always said, "Cool, we can go grab something to eat or maybe go fishing at one of the forest preserves." He always said, "Yeah, that sounds good," and for days after we'd made those promises, he would inhabit almost every one of my thoughts. Each time the phone rang, I had to force myself not to run to it, not to listen to whoever answered it. But if I were in my room when it rang and my stereo was on, a CD playing loudly as I flipped through a skate magazine, I rushed to turn the volume down and stood by the door, listening. I stood absolutely still as I waited for someone to say, "Yeah, he's right here. Hold on a sec." But it was almost never him. And as the days after we met stretched into weeks, and those weeks stretched into months, I pretended that it didn't matter that rather than beginning to know him we were becoming strangers once again.

I didn't know what to do with how I felt back then, or how to resolve the feelings that burned inside me, and so my teenage emotions did what so many unrealized male emotions do—transformed into a crushing and self-destructive rage.

T W O

When I look back at my teenage self, at that skinny, brown-eyed boy who grew his hair long and got earrings against his parents' wishes and skated and played soccer and rebelled with a fierceness that emanated from his very core, I can now see there was a layer of anger, of violence, infused into nearly everything he did. At the time, I might have called that anger passion, but I think of it now simply as fuel—the octane that powers rebellion.

After my relationship with my father began and then ended over the course of two short summers, that anger became the most powerful force in my life—and because of it, the fights my parents and I had in my adolescence often crept up on us like a fever might creep up on a sick child overnight. I would walk into the living room on a Saturday afternoon while my mother read a book on the couch and my stepfather dozed in the recliner, and one of them might ask me about my homework, and that simple question would speed up the emotional current that ran just beneath my skin until my mother and I were inches away from each other, screaming.

Over the previous year or so, our fights had become predictable. My stepfather would remain patient and calm. My mother would support him. And I would remind and accuse my stepfather, usually by shouting, that he wasn't my father, and I wasn't his child, and that I knew he loved his other kids, his real kids, more than me. But even as I yelled at him, even as I hurled accusations at him like fastballs, I knew in my heart it wasn't true.

Our most significant fight came during the summer of my freshman year. I walked down the short hallway that led from my bedroom to the kitchen, past the family photos that were hanging on the wall, the floorboards creaking under my feet, to rummage through the refrigerator in the way hungry, growing teenage boys can. My stepfather and mother were both in the living room, talking softly to one another, when my stepfather's voice wrapped around the doorway.

"Tim, come here a minute."

I popped a cookie in my mouth and took a bite, crumbs falling to the cracked kitchen laminate as I walked into the living room and leaned against the drywall archway.

"What's up?" I asked him, my words muffled from my chewing. My mother watched me from her seat on the couch, the book she was reading lying open on her lap. Above her hung a dime-store painting that showed a forest and a lake painted mostly in browns.

"You're supposed to mow the lawn this week, and it looks like it's going to rain the next couple of days. You need to get out there and do it today."

I swallowed. "Yeah, I'll get to it later."

My stepfather leaned forward in his recliner. Took off his glasses. "Okay, when?"

I popped the rest of the cookie in my mouth. Turned to walk back to my bedroom. "I don't know, Dad. Today sometime."

His voice grew a hair louder. "Why don't you just go out there now and get it done so we don't have to worry about you doing it later?"

I turned around, walked back into the doorway and stared at him. "Why don't you just get off my back? I told you, I'll do it later."

My mother looked at my stepfather, then settled her eyes on me. She seemed tired—perhaps exasperated from all the arguing we'd done in the last few months. "Tim," she said, "we don't want fight with you again. We just want you to pitch in and do your part around here. We agreed that mowing the lawn is your responsibility."

I rolled my eyes. "Mom, *geez*, I know. Don't talk to me like I'm a five-year-old. I said I'll do it later."

My stepfather sighed and stood up. "I don't want you to do it later, Tim. I want you to do it now." I could see the frustration on his face and I felt a sense of satisfaction knowing I had penetrated his seemingly endless patience. "For once, can't you just do what I want you to do without arguing with me about it?"

I narrowed my eyes, felt the blood rushing through me, a current as familiar to me as my shoe size. The storm began cycling through my chest. I absolutely hated when he told me what to do. "How about this?" I said, poking my finger in his direction. "How about *you* fucking do it?"

"Tim!" my mother eyes shot wide. "Stop being disrespectful and watch your language! How many times do we have to tell you that? Your siblings are upstairs. For goodness sake, it's not that hard." She got up from the couch and the three of us stood there, facing off in a triangle, all of us knowing what was coming next and none of us able to stop it.

"Yeah," I said. "My siblings? *My siblings?* You're always worried about them, right? Afraid I'm going to ruin your perfect little family?" It was a tired line that I used often, but the truth was I felt like an outsider. I was the only one with a different last name and a different father. I reached for some version of that line in nearly every fight.

My mother tossed the book she was reading onto the coffee table where it landed with a smack. "We're not doing this again, Tim. Just go to your room and cool off—and don't come out until you're ready to mow the lawn like your father told you to." She let out a frustrated sigh and looked at my stepfather, shook her head side to side.

I took a step forward, lessening the distance between all of us. "My father?" I was nearly screaming. "*My father?*" I pointed at my stepfather again and glared at him. "All I see is this guy and he's not my fucking father."

I could see him flinch from my words, could see that I'd hurt him, and I fed off it.

My stepfather took a step forward and we were now a few feet apart. Outside, the gates by the train tracks had come down, and the steady ringing of warning bells drifted in through the windows.

He spoke slowly. Decisively. "Tim, I mean it. Stop. You're not going to do this again. You're not going to continue to disrupt this family. I know you're mad. I know you don't ever want us to tell you what to do." He glanced at my mother. "But, guess what? That's life, and I don't really care how you feel about it anymore. You don't get to act however you want. Because you're not the only one who lives here."

"Yeah, I know," I said. "You remind me every fucking day. You and your perfect little family."

He glared back at me. "Yeah, well, you know where the door's at."

The words were barely out of his mouth and I was lunging forward, pushing him with my palms trying to topple him. He held his ground.

"*Fuck you!*" I yelled, realizing he'd braced himself and wasn't going to fall. I turned and rushed out of the room, hitting the drywall near the doorway as hard as I could with the palm of my hand, screaming; and then I was racing down the hallway, grabbing the family portrait off the wall as I passed it. I slammed the door to my room, locked it, leaned against it. "Fuck!" I yelled to no one, to everyone, whipping my head back so it cracked against the door. There was a flash of white. Nausea. Floaters. I scanned the room and saw a scissors sitting in a cup on my desk with pens and pencils fanning over the brim like a bouquet. I walked to the desk and slammed the picture frame on the wooden desktop. Pulled the backing off the frame and yanked out the photograph. I flipped it over and stared at it, seething, my eyes leaking tears as I looked at all of us—me, my mother, my stepfather, Heidi, Aaron, and Jillian—sitting there in the Olan Mills portrait studio that I had worked at the summer before, all of us smiling. I grabbed the scissors, held it in my hand like a knife I was going to stab someone with. Started scratching my face out of the picture with its sharp tip. The scissors poked through and dug into the wood, small strips of oak curling up from the surface. I threw the scissors into the corner of the room, and it bounced off the wall and landed on the floor. I held up the picture, saw my scratched-out face, started crying harder.

I heard knocking, then my stepfather's voice. "Open the door, Tim." I looked at the door, focused on the bronze latch that held it closed. My stepfather had installed it after I told him I needed privacy.

He was yelling now. "Tim! Open the door *right now*! What are you doing in there?"

I walked to the door and pounded back at him with both fists. My lips touched the door's paint as I yelled into it. *"Leave me the fuck alone!"* I could feel my own hot breath bouncing back at me.

I walked over by the windows, my face contorted from anger and crying, and looked outside at my neighbor Marie's house. I saw the fence in between the properties and remembered how I painted it for her when I was younger. She gave me one penny for every bare spot I found. I stayed out there painting for hours.

"Tim, open this door right now or I'm breaking the lock."

"Break it then!" I yelled. *"You think I give a fuck? Break it like you've broken everything else in my life!"*

My chest was heaving now, rage and pain causing my throat to hurt and my forehead to sweat and my right hand to clench into a fist. I screamed. Threw a punch at the window in front of me and watched the glass exploded as my fist broke through to summer air. And then my stepfather lowered his shoulder and forced his 280-pound frame through the bedroom door, the brass lock bending immediately, the door flying open and slamming against the wall. And then he was staring at me as I stood there among shards of glass, sucking wind through clenched teeth, staring back at him defiantly with blood leaking from my hand in vines.

* * *

I sat on the edge of the couch holding a wet paper towel around the fingernail-sized slice in my thumb. I could hear Heidi and Aaron walking around in the bedrooms above us and I wondered what they thought of it all—the constant fighting, the tension, the way the violence hung in the air after every slammed door.

My mother leaned forward and motioned toward my hand. "Let me see it again."

I pulled back the paper towel and bright red blood immediately filled the wet crease in my skin. She looked at my stepfather. "Tom, he's going to need stitches."

My stepfather's face remained pensive; he seemed to be contemplating what he wanted to say next. He turned and walked over to the window, looked outside at the long grass in the front yard that would likely now go uncut. He spoke with his back to us.

"Fine, I'll take him over to the ER at Christ Hospital. You can stay here with the other kids. Let them know everything's okay."

I stared at my stepfather's back, traced the broadness of his shoulders with my eyes. He was so much bigger than me. So much bigger than I would ever be. He once gave me a piece of printer paper from the word processor he bought for me to do homework on, and told me to wrap it around my bicep—to see if one end would touch the other. I'd tried it and both ends had touched easily. "You try it, Dad," I said, and he laughed, and then watched my reaction as the paper made it less than halfway around.

My stepfather turned and the expression on his face told me all I needed to know: he was doing all he could to keep himself from losing control and pinning me up against the wall by my throat. I knew I had an opening, a way to really get under his skin. I wanted to hurt him, to anger him, to make him lose control.

"Let's go then, Tim," he said.

It was subtle, but I could hear it in his voice, and it was all I needed to feel the anger fire up inside me again. The sarcasm in my response was palpable. "Oh, sorry, *Tom*. Sorry if it's too much fucking trouble to take your son to the emergency room." I clenched my teeth together. "That's what you keep saying I am, right? Your son? Just like Aaron, right?" I pulled the paper towel off the cut again and made a fist so the blood flowed over my thumb and dripped onto my jeans. "Bet you if Aaron was hurt, you and mom would already be in the car." I had the sudden urge to flick blood all over the wall, to jump up off the couch and kick the television over. I wanted to break something. To hurt something. To inflict pain on someone. To *keep* inflicting pain. "What, am I not hurt enough for you? Do you want me to really hurt myself? How about that, *Tom*? How about I grab a piece of that glass and fucking end it all right now, make it easier for everyone? It's not like my life even has a fucking point anyway." I'd started crying, and I hated that I had. I was sick of crying. Sick of looking weak. Sick of not even knowing why I was so mad at my stepfather. All he'd ever done was try to help me, but I hated him for being so patient. For trying to help me. For loving me.

I stood up and started for my room, but he moved quickly and blocked my way.

"You're staying right here where we can see you."

I stopped. "Or what? You think you can stop me, motherfucker?"

Neither of us moved. "Yeah, Tim. I can." He looked at my mother who had backed up against the wall, bracing for my stepfather and me to collide. "Lor, I need you to get the phone and call the police."

She looked at her husband, at my stepfather, at the man who provided the house that I lived in and constantly damaged. "The police?"

The tone in his voice was even and he spoke slowly. "Yes. Our son has threatened to hurt himself, to possibly take his life. He's broken a window. He's injured himself and needs stitches." His eyes stayed locked with mine as he addressed my mother. "Now go in the kitchen, Lor, pick up the phone, and please call the Oak Lawn police."

* * *

The police came, and I treated them disrespectfully until they threatened to arrest me, and then I rode in silence with my mother to the hospital, where the cut took four stitches to close. We were both exhausted by the time we got there—tired from the latest episode, but also tired from all the episodes that came before it.

Back then I wasn't mature enough to understand what I was really doing—testing them, daring them to abandon me. Because if I pushed him and he moved, if I hurt her and she pulled back, then I was right, and they confirmed what I truly thought about myself: that I was damaged and unworthy of their love.

At the hospital, my mother sat on the foot of the bed. "Maybe you need to be somewhere where someone can help you deal with whatever it is you're feeling. Somewhere you can get professional help from people who are qualified to deal with the anger bottled up inside you."

I looked in my mother's eyes and could see how badly I'd hurt her. The anger I felt at the house was gone now and all that remained was shame. For perhaps the first time, I wondered what it was like for her, for them, to have me as a son. I knew it wasn't easy. There were times in our disagreements when things would start to get out of control, and I knew that no matter what they said, no matter what they did, even if they gave in to whatever it was that I wanted, it would never satiate me. Most of the time I just wanted to fight. I wanted to ensure that someone else was hurting as much as I was. There was simply nothing she or my stepfather could do—no matter how many approaches they tried—to prevent the anger and rage inside me from roiling over and into their house.

* * *

The memory I have of that incident becomes cloudy in the moments after I agreed to give the mental hospital a try. Because that's what it was, a mental hospital, no matter how nice my mother tried to make it sound. A doctor came in and told me what I could expect when I got there. There were forms that I signed and questions that I answered, and then my mother and I were both in the back of a medical transport van, my thumb bandaged in stark white gauze and beginning to throb as the local anesthetic wore off, riding down Ninety-Fifth Street to the Dan Ryan Expressway, driving into the city.

We arrived at the facility, and after I was admitted, I said goodbye to my mother in the waiting room, her eyes soaked from tears. The intake nurse then asked me dozens of questions all designed to assess my threat and suicide level, and then showed me to my room. It had one window with cream-colored metal bars on it that looked down on the street below. We were in the city somewhere, but I didn't recognize the neighborhood. The walls around me were white and barren, the room big enough to hold two twin beds and two nightstands and nothing else. My roommate was a kid who was younger than me by a few years, maybe eleven or twelve. He was sitting on his bed reading a book and he looked up as I walked in.

"Hey," he said.

"Hey," I replied, walking over to the empty bed and sitting on the edge of it. "I'm Tim."

He laid his book on his chest. "David."

I nodded and swung my feet onto the bed. Laid back. Reached my hands under my neck to adjust my pillow. "You been here for a while?"

"About a month."

I rolled my head to the side and raised my eyebrows. "A month?" As the nurse had walked me to my room, he pointed to a line painted on the ground and said that when patients walk down the hall they need to stay on the line at all times, and they aren't allowed to converse. Everything we did was monitored. I couldn't imagine being in the facility for a month. "Why are you here?"

He folded his knees up and studied them. "Because I accidently shot my brother."

I rolled my head back and stared at the ceiling, not knowing what to say, not knowing if there was anything I could say. Somewhere in the facility the air-conditioning turned on. The sheet metal buckled and a soft, hollow boom drifted into the room. He accidentally shot his brother. I couldn't even begin to imagine what that was like.

I kept my eyes on the ceiling as I spoke, the last slices of afternoon light carving their way through the room. The bars on the windows cast shadows like piano keys over the bed. I looked over at David. "I'm sorry," I said, my voice a notch louder than a whisper, the first apology in a long time that I'd given and actually meant.

* * *

My stay in the mental hospital didn't last long, but neither did the effect it had on things at home. At first, we were all on our best behavior—none of us wanted to repeat what had happened—but nothing was really fixed, and so nothing had really changed, and soon we were right back where we always were: arguing and fighting and frustrated.

One night not long after I'd gotten home from the hospital, in yet another fight, I punched a hole in the drywall and screamed at my stepfather and ran out of the house with the keys to his Oldsmobile station wagon dangling from my fingers. It was after ten o'clock on a school night, but I couldn't be there anymore, in a house where all we ever seemed to do was fight, and so I started the car and backed out of the driveway like a maniac, the tires screeching when I hit Central Avenue, the engine of the Olds roaring underneath the dark blue hood.

Sometime the previous year, before things with my parents had deteriorated so badly, I'd begun dating a girl named Katie, who was a year older than me. Her family lived a few blocks from the high school we both attended, and that night, when I bolted out the door and into the midwestern darkness, I knew her house was the only place I could go.

I'd fallen hard and fast for Katie, into the sort of teenage love that felt all-encompassing and weighty and permanent. We were opposites in many ways—I was a skater, she was a prep; my family was blue collar, her family was white collar; our parents belonged to different tax brackets—but those differences didn't matter, and we connected in a way that made me think we would always be together. She was the person I turned to when I didn't know how to pick up the pieces left from all the things that were breaking at home. I'd show up at her house raging about school or my parents, and she'd take me by the hand and lead me upstairs to her bedroom, where I'd flop down on her enormous bed, and she'd turn on music and listen to me try to make sense of the chaos. I never knew exactly what she was thinking, or if she thought my problems were as unique or complicated as I thought they were, but she gave me honest, compassionate feedback and loved me, I felt, more than I deserved.

When I arrived at Katie's house that night, I rang the doorbell and her mom answered, her face filled with curiosity at first, and then concern.

I looked down at my shoes. "I know it's late, Mrs. O.," I said, "but it's just that . . ." It was suddenly hard to finish my sentence, hard to put into words how I felt. The anger I'd felt earlier was gone now, replaced instead by a feeling of awkwardness. I stood on the concrete porch fighting tears, embarrassed that I'd showed up to their door so late.

Mrs. O. reached out and touched my shoulder. "Tim," she said, "come in. Katie's upstairs." She stepped back and motioned for me to come through the doorway. "I'll get her in a minute, but let's talk about what happened first."

I followed Mrs. O. past a pile of shoes that had been kicked off near the door and down the hall, past her bedroom, where I could see light from the television slicing through the crack of the almost-closed door, and into the kitchen. "Here," she said, pointing to a stool next to the counter. "Sit. I'll make you some tea."

I didn't even drink tea, but the idea sounded good in the moment, like somehow tea might be the answer to all the questions I had, to all the problems that needed tending to. Maybe if I drank enough tea I could figure out how to calm down, how to stop punching walls, how to tell my parents what was going on inside my head.

Mrs. O. filled the kettle with water and set it on the burner. She turned the dial and the stove clicked a few times and then lit. "What happened tonight, Tim?"

I wasn't sure how much Mrs. O. knew about my home life, but I assumed that Katie had probably filled her in on some of the details. I shifted on top of the stool.

"I don't even really know. I just had another huge fight with my parents, and before I knew it I was yelling and running out the door with my dad's car keys."

Mrs. O. pulled opened a cabinet and grabbed a mug from the middle shelf, set it on the counter, and dropped a tea bag in it. "What were you fighting about?"

"What don't we fight about?"

"You tell me."

I suddenly wanted to tell her about everything—how I felt like my stepfather was always on my case because I wasn't truly his son, how I felt like a disappointment and burden to my entire family, how, even though I had never actually admitted it to anyone, my biological father and I not having a relationship crushed me to the point I sometimes found it hard to breathe.

I looked at Mrs. O. and sighed. "I just feel like they don't understand me. I'm not the perfect kid they want me to be. I'm never going to be, either."

Mrs. O. leaned back against the counter. "I doubt they want you to be perfect, Tim. They probably just want to figure out what's going on with you. How to help you stop getting in trouble at school. You know," she paused, "just connect with you in some way."

It was possible she had a point, but connecting with my parents seemed anything *but* possible. How could they understand what it was like for me? How could they truly understand? Everything I was feeling, all the hurt and anger, the abandonment, the rebelliousness—it felt like something no one else had ever experienced before, certainly not either one of them.

The kettle began whistling and Mrs. O. turned off the burner and poured hot water into the mug she'd set on the counter, just as we heard footsteps coming down the stairs. Mrs. O. walked over and set the mug in front of me as Katie came into the kitchen.

"Hey," she said, her eyes widening. "What are you doing here?"

Mrs. O. looked at Katie. "Why don't you guys go upstairs for a bit, and I'll give Tim's mom a call and let her know he's here, and that he's safe." It dawned on me that I still had my stepfather's car, and that he was going to want it back immediately. My stomach dropped.

"My parents are going to freak out because I have their car," I said.

"I'll talk to your mom and figure something out." She shook her head ever so slightly. "Something's got to change, Tim. For the sake of all of you."

I nodded and stood up, and the stool scraped across the tile floor. "Thanks, Mrs. O. I really appreciate it. Really."

A few minutes later Katie and I were upstairs in her bedroom, and I sat on the edge of the bed with both hands wrapped around my mug of tea. Her stereo was turned low and there were two piles of papers on the floor and a couple of pens—she must have been doing homework. A candle burned on the nightstand and the air smelled like sugar cookies.

Katie sat down next to me. "So, what happened?"

"Same shit. Different day."

"I get that. But seriously, what happened?"

I thought back to earlier in the night, but I couldn't even remember what had started the fight, or who had said what. I shook my head. "I don't know. One second we were fine and the next we were screaming at each other."

Katie got up and walked over the stereo, turned the volume down a little. A few strands of straight blonde hair fluttered behind her, and I wanted to get up and wrap my arms around her and never let go. For a second, I could see our future together—just her and me living in the city and taking the L to work together, or maybe living near the beach somewhere, being young adults with important things to do. I wondered if she knew how much I loved her, how badly I wanted to figure out a way to fast-forward through the next few years and start a life together.

Katie turned to me and smiled, but it was faint, just enough to round out the corners of her mouth. "I definitely don't have all the answers, but I'm pretty sure that everything that's going on for you—all that stuff we always talk about? Maybe you need to talk to someone else about all of it. You know, like a counselor?"

I set the mug on the nightstand and flopped onto my back and closed my eyes. I'd done the counseling thing with my parents when I was younger. I'd gone through quite a few of them in fact, and I absolutely hated every second of it. It had always felt like a game or a trick, like a way to get me to put my guard down, so they could fuck with my head.

"Or," I patted the bed next to me, "you could just come over here and we could forget about all this shit."

Katie smiled, but stayed where she was. "I'm serious, Tim. You need to talk to someone. You need to get a handle on what's going on with you. You can't keep getting in trouble at school and fighting with your parents and expecting all this is going to go away."

I couldn't tell whether she was angry or scared or bored or none of those things, and so I closed my eyes and lay on her bed, the down comforter soft underneath my back, the music playing quietly from the speakers. I promised myself that from there on out I would try harder, even if it was just for her.

What I didn't know that night was that in just a few months' time, after I'd lived in her basement for a couple of weeks to let things cool off with my parents, after we'd poured milk on our cereal together in the morning and I'd fallen even harder and more recklessly in love, she would break up with me, and my heart would crack in the way only a teenage heart that's never been broken before can. I would cry in her driveway and my entire body would shake and it would be hard to stop. I would feel stupid for doing so, for crying so intensely, and when I would tell certain friends about it, I would act like it didn't matter, as if she wasn't always occupying space in my mind, as if I wasn't missing all of those times that I lay in her bed looking out her window, while oak tree branches parted the sky like cracks in an acrylic landscape.

THREE

Throughout my childhood, my stepfather operated heavy equipment for a living, paving streets and sweeping them, resurfacing them, plowing them, creating and clearing new paths each day he woke up and pulled his boots on. I watched him walk to work dressed in his creased blue slacks and light blue dress shirt, cars streaking by him on Central Avenue, and wondered how he could do it, how he could get up no matter how hot or cold it was and go to the same place to clock in, work with the same people day after day.

Not long after I turned sixteen, I began working at a restaurant called Baker's Square. Situated just off Ridgeland Avenue six blocks from my high school, it was a coffee spot favored by teachers and AA groups and teenagers who sat near the back smoking and ordering french fries, paying their checks with change.

I started by hosting on the weekends. I greeted people at the door and sat them at their tables, watched them as they talked to one another and ate sandwiches, blew on hot soup, absentmindedly stabbed at the ice in their cups with straws. I was immediately comfortable there, and within a month or two I was promoted to server, wearing a dark maroon apron filled with extra Saltine crackers and pens, waiting on tables with a smile on my face and charisma in the air. Serving tables gave me a new identity, a way to present myself to people, and perhaps myself, in a different, more favorable light. I could make people laugh and feel useful, and I took a great deal of pride in the busyness of it all, in being attentive to the needs of twenty or thirty people at once. It was transactional, of course, but it was a transaction that I craved: I would be charming and polite and observant; in return, I would be compensated with cash and compliments and gratitude. I found self-worth at Baker's Square, and I also found that I could settle into the repetitive comfort of serving food in a way that I'd never felt in any of the other jobs I'd had. I'd worked at my aunt's pet store, cleaning hamster and gerbil cages, mopping up after puppies, stacking bags of dog food, coming home each afternoon smelling of bleach and pine shavings and ammonia, and with the two Virginia Slims I'd sometimes pinch from her purse. After the pet store, I stocked shelves at a mini-mart near my house, lifting cases of beer and pop and Doritos until my biceps ached and my shoulders burned, sometimes hiding a few longneck bottles from the damaged cases of beer waiting to be returned. My friends and I would ride our bikes there later that night or the next day, find the warm beers where I'd stashed them behind a stack of cardboard in the alley, and ride over to Stony Creek, twisting open the tops and taking sips while we sat on rocks by the water, laughing and cringing and making faces from the taste.

I did whatever I could to earn a few dollars: washed cars, shoveled snow, mowed lawns all over the neighborhood—which is painfully ironic, since it was refusing to mow my parents' lawn that had landed me in the mental hospital. I knocked on doors of houses whose grass was long and wavy, smiling, asking if they would hire me. For ten dollars, or even eight if they bargained, I rolled my stepfather's grease-caked lawnmower down the sidewalk, clumps of wet ryegrass falling behind me as the wheels squeaked loudly on the cement, and pushed the mower back and forth in straight lines until sweat dripped down my neck and formed dark circles on my T-shirt.

But waiting tables at Baker's Square was different than all those other jobs. There was a contentment I found in it that had previously been absent. I loved the humanity in serving people, the compassion

I could hear in how wives talked with their husbands, how the smile creases in a grandfather's face would deepen as he showed me pictures of his grandkids. I loved how people deconstructed their lives with one another over chicken potpies and bacon cheeseburgers, how a son's bad grade in geography or a daughter's failure to make the volleyball team seemed suddenly solvable and manageable once their stomachs were full.

Baker's Square was just a typical, run-of-the-mill American eatery serving average food to average people making average salaries, but it gave me a sense of purpose, of security, of significance. There was also a profound familial sense within the restaurant. Like most middle-class restaurants across America, Baker's Square had a way of giving back to those of us who hadn't gone to college, or had crappy husbands, or had small mouths to feed with no other means to feed them. We had customers who cared about what we did on our off days and asked about our kids and our hobbies and our girlfriends. We had coworkers that we genuinely bonded with, because even though we lived in different places and faced different problems, we were all in the trenches together. Each time we snatched three singles and two quarters, or a five-dollar bill, off a crumb-filled table and put that money in our apron pocket, we felt validated.

After a year of working there—during which time I finally received my driver's license—I realized that I knew some of the people that I worked with better than I knew the kids I grew up with. I knew that Sheila, the hostess who gave me the application to fill out when I first walked through the doors, was old enough to retire but couldn't quite afford to yet, even though she wanted nothing more than to spend her afternoons chasing after her grandkids. I knew that Dawn, an attractive mother of four with bleach-blonde hair that was darker by the roots, bounced from one perpetually bad relationship to the next, sometimes walking in on Sunday mornings with eyes bloodshot from arguing with one of her boyfriends long into the night. And I knew that Karen, a waitress I worked with regularly, sometimes drank a beer or two before her morning shift just to make the day go by a little easier.

Dysfunctional as it may have been, Baker's Square was a family. So when everything around me began to change, when the skate team began to show signs of breaking up—Dan was getting ready to head off to college; a few of the other skaters were moving too—it was my Baker's Square family that I turned to. They saw me differently than my own family did, or perhaps it makes more sense to say that *I* saw me differently when I was with them, and they were there to pick up the pieces as my dreams of skating professionally fell apart around me.

For most of my teammates, skating was always just a hobby, a unique way to bridge the gap between youth and young adulthood. It was never a permanent thing for them, while for me skating was a way of life, or at the very least, a way to permanently enhance it, a springboard that would allow me to jump over all the things that weren't working out. I wanted to grow the team, to get better and bigger, to start booking shows all over the country and figure out a way to skate my way to happiness.

And when I skated, I was happy. *We* were happy. My mother and stepfather had attended my shows on a number of occasions, standing at the front of the crowd, clapping and cheering as I blurred past them. After landing a trick I would glance over at them and see the pride on their faces, feel the pride in mine. But the show would eventually end and their smiles would fade and the crowd would quiet and I'd be faced with the truth of what it was: a moment. And a fleeting one at that.

* * *

On a fall day during my junior year of high school, after I had come to understand that my relationship with my father would never take root the way I had hoped it would, the cool wind blew color-rinsed leaves across Route 83, the tree-shaded road I took to high school every day during the academic term. In the station wagon I borrowed from my stepfather, my arm resting on the door as my fingers flicked ashes from a cigarette, I drove over two sets of train tracks, past two cemeteries, where large statues of Mother Mary stood watch over the graves, arms outstretched in blessing, and turned right by the gas station my friends and I stole candy and pop from after a high school football game my freshman year.

I pulled into the parking spot that day with the smell of smoke still lingering in the car, and stared at the brown brick building in front of me. As I watched students filter into the small Christian school my mother and stepfather paid for me to attend, I wrestled, once again, with whether or not to go in. There were times that instead of pulling the doors open and walking to my first period class, I put the car in reverse and drove to one of the nearby forest preserves. There, I'd sit with my head against the headrest or sprawled on my back on a picnic table, the smell of the car's cooling engine mixing in with the forest, inhaling cigarette smoke and blowing it toward the swaying leaves of the maple trees above me.

But on that day, a day that seemed no different than the one before, I stayed—and halfway through the day my life surged and throttled forward. I was walking down a long hallway toward my fourth period classroom when Marcus Andrews, a student I'd never held more than a two-minute conversation with, stopped me with an outstretched hand. "We've got a sub for fourth period," he said. "You ditching?" The idea hadn't crossed my mind until that exact moment, but as soon as the question was asked, something inside me shifted.

It was a shift I'd felt before—the same shift I'd noticed during the previous summer when I'd hiked the bluffs at Starved Rock State Park with a few of my friends. High above the Illinois River we stood on the edge of a cliff, the wind rustling through the trees, the water below us reflecting the sunlight, and I felt my heart beat faster as I thought about what it would be like to jump, to feel the freedom of weightlessness, as I fell the seventy or so feet to the water.

"You won't do it," my friend said. And I thought he was right, but then I felt the shift inside me and I was taking my jeans off and people were watching, egging me on, and the water below was rushing, quick and fierce and cold. And then I was sprinting toward the edge of the cliff, shirtless, propelling myself off the granite and into the air, my arms and legs swinging like a runner, free for a moment as I fell to the glimmering river below.

After I hiked back up, my hair matted to my forehead, beaded water dripping down my summer-tanned shoulders and back, my friend asked me how I knew the water was deep enough to jump into. "I didn't," I said, shrugging before I sat down to pull my jeans back on. "That shit never even crossed my mind."

In the hallway of the school, Marcus Andrews was waiting for my response, but instead of answering, I turned into the shuffle of students around me. The squeak of their shoes on the lacquered tile, the smell of cookies baking in the cafeteria, the expectant look on Marcus's face all consumed me, and I disappeared into the noise. Marching away from Marcus, toward what I didn't know, I suddenly loathed the constrictions of high school with an intensity that I'd never felt so acutely before. It immediately became clear that I would leave school and walk through the gray doors to my stepfather's blue Oldsmobile station wagon waiting outside in the parking lot. I would get in the car. I would go.

That night, as I lay in the wooden bed my stepfather had made for me when I younger, fingering the smooth, steel bolts that held it together, my mother came into my room and informed me that the school had called. Her voice had worry in it, or maybe it was desperation or disappointment or sadness, but it wavered as she stood in the doorway, one hand clasped around the doorknob.

"Why did you leave today, Tim? What happened?" she asked.

I wanted to say something that she would understand, to somehow make her feel what I'd felt in the hallway earlier that day. I wanted to tell her about the shift inside me, about the pull I'd felt that I had been helpless to ignore, but I just stared at the ceiling, unable to speak.

This wasn't the first time I'd done something like this. I'd left school dozens of times before, and been in trouble for other offenses as well. I'd been caught smoking outside the C-Hall doors, finishing my cigarette defiantly, slowly, before reluctantly obeying the administrator who had caught me and going to the disciplinarian's office. I'd told my biology teacher to go fuck himself, screamed at him from the middle of the classroom as the vein in my neck plumped with blood, stomped past him while the rest of the students watched in stunned silence as I barreled through the doorway, slammed the door, and threw the aluminum coatrack in the hallway crashing into the wall.

The silence lasted for a minute before my mother exhaled slowly and continued.

"Principal Dekker just called and told me that the decision as to whether or not they're going to let you come back is being put to a vote by the school board. They might not let you go back, Tim."

I rolled over onto my side and stared across the room through the window that looked out over the backyard. The light from the garage illuminated just enough of it that I could make out the silhouette of the swing set my stepfather had brought home from one of the public parks in the neighborhood that was being renovated. It was the biggest swing set I'd ever seen in a backyard, and I spent hours when I was younger pumping my legs as hard as I could, the chains squeaking as I swung higher and higher, before launching myself into the air. Years later, as I hung from the side of a small plane twelve thousand feet above the earth and prepared to let go, I recognized the feeling of weightlessness, the freedom there was in falling away from something—that was what I was always after. But I didn't have the words to explain how I felt back then, and so as my mother softly closed the door to my bedroom, and I heard her footsteps retreating down the hallway, the gravity of not being allowed back into school slowly sinking in, I thought that maybe this time it wasn't the falling away that I craved, it was the crash.

The day Marcus Andrews asked me if I was going to ditch, I knew it would change things. I knew—or at least felt—that I had only one chance left and decided to walk out the doors anyway. Everything that had been happening in my life had been leading up to that moment, and once the choice had arrived—to leave school or not—it felt like the decision had already been made.

* * *

After the school board voted, I was informed I couldn't return. Although I wouldn't admit it, I missed high school dearly. I missed the familiarity, the structure, the security. I missed seeing my friends, playing soccer, driving to the parking lot behind the neighboring restaurant after school, so we could smoke and laugh and talk about the girls we were chasing.

But I also missed it because there was a palpable division between my friends and me now. Navigating adolescent friendships without a high school anchor was more difficult than I'd ever imagined. Without classes to break up my days, without soccer and skating to dispel the unrest inside me, without the regular interaction of my friends, I began drinking more than I ever had before, cherishing the way vodka and beer burned my throat and lessened the feeling of failure. I bought weed from the cook at Baker's Square, sometimes meeting him in a neighborhood a white stoner had no business being in, other times rolling blunts with him in his car in the parking lot. We listened to hip-hop as the smoke drifted toward the velvet ceiling, the bass and anger and weed acting as a catalyst to my restlessness.

After leaving work most nights, I took the money I made and walked across the parking lot to the bar that sat on the corner, directly across the street from the store I'd rented my tuxedo from for my homecoming dance freshman year. Although I was three years under the legal drinking age, through a coworker who'd introduced me, I'd become friends with the bar's owner, and he turned a blind eye to my youth. I drank bottles of Miller Lite and did shots of Jagermeister or Goldschlager while chain-smoking Marlboro Lights, eventually giving all the money I made that night to the bartender on duty. I then got in the car, drunk and comfortably numb, and drove home, swerving and nodding to the sounds of hip-hop drifting from the speakers. Once there, I stumbled to my room, sometimes tripping on the stairs, or rummaging through the refrigerator for leftover pizza, before passing out and waking up to do it all over again.

One day after a lunch shift at Baker's Square, I came home to my stepfather sitting at the kitchen table with the *Southtown Star* newspaper spread out in front of him. He took off his reading glasses and addressed me as I walked into the kitchen.

"If you're not going to school, Tim, then this living arrangement is no longer free."

I stood next to the refrigerator with my hand in my pocket, fingering the sixty or so dollars I'd made. "What does that mean? You're going to charge me to live here?"

"It means that if you want to be out of school and working like an adult, then you're going live by the rules that all the other adults do. If you want to stay here you're going to start paying rent."

I shook my head. "That's bullshit, Dad. Isn't it your duty as a parent to give me a place to live?"

"No, son, it's not. Not when you're making all your own choices." He pushed his chair back from the table with his legs and rubbed his eyes. "You're eighteen, Tim. Legally, you're an adult. I'm not going to tell you what to do with your life, but I'm also not going to finance your apathy."

"Apathy?" The word stuck in my mouth and I glared at him. "Whatever, Dad. Just let me know how much it's going to be."

* * *

The rent was small—a hundred dollars if I remember correctly—but it was all I needed to resent my stepfather more and wish to spend even less time in his house. I found myself working as much as I could, staying away from home. I had begun hanging out with an older crowd, too, one made up of guys who could buy beer legally and afford better weed. They had jobs—as painters or electricians or plumbers or carpenters—and they had apartments or condos where the nagging of disappointed parents was, at least to me, distinctly absent.

Unlike me, however, the guys I was now hanging out with had all earned their place in their lives. They'd all finished high school, made the decision to work instead of going to college, and grown into the lives they were living. At the time, though, I didn't understand that. I didn't think about the journeys they'd taken to get to that place in their lives. Instead, I just assumed they arrived there; that I could arrive there too if I just hung out with them long enough, did some of the same things they did. I didn't realize that simply not being a high school student anymore didn't qualify me as one of them any more than watching a Mike Tyson fight made me a boxer.

One of the guys I was hanging out with regularly, Travis, the wiry, long-haired older brother of one of our other friends, had started talking about moving out West, to Colorado. "I just want to smell the mountain air," he said late one night as we sat in the living room of a friend's house drinking beer and smoking. "I want to feel the open space, see the mountains. Snowboard every day." He went quiet after he finished, staring into the cloud of smoke he'd just exhaled at the ceiling. I wondered if what Travis wanted was something I wanted too.

Growing up, I snowboarded about as much as a midwestern kid could, taking trips to the local ski resorts, most of which were nothing more than hills, not real mountains. But I took to it like

I took to skating, and it came easily. I loved the movement and speed in snowboarding, the dance between chaos and control, the way my body felt so in tune with the ground and the sky and the air and the snow.

I'd been to a real mountain only once—with my high school girlfriend Katie's family—but I thought of it often. They took me with them to the Whistler Blackcomb resort in British Columbia, and I stood on the hard pack at the bottom of the gondola, a midwestern kid who knew only skyscrapers and great lakes, staring up at an impossibly big mountain. After I took my first ride on the chairlift, the small ski town getting even smaller as we climbed, the ride down seemed to last for hours. When I finally unstrapped my board at the bottom of the mountain, my cheeks were red and my lips were chapped and I knew I needed to have that feeling again. When I was on the mountain leaning hard into turns, the edge of my snowboard vibrating with each imperfection in the snow's surface, speeding until I was hovering right on the edge of disaster, I felt completely at peace. If I wasn't pushing myself to the point where losing control was at least a possibility, I simply didn't feel like I was living.

I took a drag of my cigarette and felt the smoke pass over my tongue, down my throat, into my lungs. "That sounds pretty damn good," I said to Travis, exhaling. "Colorado could be amazing."

He looked at me through the haze, smiled. "You should go, man. I mean, why not? There's not really anything keeping you here, is there?"

He was right. There wasn't anything tying me to Chicago. Since the skate team had broken up and high school was now over, every day felt like a waste of time. Maybe moving was what I needed. A fresh start. Distance between me and everything else.

I shrugged and he continued. "I was talking to Kevin the other day and he told me he was thinking of moving out there too. You should talk to him. I'll be heading out there at the end of August. I'll have a place by the time you guys come out. You could crash with me until you guys find something."

I realized I was nodding as he was talking. It sounded reasonable, doable even. Maybe I could pull it off. Kevin was a good friend of mine from high school, and if he was going, it just might work out. At the very least it would get me out of Chicago for a while. Get my parents off my back.

"You might be on to something," I said, taking one more drag from my cigarette and stabbing it into the ashtray next to me. "Who knows, man. Maybe I will."

F O U R

I think often about the days when I skated in front of those crowds, and miss the visceral feeling of satisfaction it gave me—those people cheering, their hands clapping and voices shouting, their collective praise wrapping me in a blanket of affirmation I never wanted to shed. It felt so good to be watched, to be authenticated, to be deemed worthy of adulation. I basked in the moments just after landing a huge trick, when I could literally feel the crowd's energy entering through the pores in my skin, and I wonder now whether that was the start of it, the beginning of my lifelong struggle with substances. The dopamine release and the subsequent longing for more, the adrenaline—is that where it all truly began?

I was sustained for hours and sometimes days by those moments, by the lift they gave me, by the social and emotional capital they infused me with, but as time passed the highs were progressively shorter, the lows progressively longer, the cravings for those moments progressively stronger. I was no longer satisfied with simply having those moments—I needed to live inside them, to embody them, to burn them or smoke them or swallow them, to chop them up into little white lines and breathe them into my bloodstream. No matter how good those moments were, no matter how brightly they lit me up, I always needed more. And I would crash or burn—whatever it took—to ensure that I would have them.

* * *

In the fall of 1996, a month or so after I first talked to Travis about Colorado, I slid into a red vinyl booth across from Karen, the waitress I was working the afternoon shift with at Baker's Square, and grabbed a cigarette from the open pack on the table.

"What's it like?" I asked her.

"What's *what* like?" she said, blowing smoke into the air above us.

"You know, coke. I mean, what does it do to you?"

She tapped her cigarette on the edge of the brown ashtray between us, caught my eye before looking away. "I don't know how to explain it, Tim. It's good, though. I guess it just makes everything around you just a little bit more fun."

I nodded to her and put the cigarette to my lips, inhaled. More fun sounded like exactly what I needed. Everything had become so much less fun lately. "I want to try it," I said, wiping away an ash that had fallen to the table. "Can you get some?"

I met her at the bowling alley one Friday night a couple of weeks later. She was drinking Miller Lite from a pitcher and saw me almost as soon as I walked in. "Tim!" she yelled from across the room, arms waving above her head like she was directing an airplane. I walked to her, and she poured me a plastic cup of beer from the pitcher on the high-top table and introduced me to her friends. I shook their hands and made small talk with Karen for a few minutes, but I was there for a reason. "You got it?" I asked, when it seemed like no one else was listening. "Hold on," she said. "I need to get it ready first." She grabbed her pack of cigarettes and slid the cellophane wrapper off the bottom of it, told me to wait while she went to the bathroom. I lit a cigarette and leaned back in my chair. Over the hollow crashing of bowling pins and classic rock music, I sipped my beer and watched her friends. They looked a lot like what I thought they would look like—construction workers and bikers, most of them with goatees and Harley Davidson T-shirts, a few pairs of dirty steel-toed boots under the chairs where they'd kicked them off to put on their bowling loafers. I wondered if any of them knew my father.

Karen returned from the bathroom and put her hand on the table, slid it over toward me. "Here," she said. I glided my hand over to hers and grabbed the folded cellophane wrapper, closed my fist around it, leaned back, and stuffed it in the pocket of my jeans.

"Where should I do it?" I asked.

"Just go to the bathroom. I'm sure it'll be fine, but be careful. Make sure no one walks in on you."

I stubbed out my cigarette, stood up, and walked to the bathroom. Happy to find it empty, I walked into the stall closest to the back wall. My heart, beating hard since the moment Karen had passed me the cocaine, was now galloping, knocking against my ribcage. My palms were sweating and my hands were shaking, but I managed to dump the cocaine onto the back of the toilet without spilling. The movies always made cocaine look like a fine powder, but this was more like little white chunks—little specks of crumbled drywall.

I forgot to ask Karen how exactly to do it, but I'd seen enough films to know the basic idea. I pulled out my wallet and used my driver's license to crush the rocks into a fine powder and then scraped the cocaine into a straight line. I rolled up a dollar bill, and then for a moment I simply stood there with my heart pounding and my hands shaking, looking at the line of cocaine on the back of the toilet, at the piss stains on the edge of the bowl, at the piece of toilet paper that had fallen to the floor. Outside the bathroom I could hear pins crashing and people laughing and a toilet flushing in the women's restroom, and for the briefest of seconds I wondered what I was doing. It felt like maybe something fundamental was about to change, like I was about to cross a line I couldn't come back from. But there was such pleasure in risk, such thrill in not knowing how deep the waters were and jumping anyway. So I bent over the porcelain, put the dollar bill to my nose, and inhaled.

* * *

That same fall, Dan and my good friend Rich began classes at North Park University, a small school located in Chicago's Albany Park neighborhood, on the far northwest side. We had become friends in grade school, running around the sunbaked blacktop at recess until the sound of the bell summoned us back inside. We made it through grade school and junior high together and our friendship grew, and then we spent most of high school laughing and leaning into each other, meeting up at the Pizza Hut near Rich's house in Orland Park on Sunday afternoons to eat piles of breadsticks and drink pitchers of Mountain Dew.

As soon as Dan and Rich had officially started college, I became painfully jealous of them. After my first visit to their dorm rooms, I drove home with a lump in my throat that I couldn't seem to swallow. From the Dan Ryan Expressway, as the lights of the city stretched toward the dark sky outside my dirty windshield, two white lights blinked methodically atop the Sears Tower. In that moment, I wanted to be as far away from the city as I could be. For as much as I loved it, there was an equal part of me that had grown to resent it.

I dealt with that resentment, and the rest of what I was feeling—mostly sadness from the loss of the thing I loved most, skating—by drinking and smoking weed until the world tilted on its axis. Even at 140 pounds, it was nothing for me to drink a twelve pack of beer and take pulls from a vodka bottle and still be rummaging through a fridge or cooler for more. Wherever I was, I would drink whatever I could find, knowing that at some point, with enough alcohol inside me, the pain and sadness and resentment would eventually become static. My thinking would slow and my senses would dull, and for a few cherished hours, my mind would finally go quiet.

* * *

Once the idea to move to Colorado had crept into the fabric of my psyche, it grew rapidly, spreading into every part of me until there was nothing I could do but figure out the logistics. It was insanely exciting, a fresh start in a Promised Land of sorts, and the answer to everything I felt at the time—anger at my father for leaving me, anger at my high school for giving up on me, anger at myself for not being a better version of me. I could move to Colorado and become someone else completely. I could find a job, snowboard, never look back.

But as the trip grew closer, my situation grew more complicated. On September 13, 1996, the night Tupac Shakur died, I was at a party in the far south suburbs, two hours from the city—stars and wet grass, crickets and kegs, more than a hundred people talking and drinking and smoking and fighting and dancing. Tupac was almost all I had listened to the previous two years, an artist who made me feel tougher and more alive, quicker to raise my middle finger to any sort of authority.

The news had made its way around the party, and I walked away from the crowd to escape the noise and be alone for a few minutes. I couldn't believe he had died, kept thinking it was all some sort of stunt. I lit a cigarette and leaned against the hood of the near-decade-old Chevy I'd recently bought from my stepfather for hardly any money, and tipped my head back and looked to the sky. I let the weed and beer and liquor pull me in and soften things while I listened to WGCI give tribute by playing Tupac's album, *The Don Killuminati.*

And then my pager was going off and I could feel the vibration against my legs. I unclipped it from my jeans and tried to make out the number, tried to steady my hand, squinted my eyes to focus on the digits. It was a girl I worked with, a girl I'd been out with a few times, and I knew from the code she left after her phone number that she wanted me to come over. And it sounded like a good idea, too, like something that would make me feel better. Besides, Tupac had died and the party was weak and who really gave a fuck anyway? I reached over and grabbed the unopened bottle of Icehouse beer I'd set on the hood of the car and opened it, flicked the cap into the grass, took a long drink. *I need to get the fuck out of here right now*, I thought. *Not just to this girl's house, but to another state, to Colorado, to somewhere far away from everything here, from this bullshit, from my high school that didn't want me, from my parents who are always disappointed in me, from my friends going off to college. Yeah,* I thought, *I'm done with this place.*

I got in the car and put the bottle in the cup holder and turned the key. Tupac's voice disappeared while the car's starter turned over, and then he was back, his voice louder now that I was inside, the music dark and soothing and perfect and enraging.

And then I was driving down the road past gas stations and cornfields, past houses I didn't know, trying to find my way back toward the city, toward a girl's house, toward someplace where I could feel better, somewhere I could close my eyes and not think about anything for a while. But in front of me the yellow lines of the road were coming so quickly, and they were so hard to anticipate, so hard to avoid, and they kept pulling me toward them, the beat-up Chevy drifting to the other side of the road until I jerked it back. *Fuck this place*, I thought again. *Fuck these yellow lines and these rules and all this bullshit.* I rolled the window halfway down and lit a cigarette and then a minute later I lit a joint, and I had both of them in my hands, alternately taking pulls from each of them, the street moving like the picture on a television that needed the antenna adjusted. And then there were lights inside my car, beautiful lights that were red and blue, like the Fourth of July, and they were dancing on the dashboard, bouncing off the smoke, and at first I wasn't sure where they were coming from, but then it hit me and adrenaline dumped inside my chest. *Fuck, fuck, fuck*, I thought. *Fuck.* I pulled into a parking lot, tried to play it cool, tried to convince myself I could talk myself out of what was about to happen. But then I put the car into park before it was completely stopped, and the Chevy jerked, and my head flew forward like I'd hit something. And then there was an officer at the side of the car and I was so tired and all I wanted to do was get to this girl's house, and "No, officer, I haven't been drinking."

I knew I was talking to him, to the officer, but he was so hard to see through the smoke, through my tired eyes, through the stickiness of Tupac's death. Tupac, his voice still on the radio, still rapping, still angry, but sort of sad too. And then the officer was pulling me out of the car and pointing to the beer in the cup holder and dangling the bag of weed he found in my pocket in front of my face. And it hit me, right as the officer folded me over the warm hood of his cruiser, the engine's heat absorbing through the fabric of my T-shirt, that I wouldn't be talking myself out of trouble this time, and I wouldn't be going home.

* * *

I received five charges in total that night, including a DUI, and within a week I added another charge to the list: driving on a suspended license.

My mother had always told me that things didn't have to be the way they were, that I could start making better choices and find myself in a better place. For a second I believed her. Maybe, I thought, I could wake up one day and choose the wiser thing. But when the alcohol and drugs and anger were all lined up in front of me like temptations in the desert, the actions I took didn't feel much like a choice at all.

* * *

At my family's Christmas party the night before I left for Colorado, I sat on the ledge by the big brick fireplace at my aunt's house. My uncle Bear had stepped carefully across the living room floor, over boxes and wrapping paper balls and kids, and stood in front of me looking down.

"I heard you're leaving tomorrow," he said, glancing at one of my younger cousins as he ran by.

"Yep," I said. "That's the plan."

"Scoot over," he said, nodding his head to my left. I slid over and he sat down next to me on the stone ledge of the fireplace, the flames behind us crackling and warm, the madness of Christmas all around us. The air smelled of ham and coffee, of cookies. Voices blended together in laughter and conversation, my stepfather's family filling every empty space in the house.

"You know," he said, leaning forward and propping his elbows on his knees, "I did the same thing when I was younger." I glanced over at him, then focused on the Christmas tree in the corner, staring without blinking, watching as the lights crystallized before my eyes. "I left home when I was young—younger than you actually. Just needed to hit the road, I guess. See what I was made of."

Was that what I was doing, I thought? Seeing what I was made of? Testing myself seemed a much more noble cause than running away from myself. I looked down at the carpeting, thought about Bear leaving home all those years ago. It dawned on me that I really didn't know Bear much at all. He was my aunt Jean's second husband, in his forties I guessed, and they lived in Arizona. I saw him once a year, if that, and this was the longest conversation we'd ever had.

I turned my head and looked at him, saw the wrinkles around his eyes, the stubble just starting to fade onto his neck. "So what happened?" I asked.

He paused for a second and we both watched as another screaming kid went running by, high on sugar and presents. Bear smiled. "I'm not going to lie to you, Tim. The road kicked the crap out of me. I lived in a shed for a while, worked odd jobs—whatever I could do to make a few bucks."

I thought about what Bear was saying, wondered what his family thought when he left. Wondered if he even had any family. "So what's your plan?" he asked.

I shrugged. "My friend Kevin is heading out there with me, and my buddy Travis moved out there a few months ago. We're staying with him at first. At least for a little while." I picked up a wrapping paper ball that was lying in front of me and began packing it like a snowball.

"Job?" he asked.

"I don't know," I said. "I'll look for one as soon as I get there. But I'm hoping I can just snowboard. Try to go pro." I held the ball in front of me to aim, then launched it in a high arc across the living room and tried to nestle it into the bed of a toy dump truck. It landed wide right and rolled to a stop near the Christmas tree. I glanced over at Bear. "I'm just planning on figuring it out as I go."

Bear nodded, but his smile had faded. "Listen, man. I'm going to tell you something that I wish someone would have told me back when I was your age." I suddenly felt uneasy, not quite sure what to expect from him. "No matter what happens to you out there, you have to watch who you let into your life. People will take advantage of you if you let them. They'll fucking drain you, Tim. *If* you let them." The curse word hung in the air between us, as out of place at our family's Christmas gathering as an Easter basket would be. He reached over and slapped his hand on my knee, shook it back and forth quickly before letting it go. He seemed to read the uncertainty in my eyes. "Listen, I'm not trying to scare you. All I'm saying is be careful. Be selective. The world you know is about to change, drastically."

I looked around the room, saw the little kids running around, the dishes on the coffee table filled with M&Ms and cashews and candied pecans. I saw the shiny ornaments on the tree, smelled the cinnamon from the hot apple cider in the kitchen. For a moment it seemed as if I might be making the wrong decision to leave. For a second it seemed like I should stay.

I turned toward Bear and forced a smile. "Thanks, Bear. I'll be fine."

* * *

Looking out the window of the plane, surrounded by blue sky, the world below me was divided into perfect little rectangles of land. Roads carved through cornfields until they intersected with one another, all of America's Heartland fitting together perfectly like a puzzle. Farmland stretched as far as I could see, and I guessed we were somewhere above Iowa or Nebraska.

Undoing my seatbelt, I leaned forward and reached under the seat in front of me to where I'd stashed my backpack. I pulled it onto my lap and unzipped it, felt cool air blowing on me from the vent above. Wiping away the long strands of hair that had blown into my eyes, I took out the present my parents had given me and tore off the wrapping paper. The woman sitting beside me glanced over and smiled. It was a Bible, and tucked inside the cover was an envelope that contained a letter written in my mom's handwriting, and a check for five hundred dollars. As I read the letter, I felt a tightness in my throat. I looked at the check signed by my stepfather—his signature unmistakable in small, thin letters. I looked at the way the line that crossed the T in my name curled up at the ends where my mother had written it. I missed them already. I knew I'd put them in an impossible situation. I'd always tried to make them feel like it was their responsibility to fix me, but I knew it wasn't. And they knew it too. Regardless, they were swallowing their pride and giving me money they surely could have used on something else, as well as the one book they thought could help me most.

Outside the window, a layer of clouds tumbled through the sky just below us. I knew they were just water vapor, but they looked like they could hold me, like they could suspend me high above the world, far away from whatever was happening down below. As I looked out the window, I could feel how much I would miss Chicago: the way the sun cast long shadows from skyscrapers across Lake Shore Drive in the afternoon; the way the sudden bloom of microscopic marine plants could change the lake's color from slate gray to a brilliant bluish green overnight; the way sparks cascaded off L tracks in the evenings, creating orange and copper waterfalls. But maybe I would find something beautiful in the mountains, too, something that I couldn't find at home: a new perspective maybe, or a fullness, or a way to shrink my problems down to a more manageable size. Maybe it was the bigness of life, the weight of it, that I felt pressing down on my head right where the soft spot used to be. Maybe when everyone around me was moving toward finding something to anchor themselves to—colleges or careers or relationships—maybe I needed to be less permanent, maybe I needed to take life's bigness and throw it up against some Rocky Mountain granite so I could study it, so I could see it from a clearer perspective.

Or maybe none of that mattered and what I really needed was to ride, to feel that Burton deck under my feet and lean into the mountains, into gravity, and fall away from everyone and every-thing that held me back. As we taxied to the gate that first day in Colorado, soft jazz music drifting in from the speakers above me, I stared out the small window into the vastness of that new place, into the promise it held. The engines roared and the snow blew sideways, and just as the jet bridge nuzzled up to the side of the plane, I imagined myself in that new world, successful and happy, independent and thriving, high above the tree line with a snowboard strapped to my boots, leaning hard into champagne powder turns.

COLORADO

FIVE

The Continental Divide of the Americas runs from northwestern Canada to the southern tip of Mexico, steadily carving North America in two. It's invisible of course, this line that separates east from west, but it's definitely there, definitely real, forcing rain and snowmelt west toward the Pacific Ocean, or east to the Hudson Bay and the Gulf of Mexico.

In Colorado, the Continental Divide and Interstate 70 intersect inside the mile-and-a-half-long Eisenhower Tunnel about an hour west of Denver, at just over 11,000 feet above sea level. Just west of the tunnel, where the air is thin, the interstate begins a steep descent, snaking and meandering, winding and curving, until it levels off twelve miles later, on Summit County's valley floor.

I arrived in Summit County on Christmas Day, 1996, after traveling west from Chicago and west through the mountains and west over the Continental Divide, but I didn't yet know the significance of the direction I was traveling. For Chinese Buddhists, west is the direction of enlightenment and represents a movement toward the Buddha. For Christians, traveling west represents a return to the Garden of Eden, or a journey toward Canaan, the Promised Land. West is the direction of America's expansion, the direction of Manifest Destiny, the essential direction of the vision quest. West, as it has always been, is the direction of seeking.

And what I sought in Colorado that first day, packed inside an airport shuttle van with my snowboard and luggage stored in back, dreaming of long runs down the Keystone and Breckenridge ski resort trails, was revision and reinvention. I was searching for clarity, for purpose, for the calm that comes with the imagination of a self rebirthed. But what I was truly *feeling* that first day in Colorado was simply my independence. For the first time ever I was living my life completely on my own terms, and there was an excitement that came with that freedom, an exhilaration that rivaled anything I ever felt skating or drinking or using. So as I stared out the window at the aspens and pines that sprung from the mountainside, the check my parents' had given me folded in the pocket of my jeans, my mind already thinking about the partying we were sure to do that evening, I felt the freedom of young adulthood and the excitement of not knowing what lay ahead.

What matters to me most now, though, isn't actually any of that. What matters to me now is that the Continental Divide, that imaginary contour that separates east from west, here from there, is also known by another name—the Great Divide. Looking back over the span of twenty years, I can now see that the Great Divide was indeed a division for me. It was a gulf that I had to cross, a boundary I needed to pierce, a line that existed on a map but not in the world—but was somehow as real to me as the golden sun that hung near the corner of that sapphire sky.

* * *

Travis's apartment was located in Dillon Valley, in a ramshackle apartment complex directly across from Interstate 70, where exhaust brakes on semitrucks beat noise into the air as they made the steep descent from the Eisenhower Tunnel all hours of the day and night. It was furnished with chairs and couches and tables from thrift shops and garage sales, and neon beer signs were fastened to walls painted a linen shade of white. A perpetual haze hung just below the ceiling from the cigarettes and joints and frozen pizzas that constantly burned, and the smell of boiling ramen noodles was permanently baked into carpeting stained by years of dirty snow being tracked inside.

The apartment was small and unkempt and overcrowded—Travis had three other roommates in addition to welcoming Kevin and me into the mix—but it was near-perfect for me, a place far away from my mother and stepfather, from my father, from the legal problems I had left in Chicago.

For the first few weeks, it felt like a vacation. I slept on a sleeping bag on the floor of one of the bedrooms and never unpacked my giant red duffel. I used toiletries out of a ziplock bag. Drank and smoked weed whenever I felt like it. Snowboarded with Travis and Kevin as much as I could. But the money I'd brought, even when combined with the money my parents had unexpectedly given me, dwindled almost immediately, most of it spent on beer and snacks and lift tickets to Keystone and A Basin. I needed to find a job.

Sometime near the middle of January 1997, Travis, Kevin, and I sat tucked into a corner booth in the smoking section of the Denny's restaurant in Silverthorne, where I was thinking about applying. The three of us ate and talked, smoked cigarettes, smelled eggs and bacon and biscuits and fries as they whirred past us on the tops of oval trays resting on the shoulders of servers wearing white dress shirts, maroon aprons, and Looney Tunes ties. Our voices mixed in with the classic rock and pop music that filtered in from the ceiling, the occasional crash of a cymbal raining down on us from the speakers above. There was laughter, the crinkle of a newspaper being folded over and read by an old man drinking an endless cup of coffee.

Travis grabbed a sugar packet from the wire caddy in the middle of the table, looked at me while he tore off the top and emptied it into his coffee. Sugar granules bounced off the rim and scattered. "You still thinking about getting a job here?"

"Yeah, I was going to grab an application before we left," I said, turning my head as the wooden doors at the front entrance to the restaurant opened. A young woman walked in and approached the register near the front, said something to the cashier. She stood there surveying the room and I watched her, our eyes meeting briefly when her gaze landed on our table.

The girl's blonde hair curled out in all directions and tumbled over her shoulders. She was pale, her skin freckled, and I was immediately attracted to her. She tipped her head back and laughed after the cashier said something, and her shoulders shook, and there was something wild about her, a sort of untamed quality that I was instantly drawn to.

Travis threw a creamer that bounced off my chest and fell into my lap. "Hey, Earth to Tim. You going to sit there with your mouth open or go talk to her?"

I laughed, grabbed the creamer, and tossed it onto the table. Slid out of the booth. The girl watched me as I crossed the dining room, and I could see the anticipation in her eyes as I approached. Perhaps she saw the nervousness in mine. My voice sounded unfamiliar when I spoke.

"Hey, I'm Tim," I said, catching a trace of flowers in her perfume.

She smiled, the freckles on her cheeks momentarily congregating just beneath the corners of her eyes. "Hey, I'm April."

When we talked that first night, it wasn't for long, but we connected. I told her that I had just moved to town from Chicago, and she told me that she'd been born in Summit County, had lived there her whole life. I told her I was looking for a job and she told me she worked there, at Denny's, and that they were hiring, and that I should fill out an application. I said I would and then we laughed and stood there for a minute smiling at one another, feeling the awkwardness, the connection, the possibility. We said goodbye and she walked toward the door, and I walked back to my table fighting the urge to look back, already thinking about her, about what might happen. When I sat back down I could see her through the window, her hair blowing across her cheeks, pulling the handle on her car door, and I smiled and lit up a cigarette, laughing with my friends as I told them I was going to call her, blowing smoke into the air in streams, the glow from the dining room spilling onto the asphalt in golden strips of light.

* * *

A few days later, I sat in a different booth at that same Denny's restaurant, filling out a job application. The woman who gave it to me had dark blonde hair that was just beginning to gray and a nametag pinned above her right breast that spelled out "Debra" in straight, black letters. She looked to be in her mid-forties, in good shape, and spoke every sentence as if it were a command I had to follow, even when it wasn't. I immediately liked her.

"Coffee?" she asked.

"Yeah, that would be great," I said. "Thanks."

Debra turned and walked across the carpet, disappearing through a doorway and around a corner where I could hear her heels click-ing across a tile floor. I glanced down at the application, wrote my name on the line just under the Denny's logo, and then turned to look around the restaurant.

I was sitting in the nonsmoking section, and just outside the win-dows next to me, shoppers walked down the paved pathway from one section of the Factory Store Outlets to another. Couples held hands and swung shopping bags from Nike or Tommy Hilfiger or Mikasa, and parents chased after their kids, yelling at them to stay on the path and not veer too close to the shallow creek that bubbled through the property.

"Here you go," Debra said, placing the coffee in front of me and sliding into the opposite side of the booth. "So, give me the scoop."

I laughed. "What do you mean?"

Debra smiled and glanced out the window as a jogger ran by. "I mean, what's your story? Why are you here?"

"Same reason I'm sure you've heard a million times. Snowboarding."

She nodded but didn't say anything, so I turned my body and

looked toward the back of the restaurant, which stretched for another hundred and fifty feet. "This place is enormous," I said, turning back around.

Debra looked over my shoulder and surveyed the same thing I just had. "Yeah it is. It's actually the second largest Denny's in the country. You should see this place on Sunday morning during prime tourist season." She smirked. "It's a damn zoo."

I thought back to the Sunday morning shifts I worked at Baker's Square, a place that was probably a quarter of this size, but I would still sometimes drive home in my socks because my feet were so sore from running around all morning.

"I can imagine," I said.

"The servers here make pretty good money," Debra said, "but they work for it, that's for sure. We're pretty flexible with the schedule, though, so you can probably work as much as you want once you're trained and on your own."

I nodded, thought about how much money I had left. I needed to start working as soon as possible. "When do you think I can start?"

Debra scooted back so she was sitting straight up, put her hands on the table in front of her. "Listen, Tim. If I hire you, I'm not putting up with any bullshit." Her smile faded but she didn't look angry, just serious. "The rules are pretty simple. Come in when you're scheduled. Don't come in high or drunk. Don't do drugs while you're here." I fought the urge to look away. "If you follow the rules, things will be fine. You'll make a little bit of money and have some fun. The crew here is pretty nice. I'm sure you'll like most of them."

I thought about April. I called her the day after we met, and we had plans to get together the upcoming weekend. I learned that she had a one-year-old daughter, a rocky relationship with her mother and stepfather, and lived about ten minutes from Travis's apartment by bus.

"Sounds good to me," I said.

Debra slid out of the seat and stood. "All right then. Drop that application off with me before you leave. Call me tomorrow and we'll get the training schedule squared away."

"You got it," I said, smiling up at her. "Thanks, Debra. I can't wait to start."

* * *

The transit system in Summit County was free, a feature that I was forever grateful for, and it was mostly used to shuttle tourists from the swarms of rental condos and hotels in Summit County to the various ski resorts. The buses, driven by men and women who seemed considerably less stressed than the bus drivers in Chicago, were diesel-fueled and spit black smoke that felt offensive in such a beautiful place. Each bus, modified with curb-side racks used to hold skis and snowboards, would rattle up and down Summit County's hills, stopping every few blocks to pick up residents and tourists in brightly colored ski boots and Columbia or North Face jackets.

As I rode to April's house for the first time a few nights after we met, nervous and excited, I thought about all the buses I'd ridden back home in the months before I left. Since the DUI, I'd lost my license and rearranged my life according to the suburban PACE bus schedule, arriving to work at Baker's Square either too early or too late, a backpack holding my apron and order pad slung over my shoulder.

At some point I was going to have to go home and finish dealing with those pending criminal charges, but I pushed the thoughts as far away from my mind as I could. My next court date was in less than a month at the District 6 courthouse in the far south Chicago suburb of Markham. With my job at Denny's being as new as it was, I wasn't sure how Debra would react if I told her I had to take time off right away. She knew the new me, the young aspiring snowboarder who had moved to Summit County to pursue a dream, the guy who had started over and hadn't been in any trouble. Going back to Chicago for the court date would mean I would have to acknowledge the old me. I didn't want to do that. I wanted to leave him there, ignore him, maintain the distance I'd put between us.

Looking out the window of the bus as it weaved down Straightcreek Drive, the sky above Summit County big and dark and strange, I found myself thinking about my stepfather. There had been moments since I moved, walking down the street or searching for a clean pot in the cupboards of Travis's smoke-filled apartment, when I thought maybe I should call my stepfather and talk to him about what had happened at home before I left—about the arrests and my decision to move. It was possible that he'd understand things from my perspective, that he'd see that moving to Colorado was me trying to be a man, to make my own way in the world. But would he see me as a man? As an adult? Did I?

My stepfather and biological father, my only two real representations of manhood, were diametrically opposed. One had a child and then left him when things got tough, never looking back, or at least not admitting that he did. The other jumped into something he didn't need to jump into—took on a responsibility that wasn't even his because he fell in love with a woman and it was a package deal. And then when things got hard, when money got tight and he needed funds to pay for my private grade school tuition, he, my stepfather, sold the one luxury he afforded himself—the 1968 Camaro RS he'd been rebuilding that was stored in the small garage of the house he had bought us on Central Avenue.

When my stepfather parked his snowplow on the street around the corner from our house and I watched him walk through the steadily falling snow up our driveway after an eighteen-hour shift, just to eat a sandwich and fill his thermos to go out and work some more, I understood how hard the sacrifices he made for our family could be. I saw the fatigue in his eyes and his struggle to stay awake, his head propped up by his elbow as he ate. Was that what it meant to be a man? Was it about work and determination and sacrifice? Was it about grinding it out? Was it about doing the thing you had to do no matter the cost? If it was, what did that make me, the man who'd just taken a plane ride states away in order to not have to do the work required to solve the problems he'd created?

The bus hit a bump and the sudden movement jarred me from my thoughts. I reached up and pulled the cable that signaled the bus to stop, rose from my seat, and walked to the door as the bus slowed, its brakes shrieking then hissing. The door opened and I stepped outside, the brittle snow cracking beneath my sneakers. I looked up the hill across the street toward a small apartment building that sat just underneath a wooded area that led to the Dillon dam. Just past the trees was a two-lane road that circled the reservoir, and just past that was Lake Dillon, a beautiful, manmade lake that provided the entire city of Denver with water. As I walked toward April's, pulling my jacket tighter around my shoulders, I kept glancing at the ridgeline and thinking of all the water, peaceful yet powerful, dangerous yet contained, seemingly moments away from breeching its walls and flooding the valley below.

* * *

The sole picture window in April's living room faced west, and when the sun set, it cast a kaleidoscope of fiery colors on the apartment's carpeting and walls. From my spot in front of the window, I could see the curves of Buffalo Mountain to the north of us as it reached nearly thirteen thousand feet into the sky, a blanket of dark evergreens stopping just below its peak and giving way to a carpet of white snow.

April's apartment was small—two tiny bedrooms and a bathroom that sat at the end of a short hallway—but it was clean and efficient and the nicest apartment I had ever been in. She'd decorated her walls almost entirely with eight-by-ten pictures of her one-year-old daughter, Maddie, smiling in various outfits—a headband in one, a frilly pink dress in another, Maddie's big brown eyes bright and wide and curious. Against the wall near the dining room table were two trunks overflowing with dolls and toys, and fanned across the top of her entertainment center, just above the television we were about to watch a movie on, were collectible Winnie the Pooh plates. They were ceramic and painted with meticulous detail—the yellows of Winnie and grays of Eeyore and oranges of Tigger vibrant and warm and welcoming.

April offered me a beer, and I sat in an old wooden rocking chair sipping from a brown bottle and watching Maddie as she stood in the middle of the living room watching me, the fingers of one hand fiddling with the fingers of the other, her brown eyes almost black with her back to the fading sunlight.

"I think she likes you," April said, walking past me and sitting on the end of the couch to my right, tucking her feet underneath her. "She hasn't come bolting to me yet." She took a drink of her beer and put it on the end table next to her.

I laughed. "Give it time."

Maddie ran over to her toy bin and came back seconds later with a Raggedy Ann doll. She walked over to me and held it up.

I smiled. "Is that for me, sweetie?" I took the doll from her and put it in my lap, ran my hand over the red yarn that made up Raggedy Ann's hair.

"I had one of these when I was a kid."

"Yeah, you and just about every other child in America," April said.

I made the doll's head move while I talked in a high-pitched voice. "Well, hello there, Maddie. I'm Raggedy Ann. Do you want to play with me?"

Maddie laughed and I decided to see if she really did like me. I scooped her up, sat her on my lap, sat the doll on Maddie's lap. April watched us in amusement, and I began gently rocking the chair back and forth, immediately lulled by the rocking of the chair and the sweet little girl I was holding.

For as long as I could remember, I got along well with kids. They took to me pretty quickly, running up and grabbing my knees whenever I walked by the nursery at church, tugging at my flannel shirt until I picked one of them up and threw her into the air.

Jillian, my youngest sister, was thirteen years my junior, and Aaron and Heidi and I had found out our mother was pregnant through a game of "telephone" in the living room. We were summoned for a "family meeting," a phrase that to this day makes each of us kids cringe, and then stood in a semicircle while my mother whispered to my stepfather, my stepfather to my sister, my sister to my brother, and finally my brother to me. With each whisper I saw the eyes of the person receiving the information widen, and by the time the message, "you're going to have a new brother or sister" finally got to me, I simply didn't believe it. "What are you talking about?" I'd asked, annoyed, shooting a look at my mother. "I'm serious, Tim," she responded with a smile. "I'm pregnant."

At first it felt like a disruption, but by the time Jillian was born, I was used to the idea, and I often found myself holding her in my arms, feeling the warmth and wiggle of her tiny body, wondering how it was possible that any of us could have ever been that small. As she grew, our bond grew too, and she had a curiosity that I also recognized in myself. When Jillian was a toddler, I would put her in her stroller, strap on my inline skates, and push her down the street faster than what was probably safe, the summer wind hot against our faces, the asphalt warm beneath our wheels. We traveled the neighborhood together with the steady push of my legs propelling us down the sidewalk of Central Avenue, past the BMX trails and our grandmother's old house to Rocket Slide Park, where I pushed her in the swing or watched her, laughing and yelling, as she slid down the shiny red-and-chrome slide. We skated past the grade school I attended, the prairie that would eventually become a golf course, and the woods by Stony Creek, the place where my childhood friends and I once built a fort and a fire and blew up bottles of hairspray. And then, a little more slowly and with a little less excitement, we headed back to our house and its familiar brown brick facade, the traffic on Central Avenue whirring endlessly by, Jillian and me happy and tired and content.

Maddie turned her head over her shoulder and looked up at me, then leaned back and settled against my chest. The hair on the top of her head looked incredibly soft—yet to be styled and colored and damaged by curling irons and blow dryers. I looked over at April who sat watching us, then out the window at the unfamiliar landscape. I thought about Jillian, five years old at the time, about the way she cried when I left—big tears that slid down her blotchy cheeks to her chin before falling to the collar of her shirt. I thought about my family and what was happening back in Chicago, about what they were doing. My mother used to rock in a chair similar to the one I was in now, slowly, back and forth, lost in the pages of the book in her hand, tuning out the noise from cars driving down Central Avenue, a coveted few moments of escape from the world around her.

Right before my stepfather became part of our lives, I remember lying in bed next to my mother, rubbing her soft hair between my fingers while she read to me from the pages of a Berenstain Bears book. I wanted to do the same for Maddie, to read her a book and give her the feeling my mother had given me, to watch her get lost in a story.

I looked back over at April and smiled. "I guess maybe she does like me." April nodded, took a drink of her beer and set it back down. As we sat there rocking, this small child content to sit in my lap, accepting me, trusting me, I loved the way she felt—not heavy, but light and warm and alive.

I reached my hand over and gently moved a strand of hair from her eyes. The sun had dropped low in the distance, and the light outside was almost completely gone.

Looking around April's apartment in the last light of day, I was seduced by the order of it all, the way everything seemed to fit together so nicely—the toys and shoes, Maddie and April, their small apartment on the side of a hill in a town nestled up to the mountains.

* * *

After April put Maddie down for the night, we sat in the living room together, the television on low, smoke streaming from our cigarettes toward the ceiling, alcohol loosening our tongues and warming us up.

I reached over and stubbed out my cigarette. "You don't have to answer this if you don't want to, but where's Maddie's father?"

"You mean her sperm donor?"

I laughed. "Yeah, that's what I meant."

April was smiling, but there was something dark underneath it. "He's somewhere," she said. "Another state, I think." Her smile disappeared. "He was a bad guy—*is* a bad guy, I mean. He was mean as hell and super controlling. He was older than me by six years, and I met him when I was in high school. Things were pretty bad with my mom and stepdad at home, and he fed me a bunch of bullshit." She reached over and ashed her cigarette, took another long drag, then stubbed it out. "Of course I believed every bit of it. I quit school and moved to Denver with him, where we got this little apartment together."

"How old were you?"

"Sixteen."

This seemed crazy—even to me.

"So what happened?" I said.

"Things were fine for a while," she continued. "No parents around to give me any more shit. We had a little bit of furniture and a bed that I talked my grandmother into buying for me." The images on the television flickered and light jumped across April's cheeks. "I got a job working at an IHOP, and he worked construction jobs, but it was always something different. I'm pretty sure he was just doing side jobs because one day he was installing pools in people's backyards, and the next day he'd tell me he was pounding nails for a carpenter."

April picked up her pack of cigarettes and shook another one out. Sparked her lighter and then tossed it onto the couch next to her. "He was a short guy, but tough. He wrestled in high school and loved to fight. When he drank his temper was unbelievable."

"What would he get mad about?" I asked, using my feet to stop rocking.

"I don't know. Life. His parents. Me," she said, pulling at one of her blonde curls until it stretched to below her chin. "He would drink until he could barely talk, and then he would start crying. You know, sobbing and telling me that I didn't understand him and that I better not ever leave him." April looked ahead at the TV, then off toward the window, let the curl of hair spring back. "I should have known it was going to end badly, but of course I stayed with him. Next thing I knew I was pregnant."

I looked at the floor, taking in what she was telling me. I heard footsteps and a door slam somewhere out in the hallway and glanced at the door. April didn't seem to notice.

"He stuck around for a little while, but things got worse. I'd go to work at IHOP, and he'd show up before my shift ended and sit in the parking lot watching me through the windows. I waited on a table one night—a couple of guys who were about my age—and when they left the restaurant he beat one of the dudes senseless in the parking lot. I ran outside to try and stop him, to tell him that I'd never seen those guys before and that they weren't hitting on me, but it didn't matter. He left one guy lying on the asphalt bleeding and walked back to his truck. Before he got in it he said something like, 'Remember, even when you least expect it, I'll be watching you.'"

"Are you fucking serious?"

April nodded. "Yeah, I'm telling you, there was something wrong with that guy that was on a whole different level."

I pushed my feet against the ground and started rocking again, thought about what that must have been like, about the kid who'd gotten beat up, looking in the mirror and seeing his face—fucked up for a reason he'd never know.

I looked over at April, saw the green of her eyes and the curls in her hair and the freckles on her face. It was hard to imagine that someone that looked the way she did—normal by all accounts, pretty—had been through something like that.

"Did you ever tell your parents what was going on?" I asked.

April forced a laugh. "Yeah right. I mean, we had a couple of phone calls, but we always ended up in an argument. They were here in Summit County doing their own thing with their own little family. I've got two younger brothers—half siblings. My mom was always busy with them. She basically wrote me off after I quit school."

"Did they know you were pregnant?"

"Yeah, they knew, but it wasn't like they were going to help me."

How could they know about what she was going through and not drive to Denver and drag her into the car, even if she was kicking and screaming?

"So what happened? When did you guys break up?"

April thought for a minute. "About halfway through my pregnancy, maybe five months in or so. Things had gotten violent between us more than once. He punched me in the face a few times—a couple of black eyes, some nasty bruises. He choked me until I was about to pass out once. One night he climbed in bed next to me after he'd been out drinking. I was awake, scared to death, not knowing what he was going to do. We were both lying on our backs, looking up, and all of the sudden he extended his arm so I could see it. He was holding a gun." I stopped rocking. Searched April's face for a sign that she was exaggerating. Instead, I heard a slight shake in her voice when she started speaking again. "I was lying perfectly still. Afraid that if I moved he'd do something to me, do something to both of us." She motioned toward the back bedroom where Maddie was sleeping. "He scooted over as close to me as he could so that our heads were touching, and then he brought the gun up to his temple and I could hear the hammer click back—I'll never forget that sound, it was so loud—and then he told me that he could end it all whenever he wanted, that he controlled whether I lived or died."

"April," I said, shaking my head. "That's insane."

"I know," she said looking down at the floor. "I just laid there and he finally fell asleep. I was awake all night long, just thinking about how screwed up everything was. I was seventeen and I had this baby inside me, and this was the shit that was going on."

I sighed and again shook my head slowly. "He sounds like an absolute lunatic." My stomach was knotted and my adrenaline had begun to flow from the injustice of it all, a familiar tingle pulsing in the vein on the side of my neck. I got up and walked to the window. Turned around and leaned back against the sill. "Does he ever come around?"

April grabbed her empty beer bottle and stood up, walked around the corner and into the kitchen. I could hear the bottle drop into the garbage can—a loud clink as it landed on one of the other bottles. I heard the refrigerator open and then April came back around the corner and walked over to me, handed me another beer.

"I haven't seen him in over a year," she said, turning and walking back to the couch and sitting down again. "Not too long after the gun thing he left and never came back. I couldn't afford the apartment by myself and finally begged my mom to let me come back and live with her and my stepdad. I could tell that was the last thing they wanted, but I guess they felt like they had to, because they said yes. I stayed with them until just after I had Maddie and filled out all the paperwork for Section 8. I finally qualified for this apartment, and we've been here for a year or so now."

I took a drink from my beer and turned to look out the window. The sky was dark now and the streetlights glowed. The landscape in Colorado was so different from what I was used to back home—strange and comforting and terrifying all at the same time. I turned back to April. "Well, it doesn't seem like a bad place to be."

She smiled and I turned back to the window. In the distance, two headlights slowly carved a Z up the side of the mountain, and I wondered what it was like to grow up here—switchbacks instead of stalled expressways and smog. I thought about what April had just told me, about the gun pressed against Maddie's father's head, the way the gun's muzzle must have felt against his temple, cold and metallic, powerful. I thought about April's fear, about my own, about how someone her age, a year older than me, someone *our* age, could have seen and felt so much. I turned back to her and walked over to the sofa, read the expectant look on her face as I sat down next to her, touched her chin gently with my hand, turned it toward me, and leaned over until I felt the softness of her lips fold into mine.

S I X

There were moments while snowboarding when the world would render itself soundless, and I would surrender myself to the vacuum of a deeply fulfilling silence. It was a moment of unthinking, of erasure, of a space in time where nothing existed but the physicality of my body and my body's physical relationship to the mountain. It often happened when I was on the very fringe of control, when the paraffin wax on the bottom of my board carried me across snow crystals in a pocket of speed that existed just short of bedlam, when it seemed I was balancing on the razor-thin edge of disaster.

In the years since Colorado, and perhaps for the greater part of my life, I've sought out those moments, those fleeting instances of quiet, of purity, when my body and mind become singular, when instinct takes over and the disconnect between thought and action disappears. I've come to think of those moments as a sort of nirvana, a state of temporary enlightenment that occurs only when I give myself wholly over to the uncontrollability of life, when I willingly forfeit my ability to fear.

As a young man I couldn't articulate any of this of course. I knew only that what I felt in those moments while snowboarding, while leaning hard into turns with cold wind slicing past my cheekbones, was a kind of medicine, an opiate-like elixir that comforted something deep inside me. And so I searched for those moments as often as I could, in the softness of Colorado's freshly fallen snow, in the primitive calm of its mountains.

* * *

Keystone Resort was the only mountain in Summit County with lights that allowed it to open up a portion of its runs at night, where its snowpack glowed a brilliant, iridescent white. The temperatures would often be colder than during the day, and the runs icier, but it was less crowded and less expensive, and a month or so after I had moved west, Rich came to visit with his snowboard freshly waxed and its edges newly sharpened.

One night during his visit we sat side-by-side about halfway down Schoolmarm, Keystone's longest run, our snowboards strapped to our feet, the tree shadows created by the stadium lights reaching like dark fingers across the snow. About seventy-five yards below us was a tabletop jump we were getting ready to launch off. I looked over at Rich as he stared into the darkness in the distance where porch lights from condos spread out like stars across the black.

"Are you excited to get back to school?" I asked.

Rich pulled his knees up and tightened the strap on his binding, the plastic clicking as he ratcheted it. "Yeah, college is pretty cool. Dan and I have met a bunch of new people, and it's awesome living in the city."

I hung out at Rich's dorm a few times before I left and met some of their new friends, mostly students from other parts of the city or the Chicago suburbs. We went to parties or hung out at someone's off-campus apartment, almost always ending up at a diner near the end of the Brown Line called Huddle House, where we ate biscuits and gravy before stumbling back to Rich's dorm, cab drivers and buses honking as they drove past us.

"It sounds awesome," I said, pulling my gloves off and laying them in the snow next to me. I took the goggles off my head, unzipped my jacket and began cleaning off the condensation on the lenses with my undershirt.

Rich pulled his knees farther up and his snowboard scraped

across the snow. He reached down and brushed off some ice that was clinging to the top. "So how long are you planning on staying out here?"

I held my goggles out so I could look through them into the light. Saw a smear and went back to cleaning them.

"I don't know. I'm just planning on snowboarding as much as I can and seeing what happens. I really feel like I could go pro. Travis was telling me about a couple of contests that are coming up. I figure I'll enter one of those and see how I do—maybe get some exposure." I thought back to when I'd skated in shows with Dan, the way the cheers from the crowd had seemed like medicine. I missed it dearly. "I don't know, man. I just know I've got to do something. Show my parents and everyone else that I'm not a complete failure."

Rich stared at his snowboard. "Why, is that what you feel like?"

I hawked and spit to the side of where we were sitting, stopped cleaning my goggles and looked at him. "Hell yeah, that's what I feel like. Think about it. I didn't finish high school, so no college. I got fired from fucking Baker's Square because I showed up drunk and flipped out on the manager when he called me out. I got a DUI and then got caught driving on a suspended license. All I have back home are bullshit and problems." I looked down the mountain toward the jump, traced the corduroy in the snow with my eyes. "This is it, man. This is my shot. This is literally all I've got."

I put the goggles back over my eyes, zipped up my coat, and stood up. I ollied and turned forty-five degrees, the Burton deck slapping the ground when I landed. And then I was sliding forward, picking up speed as I carved down the mountain toward the jump, the cold wind pressed against the exposed skin on my face. I felt my body relaxing as I leaned into the final curve before the ramp, the muscles in my legs, my arms, my abdomen working in unison. And then I was fifteen feet above the ground and spinning slowly through the night, with snowflakes like fireflies glittering in my wake.

* * *

After Rich had gone back to Chicago, I walked into Travis's apartment one night after a shift at Denny's, my apron slung over my shoulder.

"We have to talk," he said.

"About what?" I said.

"About the fact that it's way too crowded in here and you need to find a new place to live."

I was angry with him in the moment because I couldn't come up with the money for a deposit on a new place. But I was also angry at myself for not saving any of the money my parents had given me, mad that even though this was probably inevitable, I hadn't seen it coming.

"I asked Kevin to leave too. Maybe you guys can find a place together," he said. "I'm sure it will all work out."

"Listen to this bullshit," I said to April at Denny's, as we stood at the soda fountain filling glasses with Coke. "I just found out that I've got to find a new place to live. Like now."

April pressed a glass against the plastic lever; it clicked and the soda started flowing. She kept her eyes fixed on the glass as she filled it.

"So what are you going to do?"

I transferred a glass to the little brown tray on the counter next to me and scooped a second glass full of ice, started filling it with Sprite. "I don't know yet. Got any ideas?"

April grabbed her drinks and started to walk away. Spoke over her shoulder. "You can stay with me for a while if you want."

"Serious?" I called after her, but she didn't hear, already halfway to her table. I watched as she walked, her slender frame swaying as she moved, the curls in her hair bouncing off her shoulders, everything about her beautiful and mysterious and irresistible. Her apartment was so nice too, so orderly, so unlike the world I was used to living in. Maybe staying with her would be good, maybe it would help ground me. Give me some structure. Maybe I wouldn't drink myself stupid every night like I did at Travis's.

April reached her table and set the glass down, smiling, and reached into the pocket of her apron for her notepad. She said something to the couple she was serving, a man and a woman with red, wind-burned faces, and they laughed, throwing their heads back in unison, looking up at April as she placed her pen behind her ear.

* * *

I took April up on her offer and moved in with her and Maddie. It was an easy transition to make, and an easy move too, since most of my stuff was still folded and packed in my duffel bag.

One morning not long after I moved in, I awoke to her gently shaking my shoulder. "Tim. *Tim.* Wake up. We're going to the zoo."

She opened the blinds and the early morning sun assaulted the room.

I blinked my eyes and rubbed them. Smiled. "Say what?"

"I'm saying get your lazy ass up so we can go see some zebras."

I rolled over and looked at April's face. Her smile was huge and genuine and I couldn't help but laugh and shake my head. "You want to go to the zoo right now? In Denver?"

"Yep."

I turned onto my back, rubbed my face again, and yawned. "What time is it?"

She grabbed the blanket that was covering me with both hands and slowly started inching it down. "I don't know, like seven or something?" Her eyes narrowed, playfully.

I smiled and grabbed onto the blanket, tried to stop her from pulling it any further. The fabric between our hands was taut as a trampoline mat.

"You pull this blanket all the way off me and there's going to be hell to pay, girlfriend."

Her smile widened. "Why, I would never think to do such a thing."

I started to say, "that's what I thought," but she jumped up, ripped the blanket all the way off, and ran out of the room laughing and yelling, "Come on Maddie, we're going to the zoo! Let's go see some freaking zebras!"

An hour later we were all in the car, the heat blasting, holding breakfast rollers from 7-Eleven and changing the radio station incessantly to find songs we could sing along with. When Michael Jackson's "Billie Jean" came on, I turned around and sang it to Maddie, snapping my fingers to the beat, making her laugh with funny faces and funny voices and by moonwalking her Bob the Tomato doll across the headrest of my seat.

At the zoo, we set up Maddie's stroller and sandwiched her in between blankets, then weaved our way through the zoo's eighty acres of exhibits. The day was sunny and our stomachs were full and all around us were animals and kids and couples pushing strollers past exhibits with names like the Primate Panorama, Tropical Discovery, and Predator Ridge.

"Hey, April," I said, stopping the stroller and pointing toward an exhibit that looked like it was designed to replicate the grasslands of Ethiopia. "What's that?"

She looked to where I was pointing and started hopping up and down. "Maddie, look! Zebras!"

A couple walking past us looked at April jumping and cracked smiles.

I took a step and bowed, copped an English accent. "Pleasure to be of service, madam. Really. It was nothing. Just a little magic."

April came over, folded her hands together, then reached over and dropped her arms on my shoulders in a hug. "You're an idiot."

"Possibly," I said, locking my arms around her waist. "But I'm the idiot that just got you a zebra."

* * *

After grabbing hot chocolates and warming up inside the primate exhibit, we walked to the car. I buckled Maddie in her car seat, folded the stroller back into the trunk, and jumped in on the passenger side, rubbing my hands together briskly.

"Back to the house?"

"Nope," April said, putting the car into reverse. "I want to take you to this place we love, this restaurant I've been taking Maddie to since she was a baby."

"Sounds good to me. I'm starving." I looked into the back seat where Maddie had already fallen asleep. She looked so peaceful, so comfortable, that it immediately made me want to take a nap too.

We made our way to Eighteenth Avenue and took it west until houses and strip malls gave way to the high rises of downtown Denver. Traffic slowed as the street became more congested and people appeared on the sidewalks, many of them wearing topcoats over suits and carrying briefcases. Looking out the window, I saw buildings that should have given me a sense of home, or at least a sense of familiarity, but I was instead struck by how dissimilar Denver and Chicago were, the buildings here not quite as tall or impressive. And because I associated Colorado with mountains and nature, seeing the sprawling city with its cars and people and man-made infrastructure took me by surprise.

We turned onto Tremont Place, and a few minutes later onto Colfax, where a large building made of some sort of beautiful white stone reminded me of Chicago's Museum of Science and Industry, or maybe the Art Institute.

"April, what is that place?"

"The U.S. Mint."

"It looks like a palace."

"Yeah, because it was modeled after one in Florence."

I laughed. "There's no way you know that."

She punched me in the arm. "Of course I know that. I'm like the second smartest woman alive."

I laughed, spun my head around. Bulged my eyes. "Can you imagine how much money is inside that place?"

"Yeah, I can. I've actually been in there. But they make coins, not dollars. They give tours, and we went on a field trip there when I was in sixth grade or seventh grade."

I looked over at her. "Was it cool?"

"Yeah, I guess. I remember this crazy statistic where they told us the U.S. Mint makes something like 65 to 80 million coins every day."

"Holy shit." I thought about how much money that was. How life changing it would be to break in there and roll even one wheelbarrow full of quarters out.

Soon we had passed the Mint and turned on Colfax, following it out toward the suburb of Lakewood, where I could see Mile High Stadium in the distance. I would have to remember to tell my little brother about it. My mother had mentioned that as soon as I moved, my brother Aaron became a Broncos fan.

Ten minutes later we pulled into a shopping area. Across the parking lot was a giant pink fountain with a distinctly Mexican design and a sign that read "Casa Bonita."

"Mexican food?" I said to April, as we pulled into a parking spot.

"Yeah, but food is only part of the fun."

We went inside, and as we waited for the hostess to show us to our seats, I held Maddie in my arms. She was still tired from her nap, and, with her pacifier in her mouth, she leaned her head on my shoulder. I rested my head against hers. "Aw, you're tired, aren't you, sweetie. Hey, you know what? Your mom says you love this place." She didn't say anything, but I felt her move as she nodded without picking her head off my shoulder.

The hostess grabbed menus and began leading us through the restaurant. We passed a sign welcoming us to the 52,000-square-foot family entertainment center, and as we walked, I looked around, awestruck by how big the place was. It was built the way the zoo exhibits were—with pools of bubbling water, colorful lights, and a thirty-foot waterfall made to look like the cliffs of Acapulco. There were sculptures of Aztec warriors, signs pointing to "Black Bart's Secret Hideout," and a gift shop called "El Mercado."

We made it to our table and I put Maddie in her highchair. We were seated right next to the huge waterfall, fifteen feet above the pool of water it emptied into.

I sat down and opened my menu, looked over at the water gushing. I almost had to yell in order for April to hear me. "This place is nuts!"

She smiled. "I know, right? I love it. Maddie and I have been coming here since she was just a baby. It's been here since the '70s. My dad used to take me."

I saw movement out of the corner of my eye and glanced toward the waterfall. Fifteen feet above me a small man in a black Speedo swimsuit was positioning his toes near the edge of the cliff. He steadied himself, jumped, and executed a perfect one-and-a-half somersault. He disappeared beneath the water.

I looked over at Maddie. "Wow! Did you see that?"

She clapped her hands together and I did the same, looking over at April. She reached up and adjusted one of her long blonde curls, tucked it behind her ear, leaned in so I could kiss her. I smiled, obliged. Behind us, another diver launched backwards into the air, his body graceful in its movement, momentarily suspended above a carefully orchestrated chaos.

* * *

Early one afternoon not long after April and Maddie and I had visited Casa Bonita, I walked into Denny's to start my swing shift. Debra was standing by the register, looking down as she punched buttons on the computer. She looked up as I walked in.

"You got a minute?" she said.

"Yep," I said, immediately self-conscious, instinctively reaching up to touch the tender area around my eyebrow. A few days before, when I was drunk, I'd asked April to pierce it. After holding its sharp tip over the flame of a lighter, she'd used a safety pin. I sat on the toilet, eyes watering, while she used all her might to push the point through the thick skin of my eyebrow. We'd put a round earring in it, but it was red and sore and on the verge of becoming infected.

"Why don't you grab us two cups of coffee and meet me in the booth in the smoking section," she said.

"Okay," I said, walking over to the booth and taking off my jacket. I laid it across the plastic seat and walked over to grab the coffee. When I came back a minute later, Debra had just sat down. I put the mugs on the table and slid one over to her, steam cascading over the brim.

"Thanks." She lifted the cup to her lips. Blew on it before carefully sipping. "So what's the deal with you and April?"

I raised my eyebrows, took a hesitant taste of my coffee. Set the cup back down on the table. "What do you mean?"

She blew on her cup again. "I mean, are you guys together?"

I looked at my mug, spun it so the handle was on the other side. "Yeah, I guess so. I'm staying with her for now. The place I was staying sort of fell through unexpectedly."

Debra nodded, put both of her hands around the cup in front of her, covering the Denny's logo with her palm. "You're probably wondering why this is any of my business." She sighed. "And I guess it's really not . . . but here's the deal. I'm from Texas, which means I always shoot straight."

I suppressed the urge to laugh. Instead, looked out the window behind her to the parking lot and saw her enormous pickup truck parked in its usual spot. Even in mountain country the truck seemed big.

She continued. "So I'm going to shoot straight with you, Tim. Because you seem like you're a good kid." I grabbed a straw wrapper that was lying on the table. Started folding it into a tiny square.

"I've managed this Denny's for a while now. I actually hired April." Debra paused, took another sip of her coffee. "I know that you've worked at other restaurants before, so I'm sure you've figured this out, but in this type of environment you learn a lot about the people that you work with."

I nodded at Debra. Wondered where she was going with her monologue.

"I don't know exactly how to say this." She paused, looked across the restaurant as a family of four came in. Two small children immediately ran toward the pay phones and put their fingers into the coin return, feeling for change. Debra smiled at them, then turned back to me. "I've seen some of the people that April hangs out with and—I don't know—it just seems like they're always in some sort of trouble. I know that April's got a lot going on, being a single mom and all." She looked right at me, waited until I returned her gaze. "Just be careful, Tim. It's easy to get lost out here."

What she was saying sounded a lot like what my uncle had said to me before I left Chicago. Did everyone know something I didn't? It felt like it.

I was partly pissed off at Debra and partly touched that she made the effort to tell me what she thought I needed to know. I held her eye until she smiled, then looked over her shoulder and out the window again. I could see cars pulling into the parking lot, people walking in and out of stores. No matter what time of day it was, there was always someone shopping, always someone buying more stuff.

"Thanks, Debra," I said. "I'll be careful."

The doors to the restaurant opened again and another family walked in. This time the kids stood next to their parents quietly until the hostess grabbed menus and crayons and showed them to their table. I nodded at the new customers, thought about the money I was missing out on by not serving them. "I better clock in and get those guys some drinks."

Debra smiled. "Yep, I guess you better," she said. "Just think about what I said."

I scooted to the outside of the booth and stood up. "I will, Debra. Thanks."

* * *

There are certain images that come back to me as I look back across the expanse of almost two decades. I remember the long hallway that led from the parking behind the building to the door of April's apartment and that my footsteps sounded hollow as I walked down it. I remember the view from the picture window in April's living room, the way Buffalo Mountain seemed close up and far away and not real all at once. I remember dropping my big red duffel bag on April's floor and hearing the thump as everything I'd brought with me from Chicago settled onto the carpeting. And I remember the level of cleanliness present in April's apartment, how foreign it felt. She cleaned the bathroom at least once and sometimes twice a week, and used bleach on everything from the counter to the toilet to the floor. She disinfected the gleaming stainless-steel kitchen sink after every use, and dishes seldom went unwashed for more than a few minutes. She shook powdered deodorizer onto the carpeting every time she vacuumed so the place almost always smelled faintly of flowers. And she made the bed every morning, the sheet pulled tight and the wrinkles carefully smoothed out of the comforter.

Part of me enjoyed the order and cleanliness, but another part was deeply uncomfortable with it. I wasn't always sure I could live up to April's expectations. She sprayed the counters until they shone wet with bleach, the odor pungent in the air, and I wondered why it was so important to her, why she was constantly pushing away the dirt. It was so different from the house that I'd grown up in, which was seldom spotless—"lived in" my mother called it—and I found myself nervous at times, for no other reason than I'd just dirtied a dish.

Living with April was easy at first, a welcomed departure from the madness of Travis's place, where the floors were never mopped and no one emptied the ashtrays, and we fell into a routine fairly quickly. If April and I worked the same shift, we dropped Maddie off at her babysitter's apartment and rode to work in April's stick-shift Mazda, listening to the radio and talking. When April worked and I didn't, I stayed home with Maddie, sitting on the floor with her in front of a plastic kitchen set, baking make-believe casseroles in the tiny oven, playing house. Which seemed like exactly what April and I were doing. But at the same time it also felt more significant than that. More grown up. More mature. More impactful. Sometimes I sat Maddie on my lap in the rocking chair and read to her until her eyes grew heavy, and then brought her to her room, lay her in the crib, and pulled the blanket up to just beneath her chin. I then stood there for a few minutes watching her, amazed all over again at just how big something so small can seem, the same way I used to be with my littlest sister. And after Maddie was deeply asleep, her breathing steady and causing her tiny chest to rise and fall in a reassuring rhythm, I sat in the living room with the TV on, smoking and drinking whatever I could find in the refrigerator, waiting for April to return.

I was doing the only thing I knew how to do—emulating my stepfather. He and my mother had gotten together when she was fresh from her divorce, he just fresh from his own. In the midst of all that relational chaos, amidst all those broken vows and broken homes, they'd somehow made it through. Like my stepfather, I'd started a relationship with a young woman who had a child. And just as he had done, I'd begun to love that child and feel the responsibility that came with that love. But unlike him, I had a full-on love for substances. There was no quit in the way I drank and used, and because I lacked temperance, because the only thing I was really committed to at the time was feeling better—or perhaps not feeling at all—there was no possible way I could be or do what I wanted to be or do.

April and I accepted each other's brokenness. She sat on the couch, after the vodka or schnapps had rounded out the hard angles of reality, while I sat next to her in the rocking chair smoking a joint and blowing clouds of gray smoke toward the ceiling as she told me stories about Maddie's father or her childhood. In one conversation she told me about the visits she had with her biological father right after her parents' divorce. "He was a fighter," she said, pride and excitement thick in her voice. "I remember that we went to a bowling alley together when I was seven or eight, and we passed a guy outside on the sidewalk. He must have said something to my dad, because the next thing I knew, my dad hit him square in the jaw and dropped him." I could see the longing imprinted on her face just above her cheekbones, and I recognized that I wanted her to feel that way about me. I wanted to be the type of man who could drop another man where he stood. The type of man who could fight and protect and demand respect.

In return for listening, April would watch silently as I drank as much as I could—beer after beer, drink after drink—until I could no longer talk in complete sentences. There were times when I would be so drunk that my words would come out as incomprehensible sounds, usually followed by uncontrollable tears that emanated from somewhere deep within. After I was spent from the purge, April would grab me by the elbow, slowly leading me toward the bedroom as I bounced from one wall in the hallway to the next, the pictures of Maddie that hung there vibrating with each collision. April would have her hand on my back, telling me over and over that things would be okay.

In the mornings after these nightly benders, when I would wake in that unfamiliar bed in that unfamiliar place, hung-over and sick and nauseous, the anger I carried with me from home would ripple to the surface. One morning I walked down the hallway into the living room, where April was sitting on the couch smoking, having already been up hours watching television with Maddie. I could see the dismayed look on her face and knew that it was justified, as I tried to recall the night before, to remember what I'd said to her. But it was all misty, lost in the stickiness of withdrawal. I walked to kitchen sink and filled up a plastic cup with cold water, greedily drank, and heard April walk up behind me. There was silence for a minute or two while I tried to steady myself with my hands on the counter, but then she said, "Don't you think you should take it a little easier with the booze once in a while?"

I turned around with eyes slitted in anger. "Don't you think you should cut me a fucking break?"

Then April's eyes narrowed, and her jaw set in anger. And we stood locked in that fighter's stare-down for what seemed like minutes, like hours, one word or second or move away from violence, until one of us turned away.

* * *

After I'd been living with April for a few weeks, I invited Travis over. He got hold of Kevin—he'd moved into a new apartment above a gas station in an area of Silverthorne called Wildernest—and a few nights later, both of them were standing in April's living room, looking around and remarking on how clean the place was. They'd both met April briefly before, but this was the first time we had all hung out. It felt good to see my friends.

April had put Maddie down for the night just before the guys showed up, and once they took their shoes off and opened their beers, we sat around talking and smoking and drinking. April and Travis talked about Summit County, about the snowboarding that he'd done since he'd moved.

"I've been riding pretty much every day since I got here," he said, packing a bowl with weed he brought with him. He looked up at April. "Did you ride a lot growing up?"

April nodded her head. "Yeah, pretty much every chance I could. Summit High School had a snowboard team and I rode with them." She paused. "Well, until the whole school thing fell apart."

Travis lit the bowl, sucked in until his lungs were full and held out the pipe for April to take.

She shook her head. "No thanks, I'm good with that for tonight."

"Here, I'll take it," I said, getting up off the couch and walking over to where Travis was sitting in the rocking chair. I lit it, then held it out to Kevin.

Kevin reached his hand out. "So you guys are both working at Denny's?" he asked.

I looked at April as I blew out the smoke and she answered. "Yep. It's cool, though. They pretty much let us do what we want and we make our own schedules."

"And we can eat whatever we want, too," I added, laughing. "You have to love that part of restaurant work."

April got up from the couch. "Speaking of eating whatever we want, I've got something. Hold on a sec." She turned and walked toward the bathroom. Both Travis and Kevin looked at me. I shrugged. April returned a few seconds later and held her open palm out.

"You guys want some of these?" she said.

We all got up and stood around her, peering at her hand.

"What are they?" Travis asked, eyeing the different colored pills.

"Vicodin. I think Percocet too. Maybe some sort of tranquilizer or something." She laughed, softly. "Basically, a bunch of pills that will numb you out."

I could feel my chest tighten and stomach start to dance, the same feeling I used to get before I tried a new trick while skating or ditched a class in high school. I looked at the pills—scared and curious. I'd never taken pills before but I definitely wanted to be numb. I *always* wanted to be numb. I could already feel the alcohol and weed in my system, could feel myself slipping into the place I wanted to be. Maybe pills would get me there faster. Keep me there longer.

"So you don't know exactly what they are?" I asked.

April looked at me, raised her eyebrows. "Does it matter? I told you—they'll numb you out." She grabbed two pills with the fingers of her other hand and popped them into her mouth.

Swallowed them without taking anything to drink. "You want them or not?"

I reach out and grabbed a couple, and then watched as Travis and Kevin did the same. "Fuck it," I said, tossing them into my mouth and walking over to grab my beer.

Travis and Kevin both laughed, but their laughs seemed uneasy and forced, more nervous than they were genuine. They each took two pills from April's palm, tossed them into their mouths, and then we waited, laughing and smoking, watching each other, drinking and coughing, anticipating. And then time seemed to compress until everything was operating in slow motion, the urgency in our conversation gone. We sat on the couch or on the floor, our limbs feeling heavy, rubbery, weighted down by a gravity much stronger than anything we'd ever felt before. I stared at the lampshade, could see a cottony halo of light had formed around it. I stared at April, and could feel affection hit me like caffeine from the first cup of coffee in the morning. I turned my head and stared at Travis, then at Kevin, and felt the security of home hug me with invisible arms while the opiates in the pills came cresting in waves, washing over each of us like warm water in the shower.

* * *

There was a certain point at Denny's, when night had fallen and the restaurant had emptied of customers, that everything in the building would quiet. I noticed it nearly every time I worked past 10 p.m. and especially when the last customer had left, a perceptible shift in the way the building felt. Without people and conversations, when the music had been turned down, I could hear the noises that made up the world I spent so much of my time in. The steady hum of electricity that came from the walk-in coolers and the occasional rattle that came from the cooks rehanging the mesh fryer basket in the kitchen. The rumble that came from the ice machine as it dumped hundreds of tiny cubes onto hundreds more. The sound of water being pulled through the thin copper pipes that sprouted from the wall and fed the industrial coffee maker. The flattop grills furiously hissing and spitting every time the line cook doused them with water. The gravelly scrub of the porous black pumice stone.

Denny's was open twenty-four hours, and there were three shifts every day—morning, swing, and graveyard. The morning shift was made up of servers that were all quite a bit older than I was, mostly women in their forties and fifties. For a few of them it was a second job, or a way to supplement their husbands' income when construction work slowed for the winter or they'd been laid off, but for most of them, career waitresses, it was their main source of income.

The shift April and I worked most of the time, the swing shift, was a much younger group of servers—mostly people in their late teens and early twenties. The shifts typically started between two and four in the afternoon, which gave ample time to ski or snowboard or sleep off the last night's hangover, and the tips were usually decent, maybe four or five bucks a table. Most nights we each made seventy or eighty dollars, sometimes ninety—enough to pay for a phone bill and a couple of tanks of gas, or maybe the bulk of a car insurance payment.

There was another couple that April and I worked with quite a bit that we started talking to—Darren and Sarah. Darren was in his early thirties and built like a football player who hadn't seen a workout since the day he quit playing. He had broad shoulders that rounded out his wide, six-foot-three frame and brown hair that was perpetually mussed, and not in a stylish way. He and Sarah were from somewhere in rural Ohio, and they had moved to Summit County about a year before I had. When I asked what had brought him to Colorado, we were standing near the coffee maker. Instead of answering, he just shrugged his shoulders, poured steaming coffee into the two mugs he'd set on the counter, and walked away.

Darren was so socially awkward that it was uncomfortable to

watch him wait on customers. When he took their orders, he always looked scared or nervous, his forehead glossy, his hand nervously fingering the pen in his apron pocket.

Sarah, on the other hand, was the opposite. Even at seven months pregnant, she was energetic and bouncy, rounding corners in her nonslip high-tops with a smile that never seemed to vanish. Her straight brown hair was always pulled into a ponytail, and her apron stretched tight over her large baby bump, eliciting sympathy, questions, and admiration with each table she served.

As we got ready for work one afternoon, I asked April what she thought of them. "Darren and Sarah?" she replied, kneeling down to tie her shoes. "I don't know. Sarah's cool, but Darren seems a bit off to me. I think he's a meth head."

I wondered how April would even know what a meth head looked like. I'd come to realize that April's life experience—at least in terms of what she'd been through and seen—far outweighed mine. Friends of hers were on trial for burglary and assault, and others were in gangs. Some friends she'd had to testify against to keep from being implicated in crimes. She'd started fights and she'd ended them. Once, outside a house party, she'd beaten a girl until the girl had begged her, crying and bloody and with bits of asphalt sticking to her face, to stop.

There was a part of me that admired her experience, her resilience, her toughness, the way she managed to get through some seemingly impossible circumstances, but there was also a part of me that was scared of it. Although I was with April and part of her world, I wasn't really sure that I understood it—or even belonged there.

One night after the restaurant had quieted down and most of the customers had gone home, I was busy bussing one of the last dirty tables in the smoking section. I could hear the lone cook cleaning the grill in the back, and by the register, the hostess on duty looked like she was running sales reports.

It was a weeknight and I was tired from my shift, tired from not sleeping as much as I needed to. Overnight, I'd become a stepfather of sorts and I was still acclimating to what that meant. Maddie would sometimes wake up in the middle of the night and crawl into bed with April and me, making it harder for us to sleep, and then she'd wake up early, smiling her adorable smile, waiting for one of us to get up and make her breakfast or play.

I walked over to a booth against the one windowless wall in the restaurant and began filling a brown bus tub with dirty dishes. I grabbed the small green rag I'd brought with me, began wiping down the table with industrial cleaning solution. I realized that though we had worked the same shift that night, I hadn't seen April for a while. We'd been busier than usual, so we hadn't talked as much as we normally did. I stopped wiping and walked over to the nonsmoking section to look for her. When I didn't see her, I walked back around the corner to the door that led to the rear of the restaurant by the stockroom and walk-in coolers.

I pushed the door open, took a sharp left, and walked past Debra's dark, empty office to the break room. As soon as I walked to the doorway, I saw that April was in the room, seated diagonal in a chair, so I could see her both her back and profile. A cigarette was burning in an ashtray on the far side of her, a thin line of smoke corkscrewing toward the ceiling. April was leaned over the counter, and it looked as if she was hunched over a book or working on a crossword puzzle, but then she snapped her head back, the curls in her blonde hair fanning like a peacock's tail feathers, then slapping silently against her back. She reached her hand to her nose and touched her nostrils with her thumb and forefinger, her eyes closed so hard that the tops of her cheeks were pressing into the bottoms of her eyelids. I looked on the counter in front of her, saw that the cellophane wrapper of her cigarette box was sitting there, containing what looked to be small rocks. Next to the wrapper was a Bic pen that had been emptied of its ink tube and cut in half.

April's eyes opened and for the first time she noticed me standing in the doorway. I wanted to know what she was doing, to ask her what was happening, but I couldn't look away from her eyes. They were still green, still hers, still the eyes I knew, but they were somehow darker now, wilder, eyes like a horse right before it bucks.

"What is that?" I asked, too stunned to say anything else. It looked like it might be cocaine, but I wasn't sure.

April smiled dryly. Looked at the plastic wrapper in front of her. "You don't want to know."

"I wouldn't have asked you if I didn't want to know." I still couldn't move. Stood in the doorway like a sentinel. I spoke slowly. "April, what the hell is that?"

April reached over and grabbed her burning cigarette. Put it to her lips and inhaled. Looked right at me as she blew the smoke out. "Crystal."

I could feel my stomach and throat wrench at the exact same moments, the same thing that happened each time I knew I was going to be in a fight. I fought the urge to swallow. Tried to stand my ground and not look as scared as I felt. "Meth? You mean crystal meth?" I wasn't sure that I'd ever even said those two words out loud before.

The tone in April's voice vacillated between annoyed and antagonistic. "Yep. That's the one." I then noticed that April had her ID lying on the counter. She picked it up with one hand, dumped the contents of the cellophane onto the counter. I could hear the rocks hit the Formica, bouncing like Tic Tacs on a table. I could hear everything around me as she covered the chemical rocks with the flat part of her ID and smashed them. The rocks cracked, the sound of twigs snapping. She rubbed the ID back and forth quickly, her eyes focused intently on what she was doing. When she lifted the ID, there was a whitish-colored powder stuck to the countertop. She used the license as a scraper and pushed the powder into a pile, then began chopping it with the thin edge of the ID, like she was dicing vegetables. She then split the powder into two lines, both about an inch long. She looked up at me. Didn't smile, just stared, her eyes either warning me to leave or inviting me to join.

I looked at the floor and my voice trembled when I spoke. "April, what the hell? You're doing crystal meth in the break room?" I was so confused and didn't know what to say or how to react. I dug the pack of cigarettes out of my pocket. "Have you done this shit before?"

"Tim, relax. It's not that big of a deal." She cocked her head and narrowed her eyes. "Don't get all worked up about it."

I shook my head and pulled a cigarette out of the box. Lit it. Tasted the smoke on my tongue. Felt the nicotine hit my system. When I took the cigarette from my lips, I could see that my hand was shaking.

I opened my mouth to yell at her, to tell her how stupid she was, but the words that came out surprised me. "If you do it, I do it."

She turned and looked at me, deadpan. "You don't want to do this."

I took a drag, blew my smoke back at her. She was right, I didn't want to do it, but I also didn't *not* want to do it. I wanted to be her equal, to be on the same level she was. To feel whatever it was that she was feeling. To not feel whatever it was she was not feeling. I wanted to matter to her, to be seen, to be taken seriously.

"Fuck it," I said. "If you're going to do it, then I'm going to do it."

April shook her head, looked at the powder. Sighed. "Fine. Suit yourself." She took the pen from the counter and held it up to me. "Do your thing then."

Was this my thing? Was this what I did now? Did I like to self-destruct? Like throwing a beer bottle against a brick wall, there was so much satisfaction in the explosion. So much familiarity in making the wrong choice.

Ever since the moment I walked in and saw April, I was aware that my heart was beating more quickly, but I could now feel the entire process as if it was happening in distinct stages: the rapid pulse of my heart, the burst of oxygenated blood circulating outward, the lifting of the skin pulled over the radial artery in my wrist. I reached my hand out and took the pen from April's fingers, felt the cold plastic against my sweaty palm. April got up from the chair, and I took her place.

"Just cover your one nostril and use the pen to snort it," April said. "You've done coke before, right? Same idea. But do it fast, so it won't burn as much."

My heart thumped, and I could hear it in my ear canal, a muffled kick drum beating against my brain. I felt the pull that I always felt, the pull toward danger, toward the unknown. I felt fear and excitement and yearning as they snowballed together, gaining momentum, driving my head lower as I prepared to do a thing I never thought I'd do. And then my finger had covered my nostril, and my lungs had pulled the powder into my airway in a violent snort, my shoulders shaking as I did, the line that once existed on the countertop now seeping into my nasal passages. And then there was a searing burn inside my head, a chemical-induced ice-cream headache that screamed at my nervous system. And then the pain was subsiding, and I was filling up with something that I didn't know existed but had somehow been searching for my entire life. In one warm sensation that washed over every part of me—from the twitching muscle fibers in my calves to the tingle in my eyelids—I could feel affirmation, awareness, excitement, affection, adrenaline, influence.

I looked at April through eyes that had begun to water from the burn. In that moment, every problem I'd ever had in my life seemed solvable.

"We need to get more of this," I said.

April nodded. In the distance an exhaust fan in the kitchen raged, blowing smoke and grease and dust high into the pristine air of the Colorado night.

* * *

Perhaps it was the drugs that fueled us. Perhaps it was youth. Or damage. Or pain. Whatever it was, though, it informed every aspect of our bond. It was an urgency, an intensity, a desperation that increased the tempo of our lives and caused everything to ignite and throttle forward.

I've often looked back at how quickly April and I moved in together, at how hurried we were to cement ourselves into a life with one another, and wondered why. Was it the convenience, the ease of not having to find my own place to live, or was it seductive because of the instant family it gave me? Or was it that meeting April and Maddie simply gave me a way of identifying myself that I hadn't had before? With them I was offered a new role to fill—one where I could be a provider, which seems delusional to me now, seeing as how I could hardly provide for myself, let alone someone else. Or was it simply because we were both so lost at the time, and so angry, and so intent on using drugs and love to make ourselves feel better that it felt like the only choice we could make?

April and I were only two months into our relationship, but at times we acted and fought like we'd been together for years and were just entering into the rough patch that so many long-term relationships go through. Our fights would escalate quickly and go from a simple disagreement about who was working what shift at Denny's to all-out verbal sparring, where phrases like, "why don't you cry about your daddy again, Tim" or "why don't you date another loser, April" would fall from our lips like breadcrumbs.

We yelled and cried and threw shoes or the phone or whatever happened to be within reach, and then, when we'd both expelled whatever it was inside of us, controlling us, we ended up on the couch together, cigarettes burning in the muddy silence that exists after a fight, apologizing and vowing never to do it again. We'll be better, we said. More patient, we said. And then, at least for a while, we would be.

Since I was already over a thousand miles away from my family and friends, isolating myself with April was easy—all I had to do was not pick up the phone, not call my parents, not tell them what I was up to. It was also just as easy to fall into April's routine, to become acquainted with her struggles as a single mom—appointments at the child support office, getting the WIC program checks from the mail, wellness visits for Maddie. In some ways it gave me purpose, forced me to live for someone else other than myself. In other ways, it just gave me a convenient list of excuses that helped me push aside the fact that my court date was coming, and I had no foreseeable way of getting back to Chicago.

* * *

Having grown up in Summit County, April knew plenty of people, but of the few of them I'd met, there were only a couple that seemed like more than just acquaintances or people she partied with. She had a friend named Lauren, who sometimes showed up at Denny's to sit in a booth and talk, and who sometimes babysat Maddie. There were two guys named Spanky and Show Biz who showed up from time to time, roughneck gangster types whom I was equal parts enamored of and scared of. And there was her friend Austin, a cowboy-like guy she went to high school with that we ran into at the town rodeo on our way to watch the mutton-busting event, the three of us traipsing through the mud with sugarcoated elephant ears in our hands, Maddie giggling from atop my shoulders. April had smiled widely and yelled his name, running over to give him a lingering hug. I watched the interaction from a distance, trying to stub out the jealousy I instantly felt.

Austin walked up and introduced himself with a firm handshake, and I immediately felt self-conscious. "What's up, man?" he said to me before reaching up and tickling Maddie's side. "Nothing, man," I said back to him, looking at his dirty Wrangler jeans and thick leather belt. The buckle on his waist was big and silver.

April invited Austin to come over to the house, and a few nights later we were sitting around the living room drinking beer and passing around a small metal bowl packed with weed. April and

Austin were catching up, telling stories about when they were younger, and as I sat there rocking in the wooden chair, watching their interaction, I couldn't shake the feeling that there had been more to their relationship than what they initially led me to believe.

"So you guys have known each other for a while, huh?" I said to Austin while he stood near the window, looking out toward the City Market grocery store down the hill.

Austin turned around. Glanced at April who had just lit the bowl, the small flame bending over the edge and causing the weed to crackle. "Yeah, it's been awhile, right April?"

April nodded, blew the smoke out in front of her. "I've known Austin and his family forever." She looked at Austin and smiled. "Hey, do you remember that time when I got bucked off that horse at your parents' place?"

Austin smiled. "Yeah, that was pretty funny. You were in some serious pain if I remember correctly. Which sort of made it even funnier."

April laughed. "You're such an asshole."

There was an easiness in the way Austin and April addressed one another, a casual pace that kept their conversation rolling along. I started to feel some of what I'd felt in the break room at Denny's the day I caught April snorting lines of meth—left out. She knew I was there, listening to her and Austin talk, but it didn't seem to matter. I felt temporary and expendable.

As the night continued, Maddie sleeping in her room while Austin, April, and I drank and smoked in the living room, the conversation turned to April's past, to things she wished she could change.

"After I had Maddie and it was clear that her dad was out of the picture for good, I started dating this one guy," April said. She was sitting on the couch in her usual position, her legs underneath her and her left hand waving a cigarette while she talked. "He was nice enough in the beginning, but, as usual, I always pick the losers." She shook her head. "He smoked crack."

I lifted my eyes at April and she looked away quickly. Austin was on the floor leaning back against the wooden shelving unit that held the television. He had an ashtray next to him, butts fanned out in all directions.

"I stayed with him way too long—six or seven months or something—I don't know why, maybe because he was really good with Maddie." She paused, stirred the ice in her big plastic cup with her straw. "But he was really into crack, and he would be geeked out of his mind half the time."

I heard the flick of a lighter and looked over as Austin took a drag of his cigarette and blew out the smoke as he spoke. "Geez, April. You really do know how to pick them."

She looked down at her drink. "Yeah, isn't that the truth." She stopped talking and I looked at her, could see that she was on the verge of saying something, but having trouble vocalizing it.

"Hey," I said. "You okay?" It was out of character for April not to be able to say whatever was on her mind. There was usually so much pride mixed in with her stories, even when they were filled with resentment and sadness. "Whatever it is, April, you can tell us. Everything's okay now. We're here for you. It's just us." I glanced over at Austin.

April blinked moisture from her eye. Put the straw from her drink to her lips and took a long pull, swallowed. "I knew our relationship was basically a dead end, but then . . ." She paused again. "But then I realized my period was late. I got a pregnancy test and took it. It was positive."

I thought about what April was saying. Did the math in my head. She already had Maddie and she wasn't even two yet, not until August. That meant that in the eighteen or so months since Maddie was born April had become pregnant again.

"So what happened?" I said.

April looked at me, but her face was blank. "I told him that I was pregnant and that I wasn't having a baby with a crack addict.

He wanted me to have it, said he'd change and quit the drugs. But I knew he wouldn't." April's voice cracked and suddenly she was crying, her emotions lubricated by the alcohol and weed. "So I left him and had an abortion and I can't stop thinking about it. My baby would be almost one by now."

I could feel the anger inside warming me, as if I'd just taken a shot of cinnamon schnapps. I could see how genuine April's pain was. I wanted to do something to comfort her, to make her feel better. To make myself feel better by defending her. I wanted to show her that I was different than that guy, that she hadn't picked another loser.

"Do you know where that motherfucker lives?" I asked, my words punctuated with bravado from the liquor. Austin looked at me, nodded his approval.

"Yeah, he lives here in Summit. Not too far." She wiped her eyes. Lit a cigarette.

I looked at Austin. "What do you think?"

Austin stabbed his cigarette in the ashtray. "Fuck it. Let's go over there."

I nodded and stood up. "I was thinking the same thing."

* * *

April had pulled Maddie's coat on and put her in her car seat. Austin sat in the back with her and I was in the passenger seat, my heart pounding, the window rolled halfway down as I smoked a cigarette. The cherry on the end glowed orange with each pull and the gray Mazda weaved around corners, dirty snow covering the curbs on both sides of the road.

Austin and I didn't have a plan for what we would do when we got there, but it didn't matter because the anger I felt stood balled up just behind the walls of my stomach and didn't demand one. I simply wanted to physically assert myself, to impose my will and make someone else feel the pain that April felt. The pain that I felt.

I was sick of fathers being fuckups, sick and tired of fathers making decisions that affected mothers—and their kids.

"I'll pull up in the complex next to his and park there to wait for you guys," April said. "Make it quick, though. It won't take the cops long to get over here if someone calls them."

I took one last drag off my smoke and threw it out the window, a firework shower exploding in the air before it flew out of sight. April pulled into the parking lot, our heads bouncing in unison as she rolled over a bump. She turned into a parking spot, put the car in park, and shut off her lights. I turned around, saw Maddie sleeping. Looked at Austin. "You ready?"

"Yep," he said.

I turned to April. "Stay here. Keep the car on. We won't be long."

I opened the door into the cold and for a brief moment, the interior light of the car lit up the rear seat, a cone of yellow exposing the animal cracker crumbs ground into the fabric by Maddie's car seat.

Austin and I crossed the parking lot together in silence, our breath coming out in clouds in front of us. We reached the glass door that led to the building's small foyer. On the wall were four rows of small, metal mailboxes with unit numbers on them. I recognized April's ex-boyfriend's name.

I pointed. "That's him, right? 3D?"

"Yeah," Austin said. "I think so."

I used the heel of my hand and hit all the call buttons at one time. Seconds later, a man's scratchy voice came across the intercom. "Who's there?"

Neither Austin nor I said anything, and the crackle cut off as the man on the other end must have let off the button. Suddenly, the door buzzed and I reached out and grabbed the aluminum handle.

"Let's go," I said to Austin, and then we were taking the stairs up two by two until we reached the top floor, heaving, our blood pumping through the veins in our arms and legs and temples. And then I was banging on the door and yelling for someone to open it. *"Open the door, motherfucker! Come get what's coming to you!"* I could feel myself giving into the rage, the rage I carried from all the way back in Chicago, from Oak Lawn, not caring what happened next or who was listening or even where I ended up that night. Because all that mattered was tapping that rage until it caught fire, until it burned, until it was gone. I was kicking the door, black scuff marks left by my sneakers that looked like exclamation points, my voice rising, getting louder, and I was screaming and pounding, and the door was groaning, the space next to the doorjamb widening each time I kicked it, and it seemed that it might break under the pressure. And then I felt someone's hand on my shoulder, and I turned, and it was Austin. He was saying something to me, his mouth opening and closing but I couldn't hear him, could only hear myself, my breathing fast and hard and violent. His eyes were wide and urgent, and then the audio kicked back on, and he was telling me we had to go. "Come *on*," he said, his grip digging into my traps. "We've got to go *right fucking now.*"

He took the stairs down the same way, two by two, with me behind him until we burst through the glass door into the silence of the Colorado night. We ran across the parking lot to where April was waiting. Her window was open and she was smoking, watching us with wide eyes as we ran to her.

"Where's his car?" I asked, the clouds from my breath dragon-like, streaming tubes from my nostrils.

"It's that one," she said, pointing to a Subaru Outback parked about eighty yards away. I ran toward the car, glancing at the door to the building as I crossed the parking lot again. Empty. I reached the car and looked inside—fast food wrappers and a snowbrush, a few quarts of motor oil lying on the floor behind the passenger seat. I looked around one more time, saw a light flick on in one of the apartments. Waited until it flicked off and ran to the front of the car and searched the snow-covered weeds. Smelled the sagebrush. Felt the cold air on my face. Found what

I looking for. I glanced back toward April, could barely make out her silhouette in the car, an orange dot from her cigarette moving up and down, glowing bright and fading. I stood next to the window, briefly saw my reflection in the glass, and violently swung the rock I'd found down and into the rear seat window. The glass shattered, and for a moment the shards of glass reflected the parking lot lights as they rained down all around me and it seemed as if it was snowing. I reached in through the broken window and grabbed two quarts of motor oil. Screwed off the caps. Began flinging the oil into the car's interior like a Jackson Pollack painting. The oil splattered against the seats and the windows, began dripping down the windshield and pooling onto the dash. When the oil was gone, I ran across the asphalt, threw the plastic containers into a pair of bushes, and jumped into April's car slamming the door behind me.

"Let's go," I said, and April put the car in reverse. I turned my head and torso around to look at Austin in the back seat. But instead of Austin, I saw Maddie, her brown eyes glinting marble-like in the light, wide-awake and staring.

* * *

It was the steady sound of banging that woke us all the next morning—a hard rapping against the door to April's apartment that immediately started my heart racing. April, Austin, and I had driven home, finished the beer in the house while recounting the night excitedly, and then passed out. Austin and I had slept on the floor, and April had fallen asleep stretched out across the couch. When the officers arrived, Maddie was still sleeping in her bedroom.

April opened the door and tried to play it cool, but the two uniformed Dillon Police officers weren't having it. "April Murphy? We got a complaint last night from someone you used to date. He says that you and some other individuals went over to his apartment, tried to gain access, and threatened him."

"We didn't go anywhere," April said. "We've just been hanging out and watching movies."

"Be that as it may, Ms. Murphy, we still need to talk about it with your guests. The officer looked at Austin and me. "Put your shoes on, gentlemen. You're coming to the station with us, so we can discuss this matter further."

* * *

Austin and I were separated into different squad cars when we reached the parking lot of April's apartment, but from where I was sitting with my hands handcuffed and folded behind my back, leaning against the sedan's door to alleviate the pressure of the metal digging into my wrists, I could see the outline of his head in the car in front of us.

Since I didn't know him all that well, I wasn't sure what he would say to the police once we got to the station. I could only hope that he would keep his mouth shut when they started asking questions. But I knew that people changed under pressure. Everyone has a code of silence after they watch a mobster movie. In real life, it's always a crapshoot.

I was relatively sure that we could walk out without charges, since it seemed the only evidence against us was that April's exboyfriend had called and identified us, which was hearsay, but it was difficult to say until the police laid out their case and started in with their questions. It was always the questions that were the most dangerous, those carefully chosen inquiries—one building upon the other.

During the arrests in Chicago, I learned the hard way that police interrogators could be extremely effective when working to build their case. The night Tupac had died, I'd been caught with a can of Icehouse beer in my cup holder and a bowl packed with weed in my car's ashtray, so the evidence was indisputable, but the officer who had arrested me was thorough enough to ask enough of the right questions to ensure the charges stuck. Before I'd even sobered up, I'd admitted to him that I'd been at a party, drinking and smoking weed, and was driving to see a girl. By the time I got to court, the case against me was so solid that the best I could hope for was a generous plea agreement.

We pulled up to the police station and the officer got out and opened the door. "Let's go," he said, and he guided me through a doorway, past the booking desk, past a couple of officers working at computers, and down a short hallway that led to another door. The officer took a key ring off his belt. "Turn around," he said.

I did as I was told and felt the cuffs on my wrists loosen and then come off completely. "Here," he said, using another key to open the door we were standing in front of. "Go in and have a seat."

I walked into the room, heard the door click behind me as the officer left, and sat down on a small metal chair beside a table. The room's walls were painted the typical industrial yellow, and the only thing on them was a clock whose second hand ticked loudly. There were no windows, and the only light came from the long fluorescent bulbs humming above me.

I leaned forward in the chair and put my head in my hands, felt its heaviness as my palms cradled my forehead. I rubbed my eyes with my fingers and then ran them through my long hair, feeling the grease and sweat left behind from the night before. I hadn't even brushed my teeth yet, let alone taken a shower, and my mouth tasted sour from cigarettes and alcohol. I could smell the faint odor of motor oil on my fingertips.

I thought back to the night before, to the rage I felt as I pounded on the door and yelled through gritted teeth, wanting so badly to hurt someone, to transfer the anger I was feeling onto someone else's face. I wondered what would have happened if April's ex had opened the door and saw us standing there. Growing up, during the few fights I'd been in, whenever it was time to throw a punch, for my fist to connect with someone's cheekbone in defense of myself or my pride, it always felt that my arm was weighed down by something insufferably heavy, somehow permanently stuck to my side. If someone had opened the door, would I have finally thrown a punch that landed? Would I have pressed through my fear and let my anger guide my hands? Or would I have stood frozen, still unable to fight?

I shook my head, tried to clear my mind so I could think. Took a deep breath and heard the second hand on the clock ticking away, the sound of time wasting. Was that what I was doing? Wasting time? Was that what I'd been doing the whole time I'd been in Colorado? The whole time I'd been out of high school?

Outside the door, I heard the shuffle of papers as someone walked past. I leaned back in the chair and folded my arms across my abdomen, tucked my head to my chest as I thought about what my parents would think of me right then, in that moment. I could see the sadness in my mother's face, the way my stepfather would shake his head slowly as he broke eye contact with me and looked at the floor. I was disgusted with myself for continually disappointing them. Regardless of what happened when the officer came back in to talk to me, even if it meant going to jail, calling them was out of the question.

The door opened and in came the same officer I rode over with. He took the chair on the other side of the table. Set a manila file folder down in front of him. Laid his hand on it.

"So you want to tell me what you really did last night?" he asked.

I remembered the way the oil glistened on the back seat of the car, the slick substance shining against the fabric. "I told you already, I stayed at April's."

"No you didn't. You went over to April's ex-boyfriend's house and banged on his door, yelling and causing a commotion. Then, when he wouldn't come out, you vandalized his car."

I shook my head. "You got the wrong guy, sir. I don't know what you're talking about."

The officer sighed. "Listen, man. I get it. You're defending your woman and all that, right? She got you all worked up and you went over there to take care of business, right?"

I sat still. Continued to look at him but didn't say anything. Studied the gold badge pinned above his left breast pocket.

"Just make this easy on yourself. Tell me what happened, and I'll see what I can do to help you. It was you guys, right? You and that guy Austin?"

"I'm telling you, sir," I said, my right foot bouncing slightly under the table. "It wasn't us. I don't know where you're getting your information from, but that's the truth."

The officer looked at me, slowly started shaking his head. "So that's your answer? You're saying that you were at April's all night long?"

I nodded.

The officer grabbed the folder off the table and opened it. Pulled out a piece of paper that had a signature at the bottom. "That's funny," he said, "because your buddy in the other room wrote this nice little note for us that says something completely different."

I stared at the paper. Stopped bouncing my knee when I realized what it was—a confession.

"You better think about who you're going to call," he said, "because you're being charged with misdemeanor counts of criminal mischief and harassment. If you can't post bail right now, we'll take you to jail." He stood up. "Seems like a pretty stupid thing to go to jail for, Mr. Hillegonds. Maybe you should rethink your relationship." He nodded in the general direction of the hallway. "And your friends."

The officer approached the door and opened it. Walked through it and disappeared around the corner. I watched as the door closed slowly, the sound of compressed air being released from the mechanism that kept the door from slamming, until the lock engaged, a final click before the room fell silent.

* * *

I called April from the station, and a few hours after I'd been arrested and charged, I was riding back to the apartment in the passenger seat of her Mazda. Austin had called someone else to pick him up, and I hadn't had the chance to ask him what had happened or why he turned me in, but I assumed that he'd received lesser charges since he'd agreed to give them the information they wanted. "Austin is such a pussy," April had said when I got in the car with her. I nodded my head in agreement, but part of me was just upset I hadn't made the deal first.

* * *

The charges against me were misdemeanors—and relatively minor ones at that—so it wasn't that I was in danger of spending a lot of time in jail, but that the charges were beginning to pile up on me. I still hadn't resolved the cases I had in Chicago and now I was in this new place, this place that was supposed to be a fresh start, a turning point, and again making mistakes that ended up with court dates.

I was due in court on the new charge sometime in April, and my Chicago court date was bearing down on me quickly. It was coming up at the end of February, less than a week away, and there was a constant feeling of dread that kept both April and me looking for any escape we could find. We made sure that Maddie had what she needed—toys and food and diapers and love—but when we put her down for the night, April and I would drink beer or mix vodka with Kool-Aid, and smoke weed or snort crystal meth. When we were high on speed, the meth coursing through our veins like gasoline through a fuel pump, the world around us seemed doable. I would go back to Chicago to explain my situation to the judge and he'd understand, maybe let me off the hook with nothing more than a fine. We'd end up okay, we thought. We'd get through it, we thought.

But then we would run out of money and drugs and liquor, and life would feel insurmountable again, and we realized that we were really just two kids with jobs waiting tables at one of the least impressive diners in America. We felt the weight of our responsibilities—the way we needed to provide for Maddie no matter what happened to us, no matter how dire our circumstances seemed, and then we were on edge, bickering with each other over dishes and television programs. The bickering escalated quickly, as if it were a chemical reaction, and then we were at each other's throats, our fists balled at our sides and our faces twisted into scowls as we thought of the most horrible things we could say. Secrets that had been told in confidence were picked up and hurled back like rocks at a window until eventually, after we'd fought long enough that the rage inside of us was temporarily dispelled, the fight was over, and we scrambled to pick up the pieces.

SEVEN

The distance between Chicago and Silverthorne, between home and away, between the place I came from and the place I went to, was just over a thousand miles. In the earliest days of my move, it was a distance I hardly noticed, a gulf that was easily swallowed up by a two-and-a-half-hour flight and the glittery promise of a new beginning. But the emotional pull of home, an intense gravity that grew stronger the longer I stayed away, became something I couldn't ignore. I lay awake in bed next to April while she slept, staring at the shadows cast on an unfamiliar ceiling, wishing I could turn my head and look out into my parents' backyard, hear the metallic groan of a freight train, the familiar creak of the old oak floors straining under the weight of my stepfather.

I'd wanted nothing more than to leave home, to leave Chicago and all that it represented to me—failure, stagnation, a steep descent into mediocrity—but once I landed in that new place and felt the feral bite in that mountain air, the pinpricks of isolation that came with my newly realized independence, I missed home dearly, and that made me feel like a fraud. I made such a spectacle of leaving— the angry lashing out, the one-way plane ticket, the nonchalance I exuded about leaving without resolving my criminal charges. I knew I could never admit, not to April or my parents or anyone else, that I missed home, even though I did. It seemed impossible and ridiculous to be both rebellious and sentimental.

Maybe that's what April sensed two days before I was scheduled to appear in court. I was in the bedroom getting ready for my shift, halfway done buttoning my white shirt, when she smiled and said, "Pack your bags, Tim. We're heading to Chicago so you can make that court date."

April was good like that sometimes, good at anticipation—a trait I attributed to her penchant for spontaneity and her motherly intuition. And so a few hours later, after I called Debra at Denny's and got permission for the time off, after I packed a bag and we stopped for gas and snacks, April and Maddie and I were headed east on I-70, the windows cracked and the music turned loud, on our way to visit Chicago.

As we sped down the highway with April behind the wheel, Maddie fidgeted in her car seat in the back, fussing or crying or staring out the window, eating bite-sized goldfish crackers and fruit snacks, finally falling asleep with a lap full of crumbs. Outside the Mazda's windows the landscape of Middle America—mostly truck stops and cornfields, Cracker Barrel restaurants, an endless parade of orange construction drums—whirred by us in the night. The stars in the distance, which seemed just out of reach, flashed yellow in the blue-black sky.

In the two months we'd known each other, I told April a lot about Chicago—usually when the liquor or drugs had mollified me and I felt the void the absence of home left inside me. I wanted her to feel Chicago in the same way I did, to feel its pull. I wanted to transfer the reverence I had for the city on to her. But of course I couldn't, because seldom do people understand the importance of something until they experience it for themselves. And even then, it's oftentimes a quickly passing proposition.

April and I drove straight through the night, stopping only for gas and coffee, across Nebraska and Iowa and Illinois, the tires beneath the Mazda vibrating across the endless ripples in the road. I called my parents' house from a gas station somewhere off I-80, and my mother answered. "Hey," I said, while watching April pump gas.

"I'm on my way home for a few days. I'm going to stop by so you can meet April and Maddie." I'd told my mother we were dating, but I hadn't shared much about what had been going on since I'd moved. "Okay," she said quietly.

When we arrived at my parents' house on Central Avenue, I felt I'd changed far more than two months should have allowed, and I thought they would see that, and be proud. I'd left their house with no identity and no purpose, but I arrived home a surrogate stepfather, a man responsible for someone other than himself.

When April was busy with Maddie in the living room, I cornered my mother in the kitchen and asked if we could stay with them for a night, just until my court appearance the following day. She looked at the floor, her disapproval of me palpable. "Let me talk to your father," she said, but I knew the answer would be "no." When she came back to me some time later, it played out exactly as I had thought. "I'm sorry, Tim," she said, her eyes filled with worry, her words filled with judgment. "But you hardly know this girl and her baby. We're not comfortable letting you stay here because we just don't approve of this whole arrangement."

I turned to walk away, frustrated, but then turned back. "Whatever, Ma, that figures. I knew you were going to say no, anyway. You've never accepted me for who I am." I knew it wasn't true, but I couldn't help but fall into the familiar pattern of lashing out and fighting that always occurred under their roof.

Back in the living room, the four of us sat on couches and chairs, all uncomfortable and aware of just how awkward the situation was, watching Maddie, beautiful, innocent Maddie as she sat on the floor and played, her brown eyes so dark they sometimes seemed black. She picked up her doll and held it up by its arm. Walked it over to me. "Baby," she said, and I smiled, nodded. Took the baby from her tiny hand. "Yeah," I said, "baby," and placed the doll in the crook of my arm and rocked it back and forth while she watched.

* * *

We left my parents after forced hugs and smiles and headed into the city to find a hotel. We drove north on Central Avenue, and I pointed places out to April as we passed them: the houses of my childhood friends; the lawns I mowed as a kid; the spot where my little brother, Aaron, had been hit by a car and almost killed, his teeth impacted into his skull with such force he needed surgery to have them removed.

We drove east on Ninety-Fifth Street, past Stanley's tailor shop and BJ McMahon's bar, past the library my mother had worked at and Palermo's Pizzeria, past the bank my high school girlfriend's father had owned, until we hit Cicero Avenue. We followed Cicero north past Ford City Mall until we passed Midway Airport, where planes flew overhead seemingly inches above the car. We then got on I-55, the Stevenson Expressway, and just around the next curve the Chicago skyline appeared, the massive Sears Tower standing taller than everything around it. "What do you think?" I asked April, filled with the same affection I'd had for the city my whole life. "Wow," she said as she switched lanes. "It's pretty cool."

We took the Stevenson until it turned into Lake Shore Drive and then we were driving north, passing Soldier Field and Shedd Aquarium and the Field Museum. I told Maddie to look out the window, and she turned her head, and then we put the windows down and Lake Michigan seemed almost as if it were in the car with us, its enormity palpable, the fresh water smell thick on the cold winter breeze. We continued north on Lake Shore Drive, the lake to our right, a parade of century-old buildings on our left, and it felt good to be home, good to be wrapped in the familiar embrace of the city I loved.

* * *

April and I found a hotel on the north side that was seedier than we had intended, but cheap enough that we could afford to stay there and still have enough money to get back to Colorado. We handed cash to the manager, an unkempt Armenian with large, dark-rimmed glasses, signed our names on the registration sheet, and received a brass key attached to a green plastic tag the size and shape of a business card. I carried our bags up the stairs to the second floor while April followed, Maddie's head folded into the space between April's neck and shoulder. Later, with Maddie tucked under the sheets and the lights dimmed, April and I sat near the window, listening to the city while we smoked a joint and talked.

"It's so much different than Colorado, isn't it?" I asked, closing my eyes and listening to dogs barking and sirens screaming and cars honking as they passed by.

April looked out the window and onto the street below. Followed a taxi with her eyes as it pulled over to pick up a passenger. "Yeah," she said. "It is." She looked at me. "You worried about court tomorrow?"

I took another long pull from the joint and looked down to the street below. A CTA bus roared by, its diesel engine growling. In the distance, I could hear the L train knocking along the tracks.

Although I didn't want to admit it, I was worried. My attorney, over coffee at a restaurant the last time we met, had advised me to get the drug and alcohol assessment that is standard in DUI cases completed without hesitation. He also told me that attending an AA meeting or two would be a huge help and maybe cause the judge to be a little more lenient with me. I'd done neither.

I turned my head and looked over to the bed where Maddie slept, the covers over her body rising and falling with each of her small breaths, a tiny ruffle of beauty in an otherwise shitty hotel room.

"Nah," I said to April, my eyes still focused on Maddie. "I'm sure it'll be fine."

* * *

The attorney representing me in the DUI and possession case was someone my parents had found through their church. Middle-aged with dark hair parted to the side, he wore ill-fitting suits that were various shades of brown, and he took my case for two hundred dollars as a favor to my parents. Both times I'd met with him he was perspiring, little beads of moisture just above his upper lip occasionally dripping into the corners of his mouth.

On the Friday of my hearing, we agreed to meet at the courthouse in Markham. I walked up the courthouse steps in baggy jeans, black-and-white Adidas shell-toe shoes, and an oversized flannel shirt that I wore untucked, hanging well below my back pockets. My hair was pulled back into a short ponytail, and I wore hoop earrings in both of my ears. I had a safety pin stuck through my eyebrow.

April carried Maddie, and the three of us walked into the spacious main hallway of the courthouse. I suddenly wished we'd just stayed in Colorado. I didn't want to deal with what was in front of me, didn't want to stand in front of the judge, where my future hinged on what kind of mood he woke up in—generous or impatient, punishing or lenient. I'd moved to get away from this feeling.

All around us, heels clicked and squeaked on the polished marble floors as attorneys and criminals and legal assistants and court employees walked and talked, decided fates over Styrofoam cups of coffee. I found the docket hanging on the wall and made my way toward the courtroom I was scheduled to appear in. As we neared it, I saw my attorney sitting on one of the wooden benches against the wall, a large brown accordion file in his hand. He waved me over.

"Hey, Tim," he said, holding up his case folder. "Let's go over this really quick."

I looked over at April. "I'll meet you by the courtroom in a couple of minutes."

"Sounds good," she said. "I'm going to grab a drink for Maddie." As if on cue, Maddie said "drink" and then looked at me. I smiled and made a face at her. She laughed. I wiggled my eyebrows just so I could hear her laugh again. It always seemed like Maddie understood so much more of what was going on than we gave her credit for. She was always paying attention, always watching what was happening around her.

As April walked away, I sat down next to my attorney. "So how do you think this is going to go?"

He opened the file in his hand and set it on his briefcase, which was laid across his lap. He read the file for a minute. Used his finger to point to a note he had made.

"Have you gotten your drug and alcohol assessment done and attended an AA meeting like we talked about?"

I shook my head. Looked at the floor.

"So what's your plan today?" he asked.

"What do you mean, 'What's my plan?'" I looked across the hallway, watched as an endless stream of people walked in all directions. "I thought you were supposed to have the plan."

"Yeah, I did have a plan, and it involved you getting the assessment done and going to an AA meeting or two. But you didn't follow it."

I clenched my fist, opened it. Set my hand on my knee. "Come on, man. I didn't have the money for the assessment and I just moved to Colorado. At least I came back for this, right?"

My attorney looked straight at me, frowned. "No, Tim, that's not going to be sufficient for the judge. He's going to take one look at this and ask you why you moved in the first place when you knew you had this legal matter to tend to." He closed his folder. Moved the briefcase off his lap and to the floor next to him. "We've already continued this case once before. I'm not sure he's going to do it again. There's a chance he might remand you into custody today."

I felt the panic building in my stomach and chest. Tried to push it back down. "I swear. This time I'll get it done. Just get me one more continuance, and I'll do what I need to do."

He checked his watch. Stood up. "I'll ask for one, Tim, but no promises. Come on, let's get in there so I can check in."

* * *

When the judge called my case, I stood up from my seat next to April and walked up to stand next to my attorney. The judge looked down at us from the bench.

"So what are we doing today?" he asked.

My attorney answered immediately. "Your honor, I'd like to request a continuance for my client." He glanced down at his legal pad. "Mr. Hillegonds has recently moved to Colorado where he feels it will be easier for him to refrain from the trouble that has plagued him here in Illinois. We'd like to ask for the continuance, so my client can find the appropriate facility to undergo his drug and alcohol assessment."

The judge looked at me. "Is this true, Mr. Hillegonds?"

"Yes, Your Honor." I suddenly wished that I didn't have a safety pin jutting through my eyebrow. Wished I had worn a suit.

The judge looked at the papers in front of him. Began talking as he read. "I see that we've already continued this case once. That makes me less inclined to grant this request." He looked up at me. "Mr. Hillegonds, is your intention to complete the drug and alcohol assessment while in Colorado?

I locked my knees. Tried to seem resolute. "Yes, Your Honor."

"And do you understand that if you do not complete your assessment by the next court date that I will have the option of putting you in jail for up to a year in addition to a fine not to exceed $2,500?"

I didn't know the jail time could be so severe, but I nodded my head anyway. "Yes, Your Honor. But the next time you see me, I promise, I *will* have it completed."

The judge nodded. "You have thirty days, Mr. Hillegonds. Do not come back into this courtroom without a completed assessment."

* * *

Leaving the courtroom that day, there was a part of me that believed that I would go back to Colorado, find an accredited place to undergo my drug and alcohol assessment, and make it back to Chicago for the court date a month later. But after we'd loaded up April's car and begun the long ride back to Summit County, after the fear and concern I'd felt in the courtroom had vanished, I realized that I probably wouldn't. There was simply too much distance between home and away, between the place I was from and the place I was going back to.

* * *

A few weeks after we returned from Chicago, April got a babysitter for Maddie and called up her good friend Lauren and one of her other friends I hadn't met yet—a guy named Abraham. At a couple of inches over six feet tall with a barrel chest, Abraham looked like he might have played football in high school. He was friendly, though, with a quick growl of a laugh and a big smile.

While we waited for the girls to finish getting ready, we each cracked a beer and talked, and I liked him almost immediately. He was a volunteer fireman at the Dillon Fire Department, and he hoped to get on with them full time after he paid his dues doing temp work. "I don't know what else to do," he said after draining half his beer in one long pull. "I mean, it's not like I'm going to college."

"Yeah, man," I said, smiling. "I'm sort of in the same boat. The whole high school thing didn't pan out all that well for me either."

Laughter floated down the hall from the bathroom, and we both turned our heads, waited for one of the girls to come out.

"So how long have you known April?" I asked him, falling back into the couch in the spot near the end table where April usually sat.

Abraham sat down on the other end of the couch, the wood groaning under his weight, which looked around 220.

"Since high school," he said. "We hung out with a few of the same people and ended up at a lot of the same parties."

"Do you know that dude Austin?" I asked, thinking back to the night we'd gone to over to April's ex's place.

"Yeah," he said. "Everybody knows Austin. That dude's been here his whole life."

I still couldn't shake the feeling that Austin and April had been more than just friends at one point, and I thought about it more than I probably should have. On the drive back to Chicago, I almost asked her directly, but I decided against it. I wasn't even sure if I really wanted to know. I thought about asking Abraham. Instead, I changed the subject.

"So what are we doing tonight?"

Abraham leaned forward. Switched his beer to his other hand and rested the bottle on his knee. "There's a party up in Wildernest that I heard about. We should head up there for a bit. Check it out."

I nodded. Took a drink of my beer and held it up to the light to see how much was left. "Sounds good to me, man."

April and Lauren walked into the room and April looked at me, then over at Abraham. "You ready?"

"Sure," he said, tipping his beer back and finishing it.

I did the same and got up. Took a long look at what April was wearing—black heels, jeans that hugged her tiny hips, a tight, spaghetti-strap shirt that stopped just above the top of her jeans. Her hair was tied up behind her head, and two curls fell down either side of her face.

April looked at me and smiled. "What about you? You ready too?"

"Yep," I said, walking past her to the garbage can to throw out my beer. I opened the plastic lid and held the bottle like a clothespin above the opening before letting it fall into the can where it cracked against the bottles and broke, shards of glass falling like Plinko chips to its base.

The four of us piled into April's Mazda and headed toward Wildernest, an area of Silverthorne that sat on the side of a lightly wooded foothill overlooking a car dealership. Wildernest was a maze of houses and apartments that could be accessed using only two roads, and I'd been up there once before. The night after I arrived in Colorado, Travis and Kevin and I drank and smoked weed until we could barely walk, and then someone suggested that we drive to the highest point on the face of Wildernest where there weren't any houses, strap on our snowboards, and ride to the bottom of the steep hill in the moonlight. Travis drove us up there, swerving, the truck rounding the corners far too close to the edge, until we reached the top. And then we dropped in, the only sounds coming from the bottoms of our snowboards as they carved through the newly fallen snow.

As I thought back to that night, it dawned on me that I wasn't doing much snowboarding, that I wasn't do much of anything now that I was living with April. Life was so different than I had imagined it, and so much more work.

I turned to April. Outside the car, the night was cold and clear, the sky a giant star-spotted canopy hanging overhead. "Do you know any of the guys that will be at this party?"

She kept her eyes on the road, both hands holding the steering wheel as we drove.

April shrugged. "Probably, but I don't really know."

I looked out the window as Lauren and Abraham talked in the back seat. We had to put Maddie's car seat in the trunk and move April's seat all the way up to the steering wheel just so Abraham's giant frame could fit in the back.

I noticed that when I was talking to Abraham earlier that night that I felt the same way I felt when Austin had come over—like an outsider. There was something about the way April interacted with him—that same easiness in their conversation—that made me question whether or not they, too, had ever been more than just friends. It felt like they were keeping something from me, that everyone April knew was keeping something from me. I felt that familiar jealousy creep up. I tried to talk myself out of it, to push the feeling back down where it came from, but it was still there gnawing on me, causing me to question everything April had told me.

I kept my eyes trained out the window. "What about you, Abraham? You know any of these guys?"

He leaned forward. "I'm sure I'll know a few of them. Summit County's a pretty small place."

The higher we drove up the hill, the easier it was to see the county laid out behind us. Abraham was right, Summit County was a small place, and at no time had it ever looked smaller than right then, looking in the side view mirror of the car at the valley behind me, where two towns connected in the space between the mountains.

* * *

The party was at an apartment complex off Lodgepole Drive that everyone referred to as Treehouse. We walked up the stairs to the third floor in a single file line, our footsteps sounding like parade drums, all of us breathing heavy by the time we reached the top.

April knocked on the door and it was opened by someone who didn't live there, the noise and music spilling into the hallway as she let us in. We walked in like it was our place, like it was our party, surveying the crowd and searching for drinks. There were twenty or thirty people crammed into the two-bedroom apartment, most of them with beer bottles or plastic cups in their hands, standing and sitting wherever there was space, or leaning against the counters. Shortly after we arrived, April and Lauren wandered across the room, and I could see her from where Abraham and I were standing. April was talking to a guy that I didn't know, laughing and throwing her head back every so often. I could feel myself tensing. Why was she even over there? Why wasn't she standing and laughing with me? I felt like she was testing me, trying to get me riled up.

Abraham caught me looking at her, leaned in so I could hear him over the music. "What's up, man? What's that look for?"

I turned to him, couldn't shake the feeling that was creeping up inside me. I took a drink of my beer. "Nothing, man."

Abraham turned and looked at April. She laughed, put her hand on the guy's shoulder. Abraham turned back to me. "Don't worry about her, Tim. That's just the way she is. She's friendly." April turned to Lauren and said something. Lauren smiled and glanced in our direction. Abraham moved his head into my line of sight. "She's into you, bro. Anyone can see that."

He could have been right, but in the moment I didn't care, so I shrugged off his comment, turned my eyes from April, and began scanning the room. Everyone looked to be around our age—the typical Colorado ski crowd, except for a couple of guys that looked a little tougher than the rest. I watched as one guy lifted his beer to drink, saw his muscled, tattooed forearm.

Abraham and I continued to talk, eventually made our way over to grab new beers. A few people asked who we were, who we knew. We told them we came with April and Lauren, pointed over at them as they stood talking to another pair of guys in the kitchen. Again, I could feel heat in my stomach as I watched her, a nervous tingle just below the surface of my skin. I wanted to say something to her, to ask her why we'd come to this party if all she was going to do was stand around and talk to other guys.

I looked at Abraham. He'd spilled some of his beer when someone had backed into him, and there was a dark spot on the front of his pullover fleece.

"This is bullshit. We've been here over an hour, and she hasn't done anything but talk to other dudes."

"Yeah," he said, shrugging. "But that's all she's doing, right? Talking?"

It was true, but it wasn't what I wanted to hear. I wanted to hear how I was right, to justify the anger I felt. I wanted to hear how April should be next to *me*. I looked around at the crowd of unfamiliar faces and suddenly wished I was home, wished I was back in Chicago with Rich and Dan at North Park at a party with people I actually knew, with a girl who wasn't ignoring me.

I shook my head. "Yeah, but it's still bullshit. I'm telling you."

I took a beat and watched as the same guy that April had been talking to earlier in the night went back over to her. He handed her a beer and put his arm around her for second, then pulled it back. I clenched my jaw. Took a drink of beer and swallowed, hard. "I'm going to fucking lay that dude out."

"*Easy*, man." Abraham looked around. A few of the guys standing next to us glanced over. One of the guys kept looking. He must have heard me. "Relax. Maybe it's just some guy she knows. Why don't you just walk over there and talk to her? Shut the dude down nicely."

"Because I shouldn't have to," I said. "She should be over here, not playing some fucking game like we're still in high school."

I felt like April was testing me, waiting to see what I would do. It felt like she was putting me in a position where I needed to compete for her attention. I didn't want to compete for her. I just wanted her. I wanted it to be easy. And I wanted her to want me the same way, with no strings attached. I wanted to go to this party in Wildernest and drink beers and hang out with the girlfriend I lived with without feeling like I needed to burn the whole motherfucking building to the ground.

Abraham shook his head again and tipped his beer back. Reached over and touched my chest with his finger. "In case you haven't noticed, this isn't our party. We don't even know these guys. Just relax, man. Drink your beer."

From across the room, it seemed like the guys talking to April might have heard me talking shit to Abraham. The guy next to April motioned to his buddy and then pointed at us. I turned to Abraham. "You better back me up if shit goes down."

"I'm telling you, man. *Relax*."

A few seconds later I felt a hand touch my shoulder and squeeze it firmly. I turned around and the guy that had been talking with April stood there with his friend.

"What's the deal, man?" he said. His voice was loud, aggressive. "This is my place. Why does it seem like all you're doing is talking shit to your boy over here? You got a fucking problem with me?"

Behind the guy who was talking to me, I could see April watching us. She looked amused. Lauren stood next to her—same amused look. She always took her cues from April.

I looked back at the guy in front of me. "Yeah, I got a problem. I'm trying to figure out why the fuck you keep putting your arm around my girlfriend over there." I nodded in April's direction.

The guy laughed. "I'm not doing shit, bro. She was talking to me. And I don't even know who the fuck you are anyway." He stopped smiling. "But don't come into my house talking shit and expecting nothing to happen." He shook his head. "You guys need to fucking bounce."

Abraham moved forward, inched me out of the way. Forced a smile. "Listen, man, we're not trying to start shit. My friend here's got a solid buzz on. Everything's fine. We'll head out." He glared at me. Nodded toward the door. "Let's go."

I saw that four or five more guys had walked over to see what was going on. Even with all the beer in my system, my adrenaline was pumping. I raised my hand and waved April over to me. As she started toward us, I looked back at the guy.

"Whatever, man. Fuck it. We'll go."

April and Lauren reached us, and I heard Abraham tell them what was going on. I stared at the guy, sized him up as he stood with all his buddies spread out behind him. He was about my size—a little taller. He had a black-and-yellow Pittsburgh Pirates hat on backward, had staggered his feet in a way that made me think we were going to fight right there, with everyone around us.

Abraham grabbed me, pushed me forward toward the door with his hand on the middle of my back. "Let's go."

The door was just across the living room from where we were standing, and people started stepping out of the way. Behind me, I could hear some of the guys starting to talk shit. *Get the fuck out of here! Fuck you guys! Don't come into our house with that shit!* The stereo was loud, thumping. Jay Z's *In My Lifetime* was weaving its way through the apartment, through all of us, the bass pumping against our faces, the air warm and filled with sweat, the smell of bodies too close together, of breath, all around us.

We reached the door and stopped. I opened it, so April and Lauren could walk through first. The yelling behind us was louder now. More faces had appeared and were following us to the door, a giant swell pushing a cresting wave toward the shore.

I handed April the bottle that was in my hand as she walked by me. Her eyes locked with mine. She still seemed amused, still seemed to be enjoying what was happening. Then she was past me, and so was Abraham, and I was walking through the door and into the hallway.

"Hey!" someone yelled, and I turned around to see who it was, and as soon as I did a fist smashed against my cheekbone and there was a flash of white, a faint buzzing in my ear. For a second, I couldn't see, but I could feel that I was still on my feet, still standing. And then the image focused and all I could see were faces in the doorway, four or five of them, twisted and angry, yelling, screaming, cursing. And then I cocked back my right hand and threw it at the first face I saw, my weight shifting as I sat down on the punch, my fist connecting with a face. I felt it crumple. Reveled in the feeling. And then I was throwing it again, my right hand, at the next face, and the next one, and the next one, as fast as I could with everything I had in me—all the anger and jealousy I'd felt for April, all the insecurity that it stemmed from, all the rage that set like acid in my gut. And then the door slammed, and I was standing there sweating, breathing and gasping, beating on the door with my closed fist, over and over, until there was nothing I could do but leave.

* * *

My heart was still thrashing as we walked across the parking lot to April's car. I looked down and realized I was holding my right hand tenderly with my left arm. I held my hand up in front of my face and tried to stop it from shaking, but couldn't. There was a noticeable bump on the top of it, near the knuckle of my pinky. It was swelling quickly, and throbbing.

I looked at Abraham. "My hand is killing me. I'm pretty sure I broke it."

"You're lucky that's all you broke," he said, opening the car door. "That one dude was trying to smash a bottle over your head. The door got slammed right before he swung it."

I got in the front seat and April did the same, and then it was quiet in the car.

April turned to look at me, her eyes wild from adrenaline, one hand on the steering wheel and one hand on the keys in the ignition. "That was crazy! I've never seen someone throw that many punches that fast in my life." She started the car. Put it in reverse. "Seriously, Tim, that was insane."

I looked into the side mirror and could see the white reverse lights illuminating the parking lot behind us. I looked at my hand again. Tried to make a fist. Closed my eyes from the pain.

"You really think it's broken?" April asked.

I grimaced as we rolled over a pothole. "Yeah, it has to be."

April looked in the rear-view mirror. Abraham and Lauren were quiet. She glanced back at me. "Well, what do you want to do? You don't have insurance, do you?"

I shook my head. "No. Whatever, though. Let's just head back to the house. We've still got booze there, right? And you've got some Vicodin?"

April nodded and I turned my head to look out the window as we drove down the steep Wildernest hill, the car slowing for each turn. I settled back into the seat with my hand resting carefully in my lap and thought about what it felt like for my fist to finally connect with someone's face. The moment had come and gone so quickly—in seconds really—but in that small moment of time there was something I'd felt, a sort of satisfaction that I'd never in my life experienced before. I'd finally shattered the fear that tethered my fist to my side, had finally felt my knuckles sink into flesh, and the vindication I felt was undeniable. I wanted more.

I looked over at April, spoke softly. "You think I won that fight?"

She glanced over at me, smiled. Put her hand on my knee. "Yeah, Tim. I think you did."

EIGHT

I think it's fair to say that by early 1997 my entire existence could have been summed up in just two words: fighting and running. I was either fighting people or charges or perceptions or bill collectors, or I was running from them. I applied the fight-or-flight response—subconsciously—to every aspect of my life.

When April and I fought, which was frequently, I would often leave, knowing April had to stay with Maddie and couldn't follow. I'd walk off into the small patch of woods behind the apartment complex and sit in the quietness of the trees, drinking, listening to the wind weave its way through the barren branches. I would tip a bottle of vodka over and over, the liquid sometimes dripping down my chin while I squeezed away the burn in my eyes, and smoke my cigarettes down to the filter. But eventually, inevitably, the air's chill would surpass the vodka's warmth, and I would return to April's, shivering and cold and dejected. I postponed it as long as I could, sometimes falling asleep in the clearing I made for myself, waking up to chattering teeth and bits of snow clinging to my hair.

For a day or two after our fights—especially the ones where dishes or toys were broken or thrown—I treated every interaction I had with April as if it too could break. I watched her carefully, picking and choosing the moments to try to make her laugh, aware that one wrong word or gesture could send us spinning into another episode. I was quick with compliments and slow to react to anything negative, always a step ahead to open a door or a step behind so she could take the lead. And then, just as quickly as our relationship had entered that state of fragility, we fell right back into our routine. We went to work at Denny's, hustling from one table to the next for quarters and dollars and fives, and then home to her apartment where she'd be a mother and I'd be a stepfather, and we would peacefully drink and get high.

Our ever-present instability was the opposite of April's relationship to Maddie. Motherhood seemed to come naturally to her, and there were times when I would peek my head around the corner, my hand resting on the white casing of the door, and look into Maddie's room when the two of them were together. April sat on the edge of Maddie's tiny blue recliner, her slender frame barely fitting into it, while Maddie sat in a small plastic chair that had been pulled in front. With Maddie positioned between her knees, April brushed her thick, acorn-colored hair slowly, pride and contentment radiating from her face. Maddie almost always sat quietly, as if staring at a beautiful painting or gazing out into the ocean from a beach, her expression changing only if April had to brush out a knot.

April was also meticulous in the way she dressed Maddie, outfitting her in OshKosh B'gosh or some other name-brand kids clothing, her shoes and shirt and jacket always matching. Almost every time April and I went to restaurants, like the Village Inn in Silverthorne or the Claim Jumper in Frisco, other mothers or grandmothers stopped April with a gentle hand on her elbow, their faces beaming, to tell them how cute Maddie was. "Adorable," they said, and April beamed right back, her eyes as bright as spotlights.

Sometimes I thought that one of the reasons I stayed with April, even when signs as bright as casino neon in Vegas pointed to the demise of our relationship, was that I had fallen so deeply in love with her relationship with Maddie, and with Maddie too. She was so full of life, so new, so utterly untainted by the world around her that I wanted to be with her endlessly. Of course she cried and threw fits like any other young child, but her tantrums were infrequent and rarely lasted. To me she seemed like a promise of sorts, a pulsing signal of hope in a world that felt to me increasingly hard and more complicated with each passing day. When Maddie was on my lap in the rocking chair in the living room, the slow motion of us rolling back and forth gently as we worked our way through the illustrated pages of a book, the rageful current inside me would slow. Sometimes, for the briefest of moments, it would even stop completely.

* * *

A few weeks after the fight in Wildernest, I finished my shift at Denny's, just waiting for my last table to pay their bill and leave—two older folks slowly sipping endless cups of decaf coffee. From the table in the smoking section where April and I routinely sat and read the newspaper, I lit a cigarette with my left hand and looked at the cast on my right, turning it from one side to the other to survey the damage. The gauze around the outside had turned from bright white to dirty gray, and there were little stain spots from condiments—ketchup and mustard and what looked like Thousand Island dressing—splattered along the section that ran up my wrist to my forearm.

Waiting tables with the cast hadn't been as hard as I feared it would be, but it was still a nuisance, and earlier in the evening I had knocked a glass of Coca-Cola into a customer's lap. The woman had been gracious about it, though, gently dabbing the corner of her napkin on her jeans while I apologized and hustled to get her a clean rag, but I was still embarrassed about how clumsy I was with the cast on.

April came around the corner and slid into the booth across from me, held out her hand so I would pass her the cigarette. "How many more tables do you have?" she said, taking the cigarette.

I motioned toward the other side of the restaurant with my

head. "Just that one over there, but they should be leaving soon. What about you?"

She shook her head, blew smoke out of the side of her mouth. "None. I just have to finish my side work and I'm done."

I nodded and held out my hand for April to pass the cigarette back. There was now a faint ring of red lipstick around the filter. April leaned back against the seat and pulled a wad of bills out of her apron. Started separating the money into denominations.

She glanced up at me. "So I've been thinking. I'm going talk to Lauren when we pick up Maddie and see if she wants to go out with me tomorrow night. I'm not scheduled to work, and I just need to get out for a little while. You know, just us girls."

I took another drag from my cigarette. "What do you mean you're going to go out? Go out where?"

She rolled her eyes. "Relax, Tim. Nothing big, we'll probably just go over to the Old Dillon Inn, that bar across the street, or maybe even the bowling alley. We know some of the guys that are bartending at both of those places and they won't card us."

Across the restaurant, the front doors opened and the wind blew one of the paper kid's menus off the counter and onto the tile. "I'm supposed to stay home with Maddie?"

"Well, yeah, that's the idea." April's expression changed, and I could see she was annoyed. "Give me a break, Tim. I want to go out for a few hours and blow off some steam. It's not a big deal. So don't turn it into one."

I took another drag from my cigarette and stubbed it out in the ashtray. All I could think about was how April had acted at the party in Wildernest, even when she knew I was watching her. What was she going to be like when I wasn't around?

"Yeah for you it's not a big deal, because you're the one going out and having fun. Meanwhile, I'm stuck at the house with the kid. Why don't we just get a babysitter, and I'll go with you?"

"Because I don't want you to go with me, Tim." She combined

the two stacks of bills that were in front of her into one pile, folded them in half, and shoved them back into her apron pocket. Stood up. "I just want to get away from everything for a minute. Don't you get that? I'm not going to fight with you about this. I'm going one way or another."

"April, seriously?" My voice was noticeably louder, and a woman making her way toward the bathroom glanced at us over her shoulder. I shot her a look and stood up. "What, you got something going on with one of these *friends* you're going to see? You and Lauren going out to slut it up together?"

April's eyes narrowed and she took a step toward me. "'Slut it up?' Keep talking like that and maybe we will."

She turned to leave, her hair whipping like tree branches in the wind, but stopped once I started talking again. "Wouldn't surprise me," I said. "It seems like everyone you know is some guy from back in the day."

"What do you expect? I grew up here."

"Whatever, April. You know it's bullshit."

She took a step backward. "No, you know what would be bullshit? Me actually getting with one of those guys. But hey—I mean, why not? You're already accusing me of it. Might as well make it true, right?"

I glared at her. "Fucking try it, April. See what happens."

She smiled. "What? Is big bad Timmy going to fight everybody now?" She looked down at my casted hand. "You got in one little fight and suddenly you think you're a badass?" She turned and started walking away. Spoke over her shoulder. "I got news for you, Tim. You're not."

* * *

My mind wandered constantly when I was with April, almost always to a place where some other guy, some man with a better job who was better looking and had more money than me, showed up and

gave her everything I couldn't. I had no reason not to trust her—
she had never cheated on me—but I *didn't* trust her, and I don't
think she trusted me either. Trust was an abstract concept we threw
around in fights, an unattainable ideal, as foreign to our relationship
as sobriety, or exercise.

So throughout the next day, from the moment I walked into the
kitchen that morning, I drank. I drained the four or five beers in
the fridge and took nips from the bottle of Gordon's vodka that
was chilling in the freezer, the frost from its glass clinging to my
fingers. I was well on my way to drunken annihilation by the time
April needed to leave for her night out with Lauren.

April walked into the living room where I was watching television.
"Come on," she said. "I'm going to get ready at Lauren's. You can
just watch Maddie there." April's perfume filled the room.

I didn't understand why we needed to go to Lauren's, and I
wanted to stay home, to sit right where I was and keep drinking,
but I decided to just go along with it. To not make it more of a big
deal than I already had. I kept my eyes on the TV. "Fine, but I'm
bringing the rest of that vodka with me."

A little while later I was sitting in the passenger's seat of April's
Mazda, Maddie buckled into the car seat in the back, staring out
the window as we drove down Highway 9, the tip of my cigarette
glowing and fading with each drag I took. I turned my head and
looked at April, saw that she'd put on some of her makeup before
we left the house. She'd applied dark eyeliner underneath each of
her eyes and was wearing a subtle shade of red lipstick. Her curly,
blonde hair filled the car with the sharp, alcohol smell of hairspray,
and it fell down the sides of her face, landing on her shoulders and
bouncing with each bump in the road.

We'd been fighting so much lately that there weren't many
moments when I even stopped to look at April anymore—to see
her as I did in the beginning. We were always at each other's throats,
locked in an endless fight about money or friends or responsibilities,

and I rarely took time to notice how beautiful she was—that mischievous look she got on her face right before she tickled Maddie; the way her eyelids drooped when she was exhausted; the way her brow furrowed in concentration when she was painting her fingernails. I'd almost completely forgotten that we were a young couple in love. We spent so much of our time criticizing who we thought the other person should be that we almost never focused on what we loved.

April pulled into the gravel parking lot in front of Lauren's apartment and got out of the car without speaking. She opened the rear door and unbuckled Maddie from her seat, whispering softly into her ear as she lifted her, and then shut the door with her hip. Maddie turned her head and looked back at me. I smiled at her but her expression didn't change.

Lauren's apartment was above a machine shop in Silverthorne—an industrial building wrapped in layers of peeling brown paint. At both ends of the building, covered staircases trapped in the machine shop's smells. Every time I climbed those stairs and caught the scent of burning welding rods and acetylene, it reminded me of my stepfather, of the year or two he'd spent working as a welder.

I grabbed the bottle of vodka from underneath the seat and took a long, fiery pull while I watched April and Maddie climb the stairs to the second floor. Their relationship was so simple. April held out her hand. Maddie grabbed it. And then they walked up the steps together, their eyes trained on exactly what was in front of them. It reminded me how April and I seldom looked at what was ahead of us. Instead, we constantly scanned back and forth, too concerned with what was happening around us, or what was bearing down on us, to grab each other's hand, fall into a rhythm, and take a few steps together.

I took another long pull from the bottle, screwed the red cap back on, and decided to walk upstairs. Maybe it was time to give in, to shut my mouth for once and let April have her night out. Maybe it was time to let my jealously go and watch TV until my eyes were heavy and I could sleep. Maybe I just needed to go upstairs and settle in on the couch. To not actually say the things I was thinking. To not give in to the anger I was feeling for once.

I opened the car door and the freshness of the Colorado air hit me just as it always did, the smell of pine trees heavy on the breeze. I stood and the horizon swayed like I was standing on a ship's deck. I stumbled backward, managed to catch myself and regain my balance before I went down.

I knew I was tipsy, but like most drunks, I didn't know just how inebriated I was. In my mind I was fine—just a few drinks past "lightly buzzed." But the reality was that basic movements were becoming difficult. Thinking was cumbersome. Balancing on my own two feet seemed as precarious as balancing on the edge of a building.

I shut the car door and faltered toward the staircase, grabbing the handrail once I got there, leaning into it as I carefully took each of the steps. By the time I got to Lauren's door, I was breathless, heaving from being drunk and out-of-shape and still not quite accustomed to the thin mountain air. I stumbled into the kitchen and immediately heard the two of them laughing from the bathroom. I saw two shot glasses on the counter, a small amount of red liquid pooled in the bottom of each glass, sitting beside a half-full bottle of strawberry Pucker.

"It's about time you came inside," April said, rounding the corner and walking over to the counter, her voice emotionless. "I put Maddie on Lauren's bed in the back bedroom. She was pretty tired on the ride over here, so she'll probably sleep the whole time we're gone."

My eyes were still fixed on the shot glasses and just hearing April's voice enraged me. Was this all I was to her? A babysitter? A live-in child-care provider and partial bump in the household income? I felt emasculated. Taken advantage of. I turned my eyes to April, my jaw clenched, and slowly looked her up and down. She'd changed into a faux-leather half-top that barely covered her breasts, a pair of black, skin-tight jeans, and lacy, black high heels that were shiny enough to reflect the light coming from the ceiling fixture above us. I could see the tattoo above her navel as clearly as I could see the bright, red strawberries on the Pucker's label.

"This is a joke, right?" My voice slurred the beginning of the sentence, and I swallowed to try and clear it.

She laughed sarcastically. "What are you talking about?"

"I'm talking about you wearing that ridiculous outfit."

"Oh, come on," she said. "Don't be so fucking insecure. If you had a baby and still looked this good, you'd want to show it off too." She grabbed the bottle of Pucker and filled a shot glass to just below the rim. "But I do look good, don't I?" She smiled and threw the shot back.

It's always this moment that I come back to in my memory—her doing the shot, me standing there—drunk and swaying, skinny, with bloodshot eyes and long, stringy hair that had gone unwashed for two days.

"There's no way you're going out with that outfit on," I said. "Absolutely no fucking way."

Lauren appeared around the corner, and April asked her if she wanted a shot. Lauren nodded, her eyes wide as they darted from April to me and back again, sensing the tension. April filled up two shot glasses, handed one to Lauren. "Here's to tonight."

Lauren smiled nervously, swallowed her shot, and set the glass back on the counter. "Oh relax, Tim. You should be happy your woman looks so good."

I glared at her. "Hey, Lauren, why don't you shut the fuck up and mind your own business?"

April stepped in between Lauren and me and dug her index finger into my chest, her painted nail drilling into my sternum. I smelled strawberries on her breath. "Why don't you watch your mouth? What the hell's wrong with you?"

She was so close it was all I could do not to push her away. I could feel my body heating up, sweat starting to bead on my forehead. "Well then put some fucking clothes on," I said. "You're not going out in that."

"Or what?" April laughed again. "You going to stop me?" She leaned back against the counter and folded her arms across her chest.

"Hell yeah I'm going to stop you."

April pushed off the counter and stepped forward so that she was inches from my face. "You couldn't even if you tried. You're nothing but a two-bit punk."

I pressed my head forward so our foreheads were touching, like two boxers at the weigh-in, then gritted my teeth and started to walk her down. "All dressed up like a slut, so you can get some fucking attention, right? Right, April? Isn't that what you always want?"

Lauren stepped over and slid her hands in between us, tried to separate us. Her voice wavered. "Stop it, you guys. Seriously. Tim, why don't you just go outside and have a cigarette? Cool off for a minute. Please."

April's eyes were wild. "Yeah, Tim. Do what you're told. Go outside and have a smoke like a good little boy."

"Fuck you, April." I walked past her, knocking her hard with my shoulder. Opened the door and stepped out into the hallway, adrenaline and insecurity and anger and jealousy coursing through me like an electric current. I turned around. "You're such a fucking bitch, April. You know that? All the shit that I've done for you and this is what you do to thank me—dress up like some fucking whore and prance around Summit County while I watch your kid." I pulled a pack of cigarettes from my pocket. Flipped the top of the Marlboro box open and looked right at her. "No wonder Maddie's dad left." I shook my head angrily and started down the hallway. There was a fire extinguisher hanging in a case on the wall I was walking toward, just to the right of the staircase, and as I stared at it, I couldn't help but think that it was exactly what I needed—something to put out the fire between April and me.

But then there were footsteps behind me, rapid and loud, and just as I reached the staircase, I turned and saw April running toward me. I backed up against the wall and felt the fire extinguisher case pressing into my back, the bottom of the box digging into my spine. My cigarette dropped from my hand as she reached me, rolling over a few times before stopping and slowly beginning to burn a hole in the carpeting. April stopped just short of tackling me.

"You think you can talk to me like that, you piece of shit?" Her breath was coming out of her mouth like race car exhaust. "You think can call me a whore and nothing's going to happen to you? You think I'm just going to let you talk to me like that?" She pushed me with both hands, and the metal box behind me dug into my spine even harder. "Well, guess what, motherfucker? You can't. Because you don't know shit about me or Maddie or anything else that happened before you." She was screaming now, her saliva splashing onto my cheeks. "You don't know shit, Tim! You're a fucking hypocrite! Your own dad didn't even love you enough to visit you when he lived right across town. What kind of fucking loser does that make *you*?"

The words hung there in the summer air, pregnant with truth. And then they sank in, stinging as they entered my bloodstream and mixed with alcohol and anger and adrenaline. I couldn't deny it. She was right. I was a loser whose own father didn't love him. Didn't want him. Didn't even want to *visit* him. And as that realization sank in for the thousandth time, all the jealousy and anger and sadness welling up from somewhere near my pelvis, there was nothing I could do to stop the tears that exploded from my eyes. And then my right hand, my cast hand, was swinging from its position next to my hip in a long arc that ended on the bone in between April's left eye and cheek, her mouth twisting in pain and surprise, in fear, all the anger I'd felt just seconds before turning to shame and regret as soon as I saw what I'd done.

* * *

After April ran down the hallway and back into Lauren's house, she locked the door and I stood outside banging on it, shouting profanity-laced apologies. "I'm sorry, April! I'm so fucking sorry! Please open the door! *Please!*"

Eventually, the door opened, and April stood there icing her eye, the swollen tissue around it already turning red and purple. In that moment I was confronted with the truth of myself, of what I was capable of doing. April was now visibly marked by my anger. In the most obvious of places she was physically imprinted with a manifestation of my rage, and I hated myself for it. If I was capable of hitting her, what did that mean about who I was, or who I told myself I was? Maybe it meant that I deserved my father's negligence and my mother and stepfather's constant disapproval. Maybe it meant that I was broken. Maybe it meant that I would always be nothing more than a drug addict, an alcoholic, a criminal.

April stood in the doorway, her eyes moist with tears, her expression floating somewhere between angry, sad, and disappointed. "I'm so sorry," I said, not knowing what else to say, knowing there was nothing I could say. "I didn't mean to . . . I just . . ." My words trailed off, inadequate and desperate. Behind me, traffic moved slowly down Highway 9 and the reality of who I was thickened the atmosphere around us, like a fog the new day's sun simply can't burn off.

NINE

After the incident at Lauren's, I was too scared to drink or do drugs, or even raise my voice, for fear that I would lose control again. A silver-dollar-sized bruise the color of an eggplant encircled April's eye, a head-turning contrast to her pale, Irish skin. Each time I looked at her I was reminded of just how untrustworthy I was, and the remorse was crippling.

I had already begun to understand, at least vaguely, that my drinking and drug use could be excessive, maybe even border on abnormal. But I'd always felt that I was hurting only myself. Now it was impossible to deny the truth of the matter: I was unpredictable and dangerous. Hurting someone I loved was no longer just a possibility. It had happened.

Two days after the incident, it occurred to me that we'd previously made plans to visit April's mother and stepfather. I begged April to cancel, pleaded with her not to make me go over there and face them after what I'd done, but April was adamant. "I don't care what you do, Tim, but Maddie and I are going over there."

I stood there in the living room, running my hands through my hair and locking my fingers behind my head. "What are you going to tell them?"

April sighed. "I don't know, I'll tell them I walked into a door or something."

Hearing her say she would lie about what happened made me feel even worse. After all, wasn't that textbook domestic violence behavior? The abuser abuses, then feels guilty, and then has the victim cover it up?

I moved my hands over my face, rubbed my eyes. Spoke while I tried to massage out my stress. "I need to call your stepfather first. I need to tell him what I did." I dropped my hands to my sides, dug them in my pockets. Stared at the floor. "He needs to hear it from me."

April lifted her eyebrows. "Are you serious? He's going to be so pissed."

"I know, but what else can I do?"

I called him from the living room, pacing back and forth with the portable phone in my hand. When April's mom answered, I asked for her stepfather, and a few seconds later he was on the other end of the line.

"Hello?"

My palms were sweating and my heart was racing and my voice was shaking. "Mr. Wagner?"

"Hey, Tim, what can I do for you?"

I pictured him standing there in his jeans, the nametag from the Safeway grocery store he worked at pinned to shirt. I swallowed, tried to steady my voice. "Mr. Wagner, there's something I need to tell you." April was sitting on the couch. She leaned forward with her elbows on her knees and watched me. The swelling in her eye had diminished some, but the area around the eye was still painted in maroons and purples. I turned and paced away from April. "Your daughter and I got in a fight the other night, and . . ." My voice trailed off. I summoned it back. "And, well, it was a pretty bad one." I had to force myself to keep talking, to fight the urge to hang up. I took a deep breath. "Listen, I don't know how else to say this, but I lost control during the fight and hit April in the face. She's got a black eye." I paused, heard my voice crack when I started talking again. "I can't tell you how sorry I am, sir. I'm so, so sorry."

Silence filled the other end of the line, and I stopped pacing. Felt April staring at my back. Held my breath until he spoke.

"I should get in my truck right now and drive over there and beat the shit out of you. See how you like it." It sounded like he was trying to subdue what he was really feeling, to keep himself calm. I didn't say anything, just stood there, listening. A beat passed and he asked, "Is April okay?"

I turned around and April's eyes met mine. "Yeah, she's okay. I mean, she's got a shiner, but she's okay." My voice was quiet; my shoulders slumped in defeat and embarrassment. "I guess I just wanted you to hear it from me, so I could tell you how wrong I was, and how sorry I am, and that it won't happen again."

"I know it won't. Because if I ever hear about something like this again, I'm going to put you in the hospital. Do you understand me?"

"I understand."

"You better."

"I do."

"Good," he said, and the line went dead.

* * *

As with all broken things, healing came with time. My fractured hand mended, and April's eye lost its kaleidoscope of colors, eventually showing no signs that anything had ever happened at all. And although the forward momentum in our relationship was filled with trepidation at first, April and I soon fell into our routine once again, the rigors of daily life helping to push the night at Lauren's to the back of our minds. I wanted to forget it for obvious reasons, and maybe April did too. We both craved a return to normalcy.

February turned into March during a snowy graveyard shift at Denny's, and two weeks later I had my nineteenth birthday. Sometime near the end of March I settled the misdemeanor case that stemmed from that night I had vandalized April's ex-boyfriend's car. I pleaded guilty to a criminal mischief charge, was ordered to pay a fine and stay out of trouble, and soon, like the fight at Lauren's, it was nothing more than a memory.

One night when April and I both had taken the night off, we sat at the kitchen table, its surface covered with bills—some paid, some unpaid, some yet to be opened—smoking cigarettes. It was nearing midnight, and Maddie was sleeping in her bedroom where slivers of light from the streetlamps outside slipped in through the cracks in the blinds.

April tapped her cigarette on the edge of brown ashtray between us. "I'm bored. Let's call Darren and Sarah and get some shit."

Instinctively, my pulse quickened. There was nothing that could get me quite as excited as the prospect of drugs. I raised my eyebrows. "Yeah?"

She smiled. "Yeah, why not?"

I laughed. "Well, when you put it that way, who can argue?"

There was a dance that April and I did whenever the subject of drugs came up. Neither one of us wanted to seem too eager—not wanting to give the other person any extra ammunition to use in our next fight—but both of us would do just about anything to get them. And once we got them, at least for a little while, everything that was wrong with us, everything in our relationship that normally took every ounce of effort we could muster to make work, suddenly fit together like blue squares on a solved Rubik's Cube.

I stubbed out my cigarette. "You give them a call and tell them we're going to stop by. I'll get Maddie bundled up."

April nodded. "Try not to wake her."

In Maddie's bedroom, as I leaned over and slowly picked her up, her beautiful brown eyes fluttering open for just a second as I positioned her on my shoulder, I knew without a shadow of a doubt that what I was doing was wrong. For the briefest of moments I wanted to stop, to lay Maddie back down in the crib and tuck the fuzzy pink blanket she slept with back underneath her chin. I wanted to walk back into the living room and tell April that I'd had a change of heart and that I wanted to get some sleep, maybe wake up the next day and take Maddie back to the zoo. But then I thought of the drug, the meth, the way it smelled like gasoline and ether and fired a path from my nostril to my brain, making every single thing wrong with my life disappear into the blackness of night. I felt that anticipatory buzz, that flitter behind my pectorals like fingers brushing against them, and I knew nothing would stop me. I was going to take this beautiful, sleeping child and wrap her up in her winter coat and drive her to an apartment across town, where we would knock on the door and ask Darren, with hunger in our eyes, if we could buy some crystal meth. While this innocent little girl slept in the car in the parking lot, its engine running, the heat turned low to keep the Colorado chill out, April and I walked through the door and into the living room and sat on the couch while Darren, someone that neither April nor I really knew beyond the small talk we shared over cigarettes at Denny's, walked into the room with a plastic bag containing a rock of crystal meth the size of a golf ball. I looked at April, and then looked at the meth, and my mouth literally salivated, causing me to swallow repeatedly. And then Darren took out a light bulb, its tungsten filament carefully bored out, something I'd never seen done before, and he dropped a small, yellow rock to the bottom where it landed with a rattle. He then handed me a hollowed-out pen to go with it. "Suck when I tell you," he said. And then he showed me how to hold the light bulb with my thumb and forefinger, touching the metal screw thread where it met the thin glass of the bulb, placing his hand on my shoulder, the weight of it somehow comforting, and then talking me through the process like a father coaching his son through his homework. "There you go. Yeah. Just like that." And when I was ready, when Darren had the lighter's flame lit and bouncing, he moved the flame under the bulb. The rock inside began to smoke, rapidly clouding the bulb, a crackle in an otherwise quiet room. "Okay, suck," he said, and I sucked through the pen, my cheeks concave, my eyes crossed as they looked down my nose at the bulb, the smoke tasting like medicine and chemicals. "Keep sucking," he said, and I did, the lighter lapping up the sides of the bulb as I drew the smoke deep into my lungs. And then before I could even articulate it, before I could even begin to register what was happening to my body, the drugs were inside me, all around me, the only thing that mattered in my entire life. I blew the smoke out in a stream as long as a yardstick, and I looked up at April. "Good?" she said. "Yeah," I said quietly, forgetting that Maddie was in the car, forgetting that I'd ever even entertained the thought of not leaving the apartment in the first place.

* * *

Time in Colorado moved in unpredictable waves. At certain points, it passed as slowly as it did in the Christian Reformed Church services I sat through as a child, and I could feel every single minute in the day. Days and nights would saunter endlessly, the financial problems and arguments and feelings of inadequacy that were ever-present in my relationship with April making the very act of existing in the same place together next to impossible. But other times, when April and I fed our habits the drugs they craved, seconds and minutes and hours seemed to disappear, and days would pass without us even noticing.

March became April and April became May, and all at once the blue Colorado sky held a yellow sun that warmed all the places in Summit County it could reach. Snow on the mountaintops that was once brilliantly white now receded, the blanket of winter finally, reluctantly, retreating to reveal deep, lively greens and the promise of a new season.

One night that spring, April walked into the living room where I was watching the television and abruptly shut it off.

"Hey," I said, glancing up at her. "What's the deal?"

The look on April's face tipped me off to the fact that something might be wrong, but so often were things wrong with us that it almost seemed normal.

"I'm late," she said.

"What do you mean you're late?"

"I mean 'I'm late' as in I haven't gotten my period yet."

It was in this moment, this space in between two sentences, right after April had spoken and just before I did, that I recognized a startling blankness inside me, a vacancy, an unsettling nothingness. I wasn't scared. I wasn't angry. I wasn't happy. I was simply barren, somehow lost in a space where I knew not how to feel.

I've often wondered why that was, how it was possible that I could feel nothing in a moment that was, looking back, so absolutely life-changing. As I've interrogated that moment over the years, in coffee shops and on train commutes and on moves in U-Hauls from one part of the country to another, I've come to the conclusion that I expected it. There was no surprise in the moment. *Of course* April was pregnant, of course she was—because getting April pregnant was the logical next step for a guy like me. I dropped out of high school and did drugs and got arrested. I was uncontrollably angry. I fought. I assaulted my girlfriend in a moment of animal rage. So of course she was pregnant. What else could have happened?

I sat there in silence with April looking at me, waiting for me to react, to say something, and even then, when most of my better judgment had yet to develop, I knew that I needed to use caution in how I responded.

"Okay. So you're late." I said. "What do you want to do?"

"I need to take a pregnancy test."

About an hour later, after we got Maddie ready and drove down the hill to the City Market grocery store, after we realized we didn't even have enough money to buy a pregnancy test, after I hid two of them in my sweatshirt and used Maddie to cover the bulge as we walked out of the store without paying for them, I stood at the picture window of April's apartment, not wanting to admit how scared I was. The nothingness I'd felt earlier was gone, replaced by a rising feeling of terror. I was barely managing my role as pseudo-stepfather. How could I ever expect to do it for real? I suddenly felt so incompetent, so unprepared, so much like the immature child I was trying not to be. I couldn't take care of people. Not really. In the short time I'd been with April, I'd proven it. Our bills often went unpaid. Our checking account rarely had enough money for rent. And as much as I didn't want to admit it, without April, I wasn't even sure I could take care of myself. What would I possibly do if April were pregnant?

I heard the toilet flush in the bathroom, and when I turned around, April was standing there. She'd taken her hair out of the bun she had it in earlier and it was falling over her shoulders. She looked young and beautiful and fragile. She held up the test. "I'm pregnant."

I leaned back against the windowsill. Nodded at her and looked at the carpeting.

"Tim, say something."

"What do you want me to say?" I walked over to the end table and picked up the pack of cigarettes lying there.

"I want you to say what you're going to do." Her voice cracked and I looked up. Her eyes flashed in the living room light, filling with tears that had yet to spill over her lids "I want you to tell me if you're going to leave, because I'm not begging you to stay. I'm not. I did that shit with Maddie's dad, and I'm never doing it again."

I lit my cigarette and took a long drag. Walked back over by the window, leaned against it. Watched her as she spoke.

"But I'm telling you this, Tim, you've got one shot. If you tell me you're going to stay, then you better stay." The tears began sliding down her cheeks, and I could see how scared she seemed. I opened my mouth to say something, to comfort her, but everything in my head seemed like the wrong thing to say. I took a drag of my cigarette instead.

"So what are you going to do, Tim?" With her thumb, she wiped a tear that had dripped near the corner of her mouth. "What are you going to do?"

More than anything, I wanted to do what I always did: run. I wanted to run out the door of April's apartment, and then out of her apartment complex, and then out of her life. I wanted to run back to 1994, to when the skate team was still together, to when every person who watched me skate could see how good I was, how valuable I was. More than anything I wanted to run back to that moment in that diner off Pulaski Avenue with my biological father and tell him that I understood now. I understood the fear he had. Why he felt he needed to leave, why things with my mother had seemed far too unraveled to ever sew back up. But I also wanted to run back to that moment in the diner so I could tell him one other thing, something I felt deep inside me: that even though we shared the same chin and the same forehead and the same hands and the same eyes, we were different in the one way that truly mattered to me.

I stepped forward and gently pulled April toward me. Wrapped my arms around her. Spoke softly into her ear. "I'm not going anywhere, sweetheart." Her arms tightened around me. "We'll figure this thing out, April. I promise. Me and you. We'll figure it out."

* * *

By the time the July heat had melted the snowcap on Buffalo Mountain down to what looked like a silver wedding band, April was two months pregnant. And even though I'd seen the small plus sign on the pregnancy test with my own eyes, I still found it hard to fathom that somewhere behind the color-soaked tattoo on April's stomach my child was growing fingernails.

I caught myself, from time to time, staring at April from the corner booth in Denny's while I rolled silverware into white napkins, or watching her while she folded Maddie's laundry, and I wondered whether the woman I was staring at, the woman who was carrying my child, would one day be my wife. I thought about Colorado and how, if we were married, it would immediately cease to be the place that I'd run away to, the place where I'd started over, and instead become my home. I didn't quite know what that meant, or what to do with that redefinition. Colorado had always been a place I thought of as temporary. It was supposed to be a respite. A haven. An extended break in the narrative of my life in Illinois. I had never intended it to be permanent.

I could never say that to April, though. I could never say how scared I was of losing my home, of losing Chicago, of losing, even, the family I had wanted to get away from so badly. It was such a small thing compared to her pregnancy. But as a nineteen-year-old living as a stranger in a place so different from the blue-collar Midwest where I had grown up, it felt like a piece of me was being wiped from existence. It caused a hollowness I tried to fill, over and over, with substances.

Since April could no longer drink or use drugs, she had asked me to do the same. I had nodded and agreed with her, told her it was only fair. But as soon as I made the promise, I broke it, smoking a joint with one of the cooks at Denny's, polishing off a few beers in the break room before going home for the night. I felt I deserved that much. To get through the seven months that were left in April's pregnancy completely sober—that was an impossible thing to ask.

* * *

Abraham stood up from the couch in his living room and leaned forward to hand me the bottle of vodka he'd just taken a swig from. "So what are you going to do?"

April and I had just had another predicable fight. We both yelled horrible things, the volume steadily rising, and I used it as an excuse to get out of there. I needed to put some distance between us, needed this bottle of vodka. I leaned back in the chair, unscrewed the cap. "I don't know." I tilted the bottle back. "Wait it out, I guess. Let her calm down a bit." I looked around the room. "Is it cool if I stay here for a while?"

"Yeah, my folks aren't supposed to be back until tonight. We can hang out here for now. We'll figure out what to do once they're on their way home."

I nodded, took another pull from the bottle. Even though we'd just started drinking, I could already feel the stress and tension loosening its grip. I held the bottle up in front of me to see how much was left. I looked over at Abraham.

"You got anything else besides vodka? Something stronger?"

Abraham got up and walked over to a black backpack that was sitting near a pile of shoes by the front door. He unzipped the bag, and I heard the unmistakable rattle of pills inside a prescription bottle. He held them up, read the label, and tossed them to me, the burnt orange bottle arcing through the air like a comet.

"Those are Vicodin 10s," he said. "They're strong, so be careful."

"Thanks." I shook three of the thick, white pills into my hand and popped them into my mouth. Took another pull of vodka to wash them down.

Abraham sat back down on the couch. Picked a beer up from the end table next to him and started peeling the label off. "Listen, man, I have to ask you this." He stopped and took a sip of his beer, glanced at me. Went back to peeling at the label. The bottle looked almost miniature in his enormous hands. "If things are as bad as you say they are with April, then why are you still with her? I mean, what's the point? Why not just call it off and save yourself the drama?"

I sighed and shook my head. "I don't know, man." I glanced around the room at nothing in particular and then settled my eyes back on Abraham. I asked myself the same question every time April and I got in one of our blow-out fights, but I wasn't sure that I could even articulate an answer that made sense. "I guess because it's not always like this. There are times when everything seems to work. We have these moments when we're laughing together and for a second or two everything seems doable, and I can see myself with her over the long term." I thought about Maddie, about how I'd gotten so used to hearing her laugh. She had nearly all of her baby teeth, and she'd recently started doing this thing where she would scrunch her eyebrows and smile with her entire face. It was adorable. There was something about her, a sense of happiness that I couldn't image not being around. "And now with the pregnancy . . ." I looked directly at Abraham. "I mean, there's no way I can leave her now. You know?"

"Yeah, I get all that, Tim. I really do. But from what I've seen and what you've told me, it sounds like you guys are miserable. How many huge fights have you guys had since the last time I saw you?"

I shrugged, got up from the couch. As soon as I stood, I could feel that the Vicodin had started to kick in, washing over me in way that made it seem I was moving underwater. I felt lighter, too, as if the ground was pushing away from my feet rather than holding them up. I steadied myself, grabbed the bottle of vodka. Took a step toward the door. "I'm going for a smoke. Come with me?"

Abraham nodded. "I'll grab a beer and meet you out front."

I walked out Abraham's front door to the rusted-out pickup truck that was sitting in his driveway. I pulled the latch on the tailgate and it groaned open. I hopped up on the edge, felt the truck dip under my weight, and lit my cigarette, smoke swirling around my shoulders with the breeze. I took another pull from the bottle. Behind me, I could hear the traffic on I-70 as it weaved its way down the seven percent grade from the Eisenhower Tunnel.

Parked next to the pickup was the car Abraham drove most of the time, an early nineties model Chevy Cavalier that had a notoriously loud sound system. Whenever he pulled up anywhere, the bass from the twelve-inch kickers thumped from blocks away, the metal from his license plate holder rattling.

Abraham appeared beside me, and I took another drag from my cigarette, looked down at my sneakers as I exhaled. "So what do you think I should do?"

"You mean about April?"

"Yeah, about her. About me living here, with her. All of it."

A car passed by in front of us. There was a woman driving, both of her hands resting on top of the steering wheel as she stared straight ahead from behind sunglasses. We both watched it pass. Abraham spoke without looking at me.

"I can't really answer that for you, man, but I think you need to think about what the future holds for you guys. Realistically, I mean. I know you've got a baby on the way, but no kid deserves to grow up in a house where the parents are fighting every second of every day." Abraham paused and took a sip from his beer.

I nodded. He had a point. Maybe I was being unrealistic, but I still felt like our relationship was salvageable. I took one last drag of my cigarette and flicked it into the street. Because of the Vicodin, things were moving in slow motion. I turned to Abraham.

"I guess I feel like I really don't have a choice." I looked down the road, saw the A-frame houses lining the north side of the street. Even the houses in Summit County seemed different from home. Colorado's wooden A-frames were flimsy, Chicago's brick bungalows so much sturdier, so much more permanent.

The phone started ringing inside the house, and Abraham walked toward the door. "I'm going to grab that a minute. I'll be right back."

He disappeared inside, and I lifted the bottle back to my lips, closed my eyes, and drank. Fought the urge to gag. I swallowed and spit into the street, squeezed my eyes shut as hard as I could before opening them and trying to refocus. It was possible that Abraham was right, that I really needed to think long and hard about whether or not April and I should be together at all, regardless of whether or not she was pregnant. But the idea of leaving her—no matter how badly I wanted to at times, no matter how much we fought or how out of control our fights became—made me feel a guilt as fierce and cold as the Colorado winter. If I was willing to leave April, wasn't I just like my own father? Didn't it invalidate all the emotions I'd felt about him growing up? How could I do to a child who wasn't even born yet what he had done to me?

I jumped down from the tailgate and turned around when I heard Abraham open the front door. "Hey," he said, holding up his right hand where car keys dangled from his fingers. "That was April. She's pretty pissed off, man. She asked me if you were here, and before I could answer, she told me that she knew you were. She said she was coming over and hung up." He shook his head and motioned like he was going to throw the keys to me. "You better get out of here for a little while. There's no point in you being here when she shows. It's just going to be a huge fight, and I don't want anything to do with that drama."

Abraham tossed the keys to me, and I tried to catch them, but stumbled and missed completely. I picked them up off the ground. Looked at them fanned out in the palm of my hand.

"Just take my car and go for a drive," he said. "Call my house in an hour or so. Swing back here once she's gone and things have settled down."

I thought about telling him that I didn't have a valid license but figured it didn't matter. I also briefly thought about telling him how fucked up I was. Instead, I thanked him.

"No problem." He smiled. "Now go."

I walked over to the Cavalier and got in, put the car in reverse, and then backed out of the driveway, careful not to back into the mailbox across the street. I put the car in drive, and then I was moving down Straight Creek Drive, past Travis's place, past houses and parked cars and garbage cans sitting near the edges of driveways. I looked in the rearview mirror and everything blurred, like I was trying to look through the condensation on the bathroom mirror after a shower, nothing but indistinct shapes and gradations of light.

I reached over to the stereo and turned up the volume, heard Tupac's voice rapping over a set of crying violins. I turned it louder and felt the bass massaging my lower back, the pain and fury in Tupac's voice, the tweeters amplifying the high hats so the cymbals were exploding just inside my eardrums. The song pulsated through me, weaving in between my fingers and toes, vibrating the hairs on my head. I rolled the window down, felt air rush in and sweep across my face, breathed deeply. I dug into my pocket for a cigarette. Lit it. Inhaled. Exhaled. Nodded my head to the beat.

Up ahead was a stop sign that I didn't feel like stopping for, so I didn't. I slowed just enough to take the corner without sliding into a lawn. *Was that someone looking out the window? Yelling for me to slow down?*

I kept driving and music spilled out of the car's windows like smoke from a burning building. The song switched to a new track, and once again Tupac was screaming at me, amping me up, his voice filled with desperation and pain and rage; and then the adrenaline inside me was mixing in with the pills and the vodka, and I was unstoppable. Unfuckingtouchable. I pushed the gas pedal down, and the wind bit my face. I took a drag of my cigarette. Coughed. Spit out the window and watched the wind capture my saliva and fling it behind the car. I thought about the fight I'd had with April earlier, the way she smiled at me when she put me down. Fuck April. Fuck the way she treated me. The way she talked to me. Fuck every motherfucking thing about her. About moving to Colorado. Fuck my parents too. My school. The judge that took my license away. What the fuck did any of those people know about me?

Tupac screamed from the speakers, and the bass notes punched the back of the seat, and I was rapping along with him, hitting the steering wheel with the heel of my hand, absorbing his anger. I pushed the gas pedal down again and the car responded, tires gripping the pavement. I wondered what the speed limit was. Decided it didn't matter. *Was that an elementary school I just passed?* My thoughts beat through my brain like a drumroll.

Ahead of me the road was curving, and I realized I'd driven through Abraham's neighborhood and was about to pass his house again. As I got closer I could see April's car. My heart pounded. She was outside standing with her hand on her hip, annoyed or angry, probably both, her mess of blonde hair blowing over her shoulder, looking at me as I approached, watching me with that look, that vengeful, hateful look she got every time we fought. I drove past her, and for a second our eyes locked—April standing in the driveway, me behind the wheel—the hatred and anger and love and violence we both felt melting together in the space between us. I pushed the gas pedal again and we disconnected. Ahead of me was the same stop sign that I skipped earlier, and I burned right through it once more, the rubber tires slipping and shrieking around the corner, spitting rocks and dust high into the air. And then I saw they were behind me, those lights, those blue and red lights—the undeniable signal for change.

I slowed the car and pulled to a stop on the left side of the road, facing oncoming traffic. With no wind to muffle his voice, Tupac was louder now. I took my hand from the steering wheel. It was shaking. I clenched my fist to make it stop. Glanced in the rear-view mirror and saw the police officer getting out of his squad car, talking into the radio attached to his shoulder. I stared straight ahead and wondered if April could see me. An older man with white hair came out of the house we had stopped in front of and crossed his arms against his chest. Ahead of me: an elementary school; kids playing outside for recess.

"Turn down the music." The officer was next to me now, and I looked up at him, saw my own reflection in his mirrored sunglasses.

I reached over and turned the music down.

He put his hand on the door and looked inside the car. "License and registration."

My words felt muddy. "Why are you pulling me over?"

"I said to give me your license and registration."

I glared up at him. "Yeah, I heard you, but I want to know why you're pulling me over."

The officer leaned in a little closer. Spoke slowly. "I'm not going to say this again. Give me your license and registration. Now."

I tried to force myself to calm down and speak slowly. Hoped the vodka on my breath would go undetected.

"I forgot my license back at my house."

The officer straightened back up. "State your name, son."

"Tim," I said.

"Tim what?" he asked.

"Tim Hillegonds."

"Spell your last name for me."

It was a simple-enough question, but the answer was impossible in the moment. I muttered. The officer asked me to repeat what I said. I muttered again. My palms were moist, and there was a headband of sweat on my forehead. My T-shirt jumped with each beat of my heart. Softly now, Tupac's voice spilled from the speakers.

"Turn the car off. And wait right here."

I nodded and reached my right hand over to the ignition, turned the key toward me. The engine died and immediately I could hear the sound of the children in front of me playing, their happy voices trailing behind them as they ran after each other, laughing.

I looked in the rear-view mirror and saw that the officer was about halfway back to his car, the lights still flashing. The white-haired man said something to the officer. The officer waved him closer. And the thought appeared inside my head like a sunburst, just behind my eyeballs, exploding. I slammed my eyelids shut. Tried to control myself. Tried to force the thought out of my head. But the urge to flee, to run, to be as far away from what was happening was overpowering.

The man and the officer were now talking, neither of them looking at me. I reached my hand to the ignition, my mouth dry and my fingers shaking, my heart pumping in my ears. I turned the key forward, heard the starter grind, and then the engine exploded to life beneath the hood. I slammed the gearshift into drive and smashed the gas pedal into the floor of the Cavalier as hard as I could.

And then the tires were spitting rocks at the officer, a look of astonishment across his face as I glanced in the rear-view mirror one last time. The tires caught, and the car lurched forward, and then I was headed straight toward the elementary school, in the wrong lane, speeding toward the kids who were playing during recess.

But then the corner was upon me, and I jerked the wheel, and it sent the back end of the car flying out from underneath the chassis, rubber peeling from the tires and adhering to the road, and then the wheels had caught again, and the car was moving straight again, and the kids were safe and staring at me with open mouths and curious eyes, a momentarily forgotten kickball bouncing to a stop against the chain-link fence. The needle on the speedometer continued to rise, and I saw that I was doing just over forty. There was a dead end in front of me, and I knew that I had to turn left or I would be stuck, the officer behind me in his car now and closing the distance between us, but the turn was coming so quickly and my thoughts were coming so slowly, and suddenly I was turning the wheel, leaning over and pulling the steering wheel to the left with both hands until the car was sliding around the corner. And then there was a tremendous crash, the sound of metal crumpling and tearing as my head slammed forward, hitting the steering wheel in the middle of my forehead, the world flashing white, then suddenly black, then white once more. I blinked my eyes quickly, tried to blink away the pills and the vodka, the moment. There was a hissing coming from under the hood, a steady exhale of steam near where the front end of the car had been evenly parted by a cement cylinder. I looked around, tried to figure out what had happened, what I should do. And then I heard it, the police siren, and I looked in the side-view mirror and saw the flashing lights again, coming closer, coming quickly, bearing down on me like a city bus. And the feeling of being trapped, of wading too deep in the cesspool of bad decisions, struck me with the same intensity that the impact of the crash had, and I knew that my life was about to change significantly. I felt that familiar, inescapable pull toward destruction, and I felt powerless to stop it.

As the squad car came closer, its engine roaring beneath its hood, I reached over and tried to put the Chevy in reverse. I fumbled to work the shifter. Could feel my heart pounding inside me, the sweat now pouring down my cheeks like tears. Adrenaline was thick as motor oil in my bloodstream. I reached for the door handle, and it stuck. I leaned back and kicked the door open. Blasted out from the driver's seat and started sprinting down the street. My feet were heavy as I ran, the opiates making me feel like I was running in sand. I could hear voices yelling behind me, policemen barking orders like soldiers—*Stop! Freeze!*—and so I tried to run faster—to where I don't know—but I was running again, literally running this time, as fast as I could away from myself and the mountains and the guilt and shame and sadness and panic. And then close behind me footfalls much faster than mine, and I knew it was inevitable, that all was to be accounted for, that it had all caught up with me. So when I felt the bony shoulder of the Dillon Valley police officer crash into the small of my back, his weight propelling me violently through the air, there was fear inside me, yes, but inevitability, too, even relief. As his large frame landed on top of me, my elbows instantly bloodied from the impact with the street, I knew that the running was over. As my arms were yanked behind me, a knee placed in between my shoulder blades to secure me, I could feel the cold metal of the handcuffs biting into my wrists. I lay with my cheek to the street, bits of dirt and gravel sticking to my temple, fighting for breath. I lifted my head and looked down the road toward Abraham's house, all the commotion behind me increasing with the arrival of other police officers and vehicles. I thought of Abraham's wrecked car, of the steam that was shooting from under the hood. And as I strained to see ahead of me, as the radios and sirens and lights all danced and raged behind me, I could just make out the silhouette of a young woman with blonde curls staring into the wreckage, her head slowly shaking from side to side as she got in her Mazda to leave.

T E N

Smells always take me back to jail—the industrial-strength sanitizer in the air of a freshly mopped grocery store aisle; the fryer grease snaking into the dining room from a restaurant's kitchen; the last bit of coffee that burns at the bottom of the pot. Each time those smells capture me, I'm there again, back in that small holding cell my first night in jail, wondering if I will make it through whatever lies ahead.

After I spent somewhere close to four hours in a holding cell by myself, I was led down a short hallway to a heavy metal door. The guard escorting me glanced up at a camera mounted in the corner of the ceiling and nodded, and then I heard a loud buzzing like a contestant getting an answer wrong on a game show. Then a loud click. A lock disengaging. A guard pulling a door open and telling me to step through.

In my hands was my bedroll—two white sheets and a scratchy, charcoal-colored wool blanket—and a plastic cup that contained a small bar of soap, a toothbrush, a travel-sized tube of toothpaste, and a comb. When the guard had handed it to me earlier, I asked him about shampoo. "Yeah right, inmate. You're lucky we give you toothpaste. The state requires we give you only a toothbrush."

I wasn't sure exactly what time it was, but I knew it was late, and when we finally made it to C Block, the two-tiered concrete unit where I would be housed for a still-unknown amount of time, the lights were off, and all the cell doors were closed and locked. The guard waved to another camera mounted to the ceiling, and the door to C Block slid open, the iron banging on its track as it moved. The guard nodded. "Upstairs."

I started climbing the stairs slowly, my footsteps echoing loudly in the otherwise soundless pod. We arrived in front of a door. "Wait," he said. A few seconds later the door clicked open, and the guard grabbed the handle and pulled. "Go inside," he said, and I did as I was told. Behind me the door clicked shut, the sound of it locking causing me to jump—a sound so final, so judgmental, so real. I turned, wanted to ask the guard what I was supposed to do now and what was going to happen tomorrow, but he was already out of sight, his footsteps growing softer as he descended the stairs.

I turned and looked toward the metal bunk beds, the bedroll and cup still in my hands, the orange jumpsuit I had changed into baggy and foreign against my skin. On the bottom bunk, I could just make out the figure of someone sleeping. I walked to the rear of the bed, climbed to the top bunk, put my cup in the corner against the wall, and pulled the sheets apart, arranging them so they covered most of the plastic mattress. I pulled the blanket tight around my shoulders and moved toward the window so I could look outside. From the sliver of reinforced glass, I could see the lights of Breckenridge ski resort shining down and illuminating the snow. Snow groomers slowly climbed the steep terrain, the beams from their headlights shooting into the pine trees. I thought about how ridiculous it was: how I could be watching the night crew of one of the Rocky Mountains' most prestigious ski resorts from the inside of a jail cell across the street. I put my hands on my face and rubbed my eyes, trying to wipe away the view, hoping that when I opened them again I would find out that it was all just a vivid dream, and that I was back in high school, or anywhere else.

I awoke sometime during the night with an upset stomach and scrambled off the top bunk, trying desperately to make it to the stainless-steel toilet that was bolted to the concrete just a few feet from my sleeping cellmate, whom I'd yet to meet. I dropped to my knees and grabbed onto the metal edges of the toilet with both hands, heaving violently into the cold water until all the liquor and Vicodin and whatever else was in my system finally left me. Behind me, I heard my cellmate adjust himself in the bed, and when I turned around to climb back up, I noticed he'd moved as close to the cinderblock wall as he could, the blanket pulled over his head. I flushed the toilet and the impossibly loud sound of rushing water filled the room, my first night in jail halfway done, the uncertainty of what lay ahead pressing down on me like a headache.

* * *

A few days later, after I called my parents to ask them to bail me out and listened to my stepfather's voice tell me "no," after I broke down and called April, apologizing for everything that had happened, begging her forgiveness, the judge released me from jail on a personal recognizance bond—something I could only attribute to a lucky break. I had to return to the courthouse in just under a month to appear for my sentencing hearing.

In the thirty or so days that I waited to go to court, while April's stomach grew larger and her pregnancy no longer felt new, things returned to the relatively normal state they always did after April and I went through a major crisis. We did our best to forget about the stresses of our lives and the chaos around us, focusing instead on the things that made us happy—playing with Maddie, going for long drives through Summit County, eking out an existence with the little bit of money we made at Denny's. During the day, I acted as if nothing much had happened. "It's my first real offense," I said to April as we sipped coffee at Denny's, even though I was thinking back to the DUI I'd gotten in Chicago, the court date that I'd missed, the Illinois warrant that had been issued. "I mean, how much time can the judge really give me?"

It turned out that it wasn't entirely up to the judge. A few days before I was set to appear for my sentencing, I got a call from the District Attorney asking me to come into the office at the courthouse an hour before my hearing. When I arrived, I was escorted into a conference room where my public defender was seated at a large wooden table surrounded by chairs that looked like they'd been there for years. For a moment, I stared at the table and wondered how many people just like me had sat in that very room, their hearts beating quickly as their fates were arranged, nervously awaiting the deal that could make or break their futures.

I took a seat at the table and a few minutes later a youngish woman entered carrying an armful of brown case files. She acknowledged the public defender, nodded at me, and sat down. She set the file in front of her and opened it.

"Mr. Hillegonds, you're currently charged with eleven offenses from the incident that occurred in Dillon last month. The state is willing to drop all but five of them in exchange for a guilty plea. You'd plead guilty to a misdemeanor resisting arrest charge, a misdemeanor traffic charge, one misdemeanor underage consumption charge, one misdemeanor criminal mischief charge, and one felony eluding charge." She looked up at me for the first time, and I could see that that her eyes were blue. "Will you accept the deal I've outlined for you?"

I looked to my public defender. "What do you think?"

He sighed. "I think you should take it, but it's up to you."

I shifted in my seat and put my hands on the table in front of me. Spread my fingers as wide as I could. They looked dry and cracked from washing them so often at Denny's, and I wished I were back there, waiting tables to the sounds of elevator music and low-volume conversations. I kept my eyes trained on my hands. Spoke softly. "The eluding charge is a felony?"

"That's correct," the District Attorney said. "But we're not asking for a lot of jail time. You'll likely serve ten days of your total sentence with the rest of it suspended. The judge will also probably give you the option of serving the remainder of your days on weekends."

I closed my eyes and tilted my head back. Opened them and studied the fractures in the drop ceiling while I thought about what it would mean, what it would be like to carry a felony around for the rest of my life. I was pretty sure the felony case would stick with me forever, but what was the alternative? Take my chances and take the case to trial? Maybe. Maybe if I had a real lawyer. Maybe if I had money. But right then, in that chair, what choice did I really have? I thought about Abraham and his banged-up car, how there was almost no chance I'd be able to pay for the damages. I thought about my unborn baby, how it would have a father who was a felon. I thought about how much had changed. I brought my head down and caught the District Attorney's eye. Rubbed my face in frustration. Shook my head and said I'd take the deal.

* * *

January 20, 1998, a Tuesday. Bill Clinton is the POTUS and dial-up internet exists and people are still talking and arguing and preaching about cloning. But I wasn't thinking about politics or technology, or science, and I'd only been on the internet a handful of times. Instead, I was playing a video game in the upstairs room at April's mother's house. The "bonus room," she called it, and it did sort of feel like a bonus of a room, because it was enormous and set up for watching movies and playing games and lying around.

I sat on the floor with my back against the sofa in front of a huge television, frantically pushing buttons on a PlayStation controller, biting down on my lip while trying to get my Tekken 2 fighter, Nina Williams, to kick the shit out of Marshall Law. Music was blaring from the TV, techno, but it also sounded like someone was calling my name from downstairs. I kept pushing buttons, trying to get Nina to do some sort of complicated tackle move.

"What?" I yelled, tapping the triangle button on the controller like a madman.

"Tim, it's time!"

"Time for what?" I yelled again, still tapping, annoyed, wondering why April couldn't wait five minutes for me to finish my game.

"Tim, I'm having the baby!"

I pressed the pause button on the controller. Sat there. Tried to figure out whether what I thought she just said was indeed what she said. My heart pounded and it sank in. I felt my stomach drop from my abdomen like I was riding a roller coaster. Everything was suddenly very real. During her pregnancy it hadn't seemed completely real. Even when I felt the baby moving inside her, I still didn't quite connect it to new life, to a new life I helped create.

I heard frantic movements downstairs. Took the stairs three at a time and heard April's mother say something about watching Maddie while we went to the hospital.

"Holy shit, April." I could see sweat had beaded on her forehead, and she held her stomach with both hands. She smiled at me. I felt nauseous.

"I'll drive us there," I said.

"But what about your license?"

"Who cares? If they're ever going to cut me a break it will be when I'm driving you to the hospital so you can have my baby."

She laughed. "Fine," she said, moving toward the front door of the house.

In the car, April rolled the window down. "Drive slower," she said. I let off the gas. Two minutes later she told me to drive faster. I pressed down on the gas.

"Are you ready for this?" she asked, staring out the window.

I tried to sound normal, but there were bricks of fear in my chest. "Yeah," I stuttered.

April laughed again. "You don't sound like it."

I merged onto I-70. Lake Dillon was blue in the distance and shining from the sun. The waves were ablaze. It's majestic, I thought to myself, and then immediately wondered why that word popped into my head. Minutes later I got off the highway. Seconds after that we pulled into the unloading area at the hospital.

I threw the car in neutral and pulled the parking brake, almost falling as I jumped out and sprinted around the hood. I lunged for the door handle, pulled April's door open.

"Okay," I said.

"Okay?"

"Okay, we're here."

"I see that," she said, not moving. "You need to let someone know we're here and get me a wheelchair."

"Right," I said, and ran inside, flagged down a nurse with a wheelchair.

Sometime later we were inside the delivery room and April was on the bed and I was thinking about how everything was going to *really* change this time, how I was about to transform from a nineteen-year-old kid to a nineteen-year-old *father*. I had no idea what that meant.

April screamed and her face was twisted up like when we fought. I stood over her, literally shaking, feeling utterly useless, looking at the door, averting my eyes from the expression on her face, from the pain. Maybe, I thought, maybe I should just run away from all of this. Was it even possible for April and me to raise a baby together? Did I have any idea what that meant? All the false confidence of the last eight months evaporated and the truth was swimming around in my head. But then April was pushing and the doctor was coaching her and April was angry because she was in pain and wanted the drugs to numb it, but it was past the point of no return. So she clamped her eyes shut and grit her teeth and saliva bubbled onto her lips as she pushed as hard as she could, using the anger she felt to fuel her body, and then she was screaming again, throaty and low.

And then the baby was there in the room with me, her body rigid as she cried and sucked in tiny lungfuls of air. She was pink and wrinkled and covered in blood and amniotic fluid, and still connected to April by the gray umbilical cord. And then I was crying too, the tears streaming down my face, happy, but scared, perhaps more scared than happy, and I realized the doctor was speaking to me, holding out a pair of scissors. "Here you go, Dad. You can cut the cord."

Dad? Was that me? The word hung in the air, undefined.

I took the scissors and they felt cold in my hand, lifeless. Out of place. The doctor pointed to where I should make the cut. "Give it a good snip," he said, and I reached down and squeezed the scissors together and the sharpened blades slid through the tissue easily, too easily, and I saw not just the newness of life, but how fragile it is.

And then my daughter was whisked away and sponged off, wrapped tightly in a white blanket while I watched. My eyes followed every move of the nurse, and then the nurse gave her to April and April rocked her, crying big, raindrop-sized tears. And then she looked up at me. "Here," she said. "Do you want to hold her?" "Yes," I said, and for the first time I held her, this new creation, this new person that I was now responsible for, a person barely the length of my forearm. I rocked her back and forth, back and forth, staring at her tiny eyelids. When she opened them, I saw her eyes were brown, like mine, like my father's. I rocked her gently, memorizing every feature on her face, every eyelash. Back and forth. Forth and back.

* * *

We moved into a recovery room, April on the hospital bed, propped up by a pillow. She looked exhausted, her eyes barely open. She smiled across the room at me where I sat rocking my daughter, gazing at her sleeping face, transfixed.

"What do you want to name her?" April said. We'd talked about it briefly but never landed on anything.

I glanced up at April, then back to my daughter's face. She was so perfect. So small. So untouched by the world. It was impossible that yesterday she didn't exist.

"I want to name her Haley," I said, looking up at April. The name reminded me of my childhood, of watching Hayley Mills movies at my grandmother's. It seemed right to me.

April nodded. Smiled. Closed her eyes. "Haley," she said, pondering, feeling the name as it fell off her tongue. "Haley," she said again, and I resumed rocking, smiling at the way the name sounded coming from April, floating across the room.

"What do you think?" I said.

"Haley Jade Hillegonds," April said. "Welcome to the world."

* * *

I called my mother from the phone next to the bed April was in. She picked up after the second ring.

"Mom," I said.

"Hey, Tim," she said.

"You're a grandmother," I said, smiling. On the other end of the phone I heard her start crying. Was she happy? Sad? I wished she was with us. Wished I could hand her my daughter so she could hold her. Love her. My mother was meant to be a grandmother. I felt like I'd screwed up by having a baby so far away from her. I knew I'd screwed up in a million other ways, too, even if I wasn't entirely sure what they all were.

"What's her name?" she asked.

"Haley Jade," I said

"Oh, Tim," she said, "that's beautiful."

"*She's* beautiful, Ma," I said. "You should see her. So tiny. These little fingers. Smaller than paperclips."

"I wish I could," she said.

"You will."

"Kiss her for me, Tim. Tell that little girl I love her."

"I will, Ma."

"Tim?"

"Yeah?"

"I love you."

"I know, Ma." I tried not to cry. "I'll call you again soon."

* * *

Not long after Haley was born, because we needed a little bit more space, we moved to an apartment complex called Sierra Madre. April wasn't working much since she was taking care of Haley and Maddie most of the time, and waiting tables at Denny's, no matter how much I loved it, just wasn't paying the bills. "You need to get a real job," she said to me one day, shortly after we moved. "My mom said she can probably get you a job at Public Service Company."

I sat at the kitchen table flipping through the *Summit Daily News*. I looked up at her. She had a laundry basket in her hand and one of Haley's onesies was hanging off the side.

"What's the Public Service Company?"

She put the basket on the ground, grabbed the onesie and started to fold it. "It's the electric company. You know, the guys who work on the power lines."

"Okay," I said, glancing back at the paper. "Ask your mom if she can set it up."

Over the course of the next few weeks, I had the interview at Public Service and got the job, thanks entirely to April's mom. My driver's license was still suspended by the State of Illinois, and having one was a prerequisite for the job, but April's mom called in some favors and they made an exception.

I asked the interviewer, a mustachioed man in a button-down work shirt, what I was going to be doing. "Officially, you'll be a lineman helper," he said, glancing at the paperwork on his desk in front of him. "Unofficially, you'll be what we call a 'grunt.' Which means you'll do pretty much anything a lineman tells you to do."

During the first few weeks on the job, I was introduced to hard labor in a way my drug- and alcohol-soaked body simply wasn't prepared for. I stabbed a spade shovel at the frozen dirt until my hands blistered and bled, listening to a goateed lineman spit tobacco in the dirt next to me and haze me like I was a fraternity pledge. "Is that all you got, you fucking fairy?" he said, leaning against the truck. "My baby daughter can dig holes better than you. She could probably beat your skinny little ass too." I wanted to say something back to him, to stand up to him, but he was so much bigger, so much meaner. So instead I kept my mouth shut and shoveled, wondering if I'd ever be as tough as I wanted to be, doubting it, feeling like a coward.

By the time I went home at night, my body hurt in ways it never had before. I wanted to go immediately to bed, to try and get some rest before I had to get up at 6 a.m. to do it again, but April would be at the end of her rope by the time I got home. She would hold up Haley when I walked in the door, her baby arms and legs moving like a hermit crab's, Maddie somewhere in the background playing. "Here," she'd say in a voice that did indeed seem exhausted. "You need to take her. I need a break."

And so I would take her. I would walk around the house, still wearing my dirt-covered jeans and smelling of sweat and cigarette smoke, and fly her around the room with my outstretched arms like she was an airplane. In the palm of my hand she felt light as paper, light as dried leaves, and she smiled and laughed as we flew across the first floor of the apartment, past the kitchen table and over the chairs, down low toward the floor, and then back up toward the ceiling. She giggled and squealed, and I did, too, and I loved the way she was fearless while she flew, the way, like me, she loved the freedom of falling away.

* * *

One night when April was sleeping and Haley had woken up, I walked to her room and leaned over the gate to her crib. She was lying wide-awake, her curious eyes taking in everything around her, her arms and legs and hands and fingers all moving at the same time, as if she'd just discovered she could control them and decided to use them all at once. I picked her up, brought her downstairs, and laid her on the light brown carpeting to change her. I knelt in front of her and took her pajamas off, and she seemed content to lie there forever while looking at me, wearing only her diaper, her skin pale and pink and new. Her fingers, barely longer than the zipper tab on my hoodie, opened and closed and opened again. Throughout the apartment I could hear the hum of appliances, the steady tick from the clock above the sink in the kitchen. Outside, the occasional swelling of a car passing by. I leaned forward to lie on my stomach and propped myself up on my elbows, my open palms cradling her head, Haley fitting perfectly into the space between my chest and the floor. I felt the softness of her hair in my hands, the warmth of her scalp. I leaned low to kiss her forehead, Haley squirming as I did, and I smelled her sweet, milky breath. I stared into her eyes—seal brown like mine—and felt the weighty push of fatherhood. "I love you, sweet girl," I whispered, wanting nothing more than to stay there, in that cottony stillness of night.

* * *

Even with a new job and a little more money coming in, the pattern of my relationship with April was relentless. We fought, made up, fought, made up, and then fought again until I would leave the apartment and make my way to a cheap hotel or the Silverthorne hostel or Travis's house for the night. Even though Travis and I had fallen out of touch over the previous year, he was still my friend, still a small piece of home that I could cling to in the shadow of the Rockies.

Upon getting the new job at Public Service Company, I opened a checking account that only I had access to, and with considerably more money coming in, I regained a sense of freedom. April and

I were partners in our relationship—at least we tried to be—but that was essentially where our partnership ended. The apartment lease and checking account and car were all in her name, and it was a source of constant frustration for me. Prior to opening my own account, any time I needed money for anything—fast food, beer, gum, cigarettes—I'd have to ask her for it, immediately feeling emasculated and resentful. Gaining financial freedom, for better or worse, enabled me to be bolder in my decision making. When April and I fought, I was quicker to leave, quicker to slam the door yelling curse words at her, no longer worried that I wouldn't have a place to stay or alcohol to drink or drugs to consume. I could afford those things now, and I became emboldened to the point where I could entertain the idea that maybe, just maybe, April and I weren't going to make it. And more so, if we didn't make it, I could survive on my own. I wasn't quite sure what a future without April looked like, but it had started to seem like an inevitability that we would fail.

One afternoon, after yet another fight, I walked to a restaurant just up the hill from Denny's called Old Chicago. I'd always gotten a kick out of the name—Old Chicago, *good old* Chicago—and every time I drove by the sign, staring out the passenger window of April's car, I'd feel a twinge of homesickness.

I called Travis from the pay phone near the front lobby of the restaurant, and a half hour later, he had picked me up and we were driving back to his apartment in his hatchback Honda Civic. He'd moved to Wildernest sometime after I'd gotten together with April, and I hadn't seen his new place yet.

"It's a lot bigger than our other place," he said, slowing for a red light. "If things are rough with April, man, you could always crash with us for a while. Maybe it'll be good for you guys to get some space."

I took him up on his offer, and two weeks later I was still there, still bumming rides to work from him in the mornings, still sleeping on his secondhand couch, still smoking cigarettes and drinking beer and convincing myself I was happy not to be fighting with April day after day. And I think I *was* happy, at least comparatively speaking, but there was also an ever-increasing feeling of guilt. April was at home in her apartment alone, changing Haley's diapers and taking care of Maddie, while I drank beer, smoked weed, and watched episodes of *Dawson's Creek*. I felt the unfairness of it all—how I could leave and she had to stay—but I also felt that I was getting a raw deal, too, that it was April's fault that I wasn't with my daughters: I missed those two beautiful little girls as much as I missed home. I missed putting Haley down at night and watching her sink into the softness of her crib mattress, the way she looked so peaceful while she lay there sleeping. I missed Maddie, too, how loving she was and how, with no coaxing from me, she had started calling me "Dad" a few months prior to my leaving. And on many nights, right before I fell asleep on Travis's couch, I thought of the books we read together, of the Berenstain Bears, of how the titles were always so perfect and simple for what was happening in our lives: *The Berenstain Bears Get in a Fight*; *The Berenstain Bears Moving Day*; *The Berenstain Bears and the Trouble with Grown Ups*.

* * *

Late one Friday afternoon at Travis's, after I'd gotten off work early and we'd already been drinking for a couple of hours, the phone rang.

Travis cupped his hand over the receiver and held it down near his waist. "Hey, it's April. You want to talk to her?"

I thought for a second and knew I probably shouldn't but nodded my head yes anyway. I hadn't talked to her in over a week, and I knew we needed to hash things out. I didn't want to admit it, but I missed her. I walked over and grabbed the phone. Put it to my ear and said hello.

"Hey, how are things?" she said. Her tone seemed light. Friendly, even.

Travis walked back over to the couch and sat where I'd been

sitting. He grabbed his smokes off the table and pulled one out. I motioned to him to throw me one, and he did. I caught it midair. Dug in my pocket for a lighter.

"Things are good. Just working and staying here at Travis's." I heard a child's voice in the background. "Was that Maddie?"

April laughed. "Yeah, she's all sugared up and running around the house like a crazy person."

I smiled. Lit my cigarette.

"Listen, Tim, we need to talk about things. Like really talk. You should come over here." She paused. "What are we even doing? With us, I mean. Are we going to figure this thing out or what?"

I stared at the end of my cigarette, watched the smoke rise and bend like the cursive letters I'd learned in grade school. "I don't know, April. I'm just tired of fighting all the time. I feel like if I come over and talk, it's just going to end up the same way it always ends up. And I don't want that. I really don't. Things are just so broken with us lately."

"Then let's go for a drive." There was urgency in her voice. "You know we like to do that. Right? That's our thing. We listen to music and drive and smoke and just talk about things. It'll be nice. Just like we used to. Come on, Tim. Just a drive?"

"I don't know, April. I feel like it's a bad idea."

She was right about the drives, though. We loved driving through Summit County together, her at the wheel, me in the passenger seat, Haley or Maddie or both of them buckled into her car seats in the back, sleeping while we drove through the mountains. We sometimes followed Highway 9 north all the way to the Green Mountain Reservoir, one of the water sources for Colorado's Western Slope, or up to Loveland Pass, where we stopped at the summit and felt how thin the air was at 12,000 feet. "Come on, Tim. You need to see the girls anyway. They miss you. Don't you miss them?"

I thought about the last time I held Haley. Immediately, I wanted to hold her again, to feel the softness of her skin against my cheek.

I reached over and grabbed my beer. Took a long drink before I answered. "Fine, April. But you have to promise me we won't fight."

Across the room Travis shook his head and mouthed the words, "Don't do it."

"I promise," April said.

"Fine," I said, turning away from Travis. "Pick me up here. I'll see you in a little bit."

* * *

We headed north toward the reservoir with Haley and Maddie buckled into car seats in the back, and our conversation progressed calmly, the way it always had in the beginning. The sun dipped behind the mountains, and the last of the late October afternoon light was fading, the air still warm enough for the windows of the car to be rolled halfway down, but the temperature slowly falling. When the breeze hit my face, I closed my eyes, breathed deeply.

April drove and we made small talk about work and the girls, and it felt good to be next to her again, to be doing a thing that felt normal again. But I didn't want to push it. I didn't want to ruin the night by staying together too long, so I asked her to turn around and head back toward Travis's. We were nearing April's apartment, which we needed to pass on the way back, and the radio was tuned to a country station. Two cigarettes burned. The smoke spread, then escaped out the window.

"Do you miss being home with us?" April asked.

"Sometimes," I said, looking down at my steel-toes. "Maybe more than sometimes."

"Then come home," she said.

"I don't know if I want to," I said. "Things are so fucked up between us."

"Come on, they aren't that bad."

"Yeah they are, April, and you know it."

She took a deep breath and let it out quickly. "Yeah, because you won't get your shit together, Tim. That's why things are screwed up. If you stopped acting like a child all the time maybe we could actually have a chance at a life."

A chance at a life. Something shifted inside me. It was as if I could see our entire relationship, everything that happened in the twenty-two months I lived there, everything I tried to disappear with vodka and beer and drugs, was suddenly laid out before me in explicit, intricate detail, as if all of my failures, all the drugs and court cases and fights and embarrassment I'd caused myself, were crushing me at once. The weight of it all. The density. It overwhelmed me.

"Things *are* that bad, April! Can't you fucking see that?"

I wanted to blame her for all of it, for everything that had happened in my life. I wanted to make her feel some sort of responsibility for the way things had turned out between us.

"It's because *you've* made them like this, Tim. Because you're so fucking selfish that you can't see that all of this," she motioned with her hand to the rest of the car, to the girls, "all of *us*, are your responsibility. You can't walk away from that. You just can't."

Was she right? Was I obligated to stay, to be with her, no matter how hard it was, no matter how much we fought, no matter the fallout? It seemed like complete insanity.

"I don't want to walk away from *them*, April. I want to walk away from *you*." I wasn't sure if I meant it, or if it was just the alcohol talking, but I was almost screaming, and it felt good. "I want to walk away from all this bullshit and fighting. Don't you fucking get that?"

My voice was loud, much too loud for the small car. The girls were awake, and they shrank into their car seats. I hated myself for doing this to them again. For getting in the car with April in the first place. Travis had known this would happen. Anyone with a pulse knew this would happen.

I shut my eyes and opened them. Asked her a question I should have been asking myself. "Why do you even call me when you know it's just going to be the same shit over and over again? Why even go through this? It's like you fucking enjoy the drama."

April's eyes were wide, but not from fear or surprise. They looked alive and alert, ready for battle, the eyes of an athlete ready to compete.

"It's like I enjoy the drama?" she said, glaring at me. "More like you do, asshole. You're the one who always gets us to this point. You're a piece of shit, Tim. Nothing but a loser-ass drunk that can't take care of his kids *or* his woman."

I'd heard it a million times before, but it always stung. "Stop the fucking car, April." She kept driving. "Stop the motherfucking car, April, stop it right now!" I needed to be out of the car and away from her. I could feel the rage banging around inside me, and I didn't want to give into it. Didn't want to ride this fucking bullshit merry-go-round with her again.

"Fuck you!" she screamed back. "Make me! I'm not stopping the car!"

I glanced at the speedometer, saw the needle sitting between thirty-five and forty. I glanced at April. Back at the speedometer. Looked at the door handle. Pulled it.

Air crashed into the car and I pushed the door against the wind. My eyes blinked and I squinted. My right eye teared up and water slid from its corner. Music played and wind whipped and the tires whirred along the pavement.

"What the fuck, Tim?" April yelled. "What are you doing?" Close the door!"

I undid the seatbelt, and April's voice barely registered. I looked down, and the road beneath was a blurred stripe calling me, an invitation to somewhere other than being in the car with April. I had no plan. I didn't care what happened. I just needed to be gone.

So I went.

I was consumed by the moment and the fury, and in one quick movement I grabbed the roof of the car with one hand and the door with the other and I hoisted myself out of my seat. I dropped onto the pavement and April was yelling and the wind was blasting past me, ripping through my hair and into my ears, and then I was outside the car and the fabric of my shirt was a flag behind me, flapping. I was free. Weightless. And for a moment, we were both going the same speed, me and the car, and then I was sliding in my work boots, the rubber peeling off the soles in layers. The car inched ahead of me. Inched some more. And then it was past me, and I was alone in the chaos, skidding across the road in my boots, knees bent like a skier.

And then I stopped.

I stood in the street, breathing hard and feeling the adrenaline beat through my temples, watching April's brake lights glow as she slowed to turn the corner. I had jumped out of the car a block from her house.

I ran down the street toward the taillights, making the same turn she had, sprinting hard toward her apartment. Why was I running toward her? Wasn't I just trying to get away from her?

My boots pounded against the ground as my arms pumped. Seconds later I was standing before her front door, chest heaving, and April was sitting in the parking lot watching me, white smoke from the exhaust pipe of her car clouding toward the sky. I was screaming again now, gesturing at her car, so angry with her, yes, but so angry with myself for knowing the night would end like this and agreeing to meet with her anyway. And being angry with myself made me even angrier with her and tears streamed down my face and I felt like I wasn't myself, like I was literally not myself, like I had somehow inhabited the body of someone who truly doesn't know what he's going to do, and worse, doesn't care. I looked at the door to April's apartment and I thought, *fuck that door*, and then I stepped back and throttled a kick into it as hard as I could. It gave way and splinters flew into the living room and it made me happy, the broken wood, the destruction, the strength I felt. I screamed in the direction of the car from the doorway, sweat and tears streaming down my cheeks. *"Is this what you wanted? Is this what you fucking wanted?"*

I charged into the house, my boots cracking splintered pieces of wood as I stepped on them on my way to the kitchen, and I tried to think, tried to calm down, tried to control myself. I was scared of what I might do, and I knew I should leave but I didn't. Instead I leaned forward against the sink and turned on the cold water and bent down and gulped straight from the faucet. I coughed. Drank more and let the water run. I knew I should leave. I needed to leave. I needed to leave right that instant. I watched the water pour against the stainless steel, splattering in all directions, and then I cupped my hands and filled them up, splashed water on my face. *Calm down, Tim,* I thought. *Calm down.*

Did I know this would happen? Deep down inside did I know that if I left Travis's house and got in the car with April that we would fight and I would lose control and this would be the inevitable conclusion? Did I know this and do it anyway? Did I want this? Was I that fucked up?

I heard April walk through the door, and I turned around to see her carrying Haley, her eyes wide, Maddie following close behind them. Maddie stared at me with her big, brown eyes, and I could see how afraid she was, how afraid I'd made her. Was there ever a bigger piece of shit than me? I hated myself for all I'd put them through. I was a coward. I was everything April had told me I was.

April said nothing and took the girls upstairs. I stayed where I was. Continued to ignore the voice inside my head telling me to leave. A few minutes later, April came back downstairs. I watched her from the kitchen. Water dripped from my wet face onto the front of my shirt. She walked over to the broken front door.

"Great," she said, trying to force the door closed. "You better pay for this. I can't even lock the door now." She glared at me.

Don't say anything, I thought. *Stay calm,* I thought. And the second

I saw her glaring at me I was angry again, and ready to fight with her again, to fight her, to fight.

I pushed myself off the counter and walked toward her. "I'm not paying for shit, April," I said, midstride. "It's your fault anyway." I stopped a few feet from her, pointed my finger. "I told you to stop the car and you wouldn't."

"So you come over here and kick my door down?" She planted her feet and shook her head. "You're lucky I don't call the police."

I said, "You're lucky *I* don't call the police, you crazy bitch."

"Yeah, see how far that gets you."

I turned and walked to the couch, fell onto my stomach and buried my face in the cushions. This was something a child would do, I thought. Is that what I was? A child? A toddler who couldn't manage his emotions?

I heard April's voice. "What, are you just going to lie there now?"

My whole body clenched, every muscle flexed. I tried to push all my emotions, all my anger, into the fibers of my muscles. I tried to expend the rage.

"Did you hear me, Tim? What the fuck are you doing lying there? You need to leave. Right now."

I squeezed my eyes shut even tighter. Tried to bury my face deeper into the couch cushion. I heard April take a few steps toward me.

"Tim! Get the fuck out of here!"

I heard her voice and I knew I should listen to her and I should leave, and I wanted to, but I also wanted to stay, and I didn't know why because I knew everything was about to go crazy in a minute or two, but I felt so fucked up and this is what we did, we went crazy. So I said, "Why don't you make me leave, April," and as soon as the words left my mouth I felt April jump on my back and start hitting me with hammer fists. That was just the excuse I needed to release all the rage I'd been trying to get a handle on, and so I pushed off the couch as hard as I could, felt the back of my head hit the bottom of her chin, heard her wince, and I loved every single second of it.

She jumped off me and walked toward the kitchen.

"Don't walk away from me!" I screamed.

She kept walking, and so I popped up and rushed her, grabbed her right shoulder and spun her around so she was facing me. I felt strong. I felt like the strongest man in the universe. I wanted her to fear me. To hate me. Or did I want her to love me? Was it all the same? What the fuck was wrong with me? Why was I still there?

I grabbed both of her shoulders and pushed her against the wall. Pushed her *into* the wall. She tried to fend me off, but I held her, slammed her against the wall again, already hating myself but feeling absolutely powerless to control it. I realized I was crying again, and I felt like a fucking madman, tears streaming down. "Get off me, Tim!" she screamed, with fear in her eyes. "Please, stop!" she yelled, her shoulders trembling. "Tim!"

I heard my name and it snapped me out of it and for a split second I glimpsed the enormity of what was happening. I released her, and the second the pressure was off she grabbed my throat and squeezed. I cocked my right hand and wanted to crush that small, fragile face directly in front of me, with its pale skin and adorable freckles—the face that I still loved but somehow wanted to hurt, and I released my balled fist, punching downward at the last second, hitting her in the arm. She cried out in pain, a loud cry that sounded so real and so terrible that I knew I'd hurt her, that I'd truly hurt her, again. And I knew without a doubt that I was an out of control wildman, a lunatic, and the shame and fear and regret was instant and paralyzing.

I stepped back from April, and she grabbed her arm and cried, and I turned and ran out the door as fast as I could, already knowing that I ran because I was a coward and a loser and a criminal and an absent father and an abuser. I ran because it's what I did, because I didn't know what else to do, because I hurt so bad in that moment and knew I didn't have a right to after what I had done. I ran because I felt so insignificant, so broken and damaged and utterly irredeemable, that I knew that I could never be normal, and I could never be good, and I could never make up for all the despicable things I had done.

* * *

From April's house, I ran for a block until I reached the Grease Monkey at the end of the street, its windows dark and parking lot filled with cars, and wished I could steal one, wished I could reach under the dash and hotwire it, drive the stolen car across the Continental Divide, across state lines, across the entire country and never return.

I ran around to the side of the building where the streetlamps couldn't reach me and fell with my back against the brick wall and slid down it until my face was in my kneecaps. I thought about the look in April's eyes, the fear they held, and the sound of her scream—an audible confirmation of the pain I caused.

After some time had passed, I heard a car coming down the street and got up to peer around the corner. As it drove by, I saw that it was April. I wondered where she was going, and then felt my stomach drop when I realized she was probably headed to the police station.

I walked out from behind the building and stopped near the edge of the parking lot. Maybe I needed to be arrested, maybe I needed to be taken off the street and put in a jail cell where I couldn't hurt April or anyone else anymore. Maybe I needed to be completely removed from the equation.

I started to walk toward Travis's house, but then I turned back toward April's. I was so exhausted I felt like I couldn't manage to stay awake for another second. I wanted to fall asleep right there on the street, my head against the pavement, and drift off into a dream where none of this had happened.

Maybe I could just wait at April's until she returned home. I could apologize. Try to make her understand that it was the alcohol that made me act that way, that it wasn't really me. Did I even believe that?

A few minutes later I was back at April's broken front door. I pushed it open and stood there in the doorway, the inside of the apartment dark and empty, the air still sticky with the residue of our fight. I stepped into the living room and shut the door behind me as far as I could. It was quiet, the clock on the wall ticking softly from above the kitchen sink. My eyelids felt unbelievably heavy, and I walked to the couch, lay down on my back. I would close my eyes just for a second, I thought, just until April came home and I could apologize. Maybe our relationship was still fixable. Maybe she would forgive me and things would go back to normal. Maybe in a couple of weeks we'd look back on what happened tonight and be grateful, because it finally meant that things between us would change.

* * *

I heard their voices first, firm and authoritative, and then the static from their radios. I opened my eyes to a flashlight, a small yellow sun burning into my retina. I squinted. Swallowed. Heard a voice tell me to stand up and put my hands behind my back. I got up slowly, and the blood from my head rushed to my feet. I felt like I might fall. An officer cuffed me, then reached in my pocket and pulled out my wallet. Looked at my bank card. Another officer asked me if April was my girlfriend. I nodded. One of the officers said, "We're going to take you over to the police station," and then he spoke into the radio on his shoulder. "Confirm one in custody. Last name Hillegonds. Suspect is being cooperative."

E L E V E N

Before every change, there comes a type of surrendering, a kind of conceding, a yielding to the idea that perhaps everything one has done up to a certain point may have been flawed. At times, this surrender comes like a sucker punch, quickly and abruptly; other times, it arrives sluggishly, like the warmer temperatures of spring after a long Chicago winter.

After I'd been arrested at April's house and brought to the police station, after I'd sat handcuffed to a table admitting to the officer in front of me all that I'd done, I arrived at the jail in the same way I'd arrived the other times, through a garage door that led into the back of the facility. I distinctly remember feeling something within me shift that night, perhaps at exactly the same time my inky fingers rolled across the ID sheet—a piece of me moving over and making way for the idea that I was a failure at everything—my relationship with April, my fresh start, being a father. I wasn't yet ready to admit it, explicitly, and I'm not certain I could have properly identified it that night, but the chaos of my life was finally beginning to soften me, to open me up to the idea of change.

My first full day in the jail, as voices droned endlessly from the television bolted high above the reach of inmates, I called my stepfather. I knew he would be disappointed in me, and likely not help, but I had no one else to call, no other numbers I thought would actually accept the collect call charges. When he answered the phone, I was quick to blame the night on April, to tell him how crazy she'd made me, how none of it would have happened if she would have just let me out of the car, but even as I told him, even as I pleaded with him to bail me out once I'd had my bond hearing the next day, I knew that I was lying, that the truth was that I could have run away from April and the fight, and instead I ran toward it.

"Please, Dad. *Please.* You don't understand what it's like in here."

His responses came slowly, and I could hear him choosing his words carefully. "I'm so sorry you're in there, son. I truly am. But you'll get through this. I promise. You need to be strong." He paused. "We're praying for you, son."

I clenched my eyes shut. I didn't need prayers. I needed money. I needed to be at work on Monday morning and fix things with April and be a father to Haley and Maddie.

My eyes welled up, and I tried to blink the tears back. "Dad, I swear I'll never ask you for anything again. Just do this one thing for me. Please don't leave me in here."

I rested my forehead on the cinderblock wall and above me, on the television, a talk show audience cheered.

"What happens tomorrow?" he asked.

I closed my eyes. "My bond hearing."

"Then call me after your bond hearing when you know more. I love you, son. You're going to be okay. You need to know that."

I opened my eyes, wishing I could tell my stepfather how scared I really was, how defeated I felt. How much I'd been drinking and using, and how bad things were with April. Were there even words for that? Was it possible for him to understand? To know the pain I felt, the self-hatred, the endless compulsion I had to be drunk and anesthetized and operating on the blurry edges of reality?

Maybe he understood more back then than I knew, but I had no perspective, and no patience. All I knew is that I was in a place that scared me, and I needed money to get out, and so instead of listening and being thankful that he had even accepted the collect call charges in the first place, I reached over and hung up the phone, his words cut off midsentence, replaced immediately by the relentless sounds of incarceration.

* * *

At my bond hearing the following day, the bailiff motioned for me to rise, and when I stood, the silver shackles around my legs and wrists clinked loudly.

"Next up, Hillegonds case number D0591998CR000313."

I made my way to a podium and stood there watching the judge, whose eyes were lowered and scanning something on the bench in front of him. He glanced up at me quickly, then back down again.

"Mr. Hillegonds, you're charged with first-degree felony burglary, third-degree assault, criminal mischief, and harassment."

It was the first time I'd heard exactly what I'd been charged with. Felony burglary? That didn't make any sense. I didn't think I'd taken anything from April's. It was probably just the police charging me with everything they possibly could, knowing it would get pled down eventually. The felony charge would give the district attorney a lot of leverage when it came time to offer me a deal.

"Given the nature of the case and the defendant's prior criminal record, bail is set at $22,200." The judge shuffled the papers in front of him and began preparing for the next case. I wanted to run up to him and beg him to reconsider, to ask him to give me a number that I could afford, a number that would allow me to bond out immediately. Instead, the judge addressed me directly. "Mr. Hillegonds, lest you forget, the court has implemented an order of protection for the victim, Ms. Murphy. You're to have no contact whatsoever with her, whether on the phone or in person. Do you understand me, Mr. Hillegonds?"

I nodded.

"Speak your answer, Mr. Hillegonds."

"Yes, Your Honor. I understand."

"Good. That's all. Bailiff?"

The bailiff came over to the podium, put his hand on my shoulder, and motioned toward the side door we'd come in. "This way," he said, and I followed him to the door, shuffling through it while my leg shackles rattled, wondering how I would ever find the money to leave.

* * *

Later that night, I called my stepfather again and pleaded with him to post the $22,200 it would cost for me to bond out.

"I'll pay you back, Dad. I *promise*."

I heard him sigh on the other end of the phone, and when he spoke, his voice sounded strained, as if he didn't want to say the words that were about to come out of his mouth. "I'm sorry, Tim," he said, "but we won't be bailing you out."

I hung up on him angrily, before he'd even had a chance to give me his reasoning. Sometime later, after the lights were off and there was only the even breathing of my cellmate sleeping below me, I agonized over the way he'd phrased it. "Won't be bailing you out" was a lot different than "can't bail you out." Which meant that he was making a conscious choice to leave me there, to grapple with my mess.

* * *

For almost the entire first week in jail, I slept. I woke for breakfast and lunch, and most of the time for dinner, but almost every other moment, I stayed wrapped in a blanket on the top bunk in my cell, my face inches from the wall, willfully escaping into sleep. Although I hadn't realized it until I was literally forced to slow down, I was physically and emotionally exhausted, tired from no sleep and no routine and no rules and too much drinking and too many pills and having no consistent place to lay my head at night. So even though my polyester-coated foam pillow was hard and my pillowcase so thin I could almost see right through it, even though my standard-issue wool blanket caused me to itch wherever it touched bare skin, I slept more than I'd slept in months, perhaps more than I'd slept the entire time I'd been in Colorado, which was a welcome change from the madness of being awake.

Sometime near the end of my first week in the Summit County Jail, I received a visit from the man who had hired me at the Public Service Company. He tried to make it as cordial as he could, but it was awkward and embarrassing. "Rough weekend, huh?" he said through the phone in the visiting area. "You could say that," I replied. I guessed he'd heard from April's mom that I had been arrested. He adjusted the phone on his ear. "Look, Tim, I don't know how else to say this, but we need to let you go." I wished there was something more I could say, some way to ask him to hold the job for me, but I knew it was pointless. So instead I apologized, thanked him for coming, and went back to my jail cell to sleep.

* * *

During my second week in D Block, just after I finished my lunch in the dayroom, the main area where inmates spent their waking hours, I got up from the table, crossed the pod, stacked my tray on the cart near the door, and heard a voice behind me.

"Where you from, bro?"

I turned and saw an inmate who I recognized during my first week in D Block when I'd come down to eat with the rest of the inmates. There were roughly thirty men in my cellblock, all of various ages, all doing time for various reasons, and this inmate, whose name I knew was Vinnie from hearing other inmates address him, always seemed to be in the middle of whatever was going on, whether it was cards, chess, or conversation.

"Chicago," I said, turning, walking back to the table and sitting down.

Vinnie followed and took the seat across the table from me. "Your name is Tim, right? I saw it on the board up front."

Near the booking desk was a large marker board where every inmate's name, booking date, bond amount, and current block assignment was written. I'd taken a look at it when I was being booked, scanning to see if any of the names had looked familiar, but none of them had.

"Yeah," I said.

He adjusted himself on the bench. "Everyone calls me Vinnie."

I nodded. "Short for Vincent?"

"Shit no, I'm not even Italian." He laughed. "My name's Charles. But everyone's been calling me Vinnie since I was a little kid." I waited for him to elaborate but he didn't. Instead, he shrugged. "It is what it is."

I laughed. "I guess so."

Since we were in a county jail and not a prison, most of the inmates were doing sentences of less than a year—a lot of them alcohol related—but there were a few inmates, inmates like Vinnie, who were awaiting trial in Summit County before being transported to a Department of Corrections facility, where they would serve much longer sentences.

Vinnie was just under six feet tall and looked to be about my age, his hair buzzed close to his head. He was stocky and loud, and always laughing or cursing, sometimes doing both at the same time, and he seemed to miss nothing that happened around him. I watched him move through the cellblock each day like a politician at a fundraiser, stopping to talk to different people, leaning against the doorframe of an open cell, addressing each guard with a nod and look that conveyed some sort of mutual understanding. People reacted to Vinnie—that much was clear. And to me he seemed like a good person to know, especially since I was unsure how long I'd be locked up.

Our first couple of conversations went well beyond the small talk that usually emerges between strangers, and I got the feeling that Vinnie and I would be friends if we had met somewhere in the outside world. Within a day or two, Vinnie introduced me to his friend William, a quiet guy seven or eight years older than Vinnie and me. William had a narrow face and a high forehead, wore dark-rimmed glasses, and when he spoke, he spoke clearly and articulately. He came across as educated, and he seemed to me to be a sort of anomaly in the jail. His jumpsuit was almost never wrinkled. He used a small canister of Vaseline he'd bought from the commissary to keep his hair parted to the side. When I walked by his cell, I could see that the few personal items he was allowed to have—three prestamped envelopes, two pairs of white boxers, various kinds of candy from the commissary, two books on loan from the jail's library—were stacked neatly on the shelf near his bed.

By about the end of the second week, the three of us had formed a tight bond, partly because time moved slowly in jail, with little to no variation in the way things progressed each day. That meant that relationships, whether with other inmates or higher powers, moved quickly. It was true that many inmates found God in jail—I found myself praying more than I had in years—but it was also true that they found each other, and many times themselves. Captivity, it seemed, made self-reflection inevitable.

Vinnie ran daily poker games that were billed "just for fun," but every single game that was dealt inside D Block was dealt for money. Commissary items were won and lost throughout the day, and for anyone who didn't have any money on his books, dollar amounts were assigned to meals—three bucks for breakfast, five bucks for lunch, eight bucks for dinner. If someone without any commissary money lost enough poker hands, it was possible—and actually happened almost daily—that the inmate would go without breakfast and lunch the following day.

William and I played, and won, quite a few games with Vinnie, who was incredibly gifted at dealing from the bottom of the deck—an unbelievably risky move inside a jail, even a small one like ours. But for as likeable as Vinnie came across, he also came across as a seasoned convict, or at least how I imagined a seasoned convict would come across, and that prompted the conversation we had late one afternoon.

I sat against the wall in Vinnie's cell while he lay on his back on the bottom bunk. William sat near the cell's door, and he had closed it to the point where it touched the frame, careful that it didn't shut completely and lock us in. We had to be wary of who saw us, because if we got caught hanging out together in a cell we weren't assigned to, the inmates who didn't belong could be charged with an "operational rules violation." It wasn't a huge deal, but it carried a maximum punishment of being locked down in our cells for seven consecutive days, twenty-three hours a day, and none of us wanted to deal with that kind of boredom.

I leaned my head back until it was resting against the wall. "I haven't asked you this yet, Vinnie, but what are you in here for?" I knew from watching movies that asking that sort of question was frowned upon, but we were friends, so I figured it was fair game.

He kept his eyes trained on the top bunk while he spoke. "It's a long story, but I got busted moving a key of cocaine in a stolen car while I was in Florida."

William jumped in. "You have to admit, Tim. A guy called Vinnie getting busted with a key of cocaine in Florida has a pretty *Miami Vice*–type feel to it, doesn't it?"

I laughed. "Vinnie, are you serious? Then what the hell are you doing in Colorado? And how much time do you have to do?"

Vinnie lifted his leg up until his foot was touching the underside of the bed. He held it there. "When it's all said and done, probably ten years. Maybe a little less with Good Time." He let his foot drop to the bed.

I tried not to show it, but his words leveled me. In ten years we'd be thirty. Vinnie would spend nearly every second of his twenties incarcerated. He wouldn't celebrate his twenty-first birthday at a bar with his friends. He wouldn't marry his girlfriend and take wedding pictures on the steps of some beautiful church. He wouldn't start a career or go back to school or join a rec softball league with his friends. He'd be institutionalized somewhere in one of America's growing selection of penitentiaries, playing poker games, and eating terrible food with ungodly amounts of salt.

He rolled over on his side and used his elbow to prop his head up. "When I got busted with the drugs, it was all pretty much coming to an end anyway. Me and a few other guys had been printing fake checks and passing them all over the country. We passed a few here in Colorado. My charges here in Summit County are actually for check fraud."

William shifted his weight and pulled his knee up, rested his forearm on top of it. He looked at me. "Any time it's a felony charge, the states want their pound of flesh, even if you're over a thousand miles away. And once you're in the system facing as many years as Vinnie and me, no one is in a hurry."

"You got that right," Vinnie said.

I nodded in William's direction. "So you're in for a long time too?"

"Yeah, ten years. Same as Vinnie." He took his glasses off and held them up to the light, checked for smudges. "It's such a waste."

I thought about how long ten years really was. It was nearly unfathomable. Ten years ago I had been riding my BMX bike around the neighborhood and setting up lemonade stands at the end of my driveway. "Damn, William. For real? What did you do?"

Vinnie sat up and swung his legs over the bed, leaning forward, so his head didn't hit the metal bedframe. "If you thought my story was good, wait to you hear this one."

William put his glasses back on. "You want the short version or the long one?"

"Are you kidding me?" I said. "I want the long one."

He laughed. "Too bad, you get the short one. They got me on bank robbery."

"Get the fuck out of here."

He shook his head. "Wish I could."

Vinnie stood up. "You at least have to tell him about the red Corvette, Willy."

"I told you not to fucking call me that, Guido."

Vinnie looked at me. "He almost sounded tough for a second there, didn't he?"

I laughed. "Come on. Seriously. William, what's up with this red Corvette?"

He straightened his leg back out on the floor and took a breath. I could sense there was some sort of confidence that had settled in on him, a subtle shift that indicated pride or reverence, something I couldn't quite identify. But it was there, and when he spoke, I was instantly lost in his story.

"What's one of the most recognizable cars on the road?"

"Well, I'm guessing—"

"Exactly. If you think of a Corvette, chances are you think of a red one. It's one of the most easily identifiable cars on the road. Plus, there's that Prince song that pretty much ingrained it in everyone's brain permanently."

Vinnie started humming the tune, and I cracked a smile.

William continued. "There wasn't anything complicated about our plan. We figured out a bank we wanted to hit. We got ahold of a red Corvette. I went into the bank while my partner waited in the parking lot in the car. I gave the bank teller a note asking for 50s and 100s. The bank teller would insert the cash into an envelope and hand it to me. I'd say 'thank you' and walk outside. My partner would be waiting for me, and I'd get in, and then we'd drive the speed limit to the nearest expressway. We'd drive a few exits down to where we had another car waiting for us. Get in the new car. Leave the Corvette. Get the hell out of there."

I shook my head. "That sounds like something out of a movie."

William didn't say anything. Just sat there looking at me like he was waiting for me to ask him something else.

I took the bait. "But why the red Corvette?"

"I already told you. Because it's one of the most recognizable cars on the road, and there are, literally, tens of thousands of them. By the time the police are onto the Corvette, we're on the way home in something else, an Escort or a Galant or something. The news breaks the story, and the police start getting calls about red Corvettes, and pretty soon that's all anyone can think about. The car eclipses any other description, even the descriptions of the people involved."

I let my eyes drift to the floor and tried to make sense of what he was saying. William, assuming he was telling me the truth, was serving a ten-year sentence for bank robbery. Vinnie, who seemed like he was telling the truth, was serving a ten-year sentence for check fraud, vehicular theft, and transporting drugs. I wasn't positive, but these two guys had to have the most serious charges of anyone locked up in Summit County. I looked back at William.

"So how did you get caught? When you were leaving the bank?"

He shook his head. "No, we didn't get caught in the act, but the feds were onto us for a while. They froze my assets. When I walked into First Bank in Silverthorne to take out money, well, let's just say it was all over with. They were literally waiting for me."

Vinnie lay back down on the bed and readjusted the pillow behind his head. "The cops always get you in the end." I couldn't tell if he was being serious or sarcastic.

William lifted his left hand and carefully slid it through his hair. For the first time I noticed that he was wearing a wedding band. I'd read in the Inmate Handbook that inmates could keep their wedding ring as long as it didn't have any stones in it.

"Are you married?" I asked.

"I am."

"Kids?"

"A son."

I thought about Haley, who was now nine months old, and how I'd already missed so much of her life. I thought about the first time

I'd held her in the hospital room, how she'd felt almost weightless in my hand, how I felt love for her in a way that was unexplainable. I thought about saying her name for first time, about feeling that beautiful name on my lips, about the little bump on her forehead she always seemed to have from accidentally hitting herself with her toys. I thought about the fight I'd had in the car with April, how Haley and Maddie had seen the worst sides of me over and over again. How scared of me they must be. How confused. How disappointed. Could children that young be disappointed? Did I make them feel unsafe? My eyes welled up.

I nodded at William, and there was nothing more to say, because the gravity of it all was suddenly so real, pulling each of us into the concrete floor of the cell. We made light of our situations—Vinnie cracked jokes and William seemed to revel in how smart he was—but here we all were, locked up in a small cell in the middle of a town where most people came for vacation. It wasn't lost on me that Vinnie and William could be versions of the future me, the me I would turn into if I continued doing the things I was doing, if I kept fighting with April and drinking until my vision blurred and vomit dripped from the corners of my mouth. In that small place at the base of the Breckenridge Ski Resort, all we had were the stories of how we got there. Vinnie was a tough guy who ran drugs in the street and poker games in jail. William was a red Corvette-driving bank robber. And I was a father who drank too much but now wanted to make things right with his daughter and his daughter's mother. Or maybe it is truer to say we were none of the things we wanted to be and only the things we were: three guys who'd committed crimes without truly understanding all the people they'd hurt.

* * *

At some point during the first two weeks of my incarceration, I realized that constantly thinking and hoping and praying that I would get out, that someone would magically show up with bail money, was doing more harm than good. I'd lost my job. April had a restraining order. And not even Travis knew where I'd landed. I was pretty sure he thought I was back living at April's place, settled into the usual routine. My absence probably hadn't sounded any alarms.

For the first time in my life, I felt truly alone. As I lay in bed at night staring into the ceiling and listening to ever-present noises of the jail, I realized that everything I took for granted had, quite literally, been taken away from me. I'd lost my freedom and my family. I was now in a place where I was told when to eat, when to sleep, when to wake up, when to shower, and the sooner I accepted that, the sooner I stopped envisioning any other reality other than the one I was in, the easier being in jail would become.

So I simply stopped thinking about leaving. I accepted the fact that I was imprisoned, that I lived inside a jail, and I began to adjust to it. Good portions of my days were spent with Vinnie and William. Whether we were playing cards or eating or sitting inside one of our cells—talking, laughing, sometimes crying—it was apparent that there was a bond between the three of us. We seemed to understand one another on a level that transcended the two weeks we'd known each other.

During those moments that we sat with our backs against the wall in one of our cells, time disappearing into the fluorescent lighting and stale air around us, we sometimes talked about what it was like for each us growing up. We were all from different parts of the country, but we had all been brought up in strikingly similar households. Our parents were married. Our fathers or stepfathers had jobs. We had all been brought up in Christian homes. It seemed ironic to us that we could be raised up in such privileged environments, in homes that met every one of our physical needs and then some, yet still find a way to rebel against all the good things we had in our lives. It would be decades before I would finally come to understand what I believe we were beginning to name in those moments, which was that our rebellion was itself a sort of privilege, one that stemmed from being white and male. That realization, that understanding, even despite the fact that it eluded me for so long, which I know is another type of privilege, is one of the most transformative realizations of my life.

On some days, we talked about our faith, about our journeys from Sunday school to jail. It seemed we'd all shelved the lessons we'd learned when we were kids—lessons about discipline and respect and about asking for God's help and forgiveness, in lieu of . . . in lieu of what? Experience perhaps. Maybe I needed to test the love I'd been told God had for me. Maybe I needed to push him away to feel him. Or maybe I just didn't understand any of it—church, worship, aspiring to live a Christian life. If God truly loved me, if there truly was a God, I needed to find him—and know him—on my own, and in my own time.

Vinnie brought a Bible into the cell one day, and we flipped through it, stopping at familiar passages. John 3:16. Psalm 23. Philippians 4:13. We read the words out loud, each of us taking turns with different verses, and it felt good to be reciting something that felt significant, something that linked us to a different time, a period of our childhoods that seemed so simple. *Believe this and be saved. Believe this and no matter how broken you think you are, you'll be fixed.* In that cell reading those verses, we were all painfully aware that there was a time before all this when we acted normally. Vinnie had played peewee football while his father watched from the sidelines. William had built model airplanes with his brother. I had watched my mother spend days putting together puzzles, awestruck at how lost she could get in the world she created with those puzzle pieces. There was a time before anger and rebellion had consumed us, and we were small, and the world around us was big, and the God who had made it felt real and loving and present in our lives. And when we read those verses from inside that cell in a state where none of us had been born, our voices soft and unwavering as they climbed over those familiar, ancient syllables, we felt at peace inside D Block, like the God we all believed in was near and giving respite to our souls.

* * *

Vinnie and I were sitting at one of the tables inside the dayroom when I heard one of the guards, standing near the entrance with both thumbs hooked on his utility belt, tell me I had a visitor.

I caught the guard's eye, nodded that I'd heard him, and slid the paperback book I'd been flipping through to Vinnie.

"Who do you think it is?" he asked.

"It has to be April." I felt my stomach tighten. "They lifted the restraining order during my last court hearing." I climbed off the bench and stood from table. "This should be interesting."

It was Wednesday—visiting day—but I hadn't expected anyone to come. I hadn't had a visitor since the Public Service supervisor had come to deliver the news that I'd been fired.

I crossed the pod and met the guard just on the other side of the large steel door. "Stand here," he said, pointing to a spot on the cement floor. I did as I was told, and he waved to a camera on the ceiling. The door to the pod clanged loudly and slowly slid shut. The sounds of inmates swearing and talking from within the pod grew softer.

The guard put his hand on my shoulder and nudged me forward down the hallway. On both sides, enclosed in shatterproof Plexiglas, were small rooms that were used for the segregation of unruly inmates. The cells were eight-foot-by-eight-foot squares that offered zero privacy, and as we passed one of them, a tall, lanky inmate known as "Flakes"—his name came courtesy of his psoriasis—walked over toward the glass and flicked off the guard. Flakes saw me looking at him, and his gaze shifted to me. His middle finger followed. I shook my head and moved a little faster as I felt the guard's hand on my shoulder again.

As we approached another steel door at the end of the hallway, the guard ordered me to stop, and once again waved to a camera in the ceiling. The familiar sound of metal on metal filled my ears, and the door began sliding open. As it did every time I was taken to the front of the jail, where the kitchen was located, the smells swallowed the space around me—that pungent mix of industrial sanitizer, fryer grease, and burned coffee.

We continued through the door, and the guard walked me up to the booking desk, where another guard in an identical uniform with a similarly sized gut stood flipping through a file.

"I've got inmate Hillegonds here for his visitation," the guard said, leaning against the counter. "Confirm restraining order status. It's a domestic case."

The guard behind the booking desk put down his file, peered at us over his glasses, moved over to the computer next to him, and began typing.

"Looks like the judge removed the order two days ago," he said. "He's clear."

The guard who had escorted me nodded, then turned. "You know where you're going?"

"Yeah."

"Third bay. You've got thirty minutes."

I started toward the door—it had to be April, because why else would the guards be looking into the restraining order?—and although I'd thought a lot about what I would say to her once I saw her, now that the moment had arrived, all I felt were nerves. I had been so out of control that night. I'd replayed it over and over in my head—the conversation, jumping out of the car, the broken door, hitting her—and even though weeks had passed, I was still spinning.

April was already holding the phone by the time I sat on the stool in the third bay. Her curly blonde hair was pulled back into a pony-tail, and she was wearing her red Tommy Hilfiger jacket. It was her favorite one—a Christmas present from her grandmother—and I had always thought she looked radiant in it. There was something about the way her Irish complexion played off the bright red nylon that always made me think she should be modeling outerwear for a department store. She looked serene, and happy, and it made me miss the way things had been in the beginning.

I caught a glimpse of myself in the reflection of the glass and wondered what April thought when she saw me. My face looked greasy and my lips were chapped. I'd been inside for almost a month.

I picked up the phone and put it to my ear.

"Hey," I said, and for the first time, I noticed Maddie standing behind Haley's baby carrier. She was wearing overalls, a long sleeve yellow shirt, and had her Bob the Tomato doll in her hand. I wanted to pick her up, to hug her, to tell her I was sorry for what I did to her mommy.

"Hey," April said through the phone. "Looks like your hair is getting pretty long." The lights above us flickered, and the steady hum of electricity filled the room.

"Yeah." I instinctively ran my fingers through my hair. "Must be all the nutritious food in here."

April smiled, and I studied her through the glass. The nails on the fingers she had wrapped around the phone were painted crimson. She looked beautiful, and I wondered if she was wearing the perfume I had bought her for Mother's Day.

April leaned down and adjusted the baby carrier next to her. I stood up and pressed my forehead against the glass. Peered down at Haley. My beautiful, sweet daughter, Haley. She was sleeping, eyes lightly closed, thumb in her mouth as it almost always was. I missed her so much and so often, but never as much as right in that moment when she was so close, yet so unreachable. I was struck by the way I was literally, physically separated from my little girl's life.

The door on April's side of the glass opened, and another woman walked in, looked like she might be in her forties. She glanced at April, then down at the two girls. She sat down on the stool in the first bay.

April spoke into the phone. "I called the jail yesterday, and they told me that your bond was finally reduced."

I had filled out an inmate kite a week or so before—the form used to contact the courts to request everything from bond reductions to public defenders to the removal of restraining orders. I'd received word the day before that it had finally been reduced. I was pretty sure I had just enough money in the bank to get out.

Maddie had wandered over near the other woman, and April called her back over.

"The girls miss you, Tim."

"I miss them too," I said, tears welling. I thought back to the night everything had happened. Maddie had looked so scared. Did I even deserve forgiveness? Did I even want it?

"I'm so sorry, April. I really am."

She brought the phone closer to her lips. "It's not okay."

"I know." I wiped my eye. "I know it's not okay. There's no excuse for what happened. For what I did."

"Just get out of here and come home, Tim. We just need you to come home, so we can fix all this."

I leaned my elbow on the small countertop. Let my ear smash into the phone as I rested my head against it.

"I lost my job."

"Yeah, I heard. My mom told me." She looked away for a second, then looked back at me. "It's okay, though. We'll figure it out." She sighed. "You'll just have to talk to Debra and see if you can go back to Denny's. I'm sure she'll let you. Just pick up as many shifts as you can."

I looked at April, then Maddie, then Haley. I loved those little girls so much, and if I was being honest, I loved April, too, but I was scared of my relationship with her, scared of the person I became in it. Could I stop it all from happening again?

The door to the visitor's room opened and an inmate I'd never seen before sat across the glass from the woman in the first bay and picked up the phone. I turned and glanced at him. Looked away when he put the palm of his hand on the glass, a sign for the woman to do the same.

I turned and noticed that one of April's curls had fallen across her forehead, a renegade strand of hair tired of being tied up with the rest of them. What had happened to us? How had we gotten so far off track? It seemed like it was just the other day that I was watching her walk into Denny's for the first time, and now we were here. I spoke into the receiver. "I've got the number for a bail bondsman not too far from here. It'll probably take me a day or two to figure it all out, but I should be out pretty soon. I'll call you soon as I know something."

"Okay," she said. "I love you, Tim."

I paused. It had been so long since we'd said those words to one another. Love? Is that really what this was? Is this how complicated love had become?

Somewhere far inside the jail I heard a steel door closing and shut my eyes. Heard the door lock. Opened them and settled back on April's face, her freckles, the mouth that had grimaced in pain as she birthed my daughter, as I'd struck her, the same mouth that now seemed to relax into a forgiveness I knew I didn't deserve.

"I love you too," I said, and placed the phone back into its cradle.

* * *

By the time I posted bail and was released, it was the tail end of November. I had spent a total of twenty-eight days in jail, but the case was still pending, and sometime over the next month or two I would be sentenced. I'd said goodbye to Vinnie and William the night before my release, asking them to stay strong while they did their time, praying with them, promising them we would keep in touch. But we all knew it would be hard once I was back in the outside world, and once they'd been transferred to prison.

Snow had begun to fall when I was locked up, and when I walked out of the jail, everything, as far as I could see, was covered in a blanket of white. Clouds hung in a low apron around the mountain, and the smoke-colored sky wrapped Summit County in an afghan of gray.

April's Mazda idled in the parking lot, its exhaust pipe spitting into the cold air, and I walked toward it. I was wearing the same clothes I had been arrested in—work boots and dirty jeans and a shirt that smelled of sweat and cigarette smoke. To the outside world it might have seemed like nothing had changed, that I was the same person, in the same clothes no less, that had walked into the jail. But inside, everything felt different.

I'd had so much time to think when I was in jail, so much time to reflect on April and the girls and my parents and the friends I was missing back home. On the snowboarding I hadn't done. On skating. On soccer. I hadn't spoken to Rich or Dan in months, and being locked up had made me realize how much I missed them, how much I yearned for their friendship. Connecting with Vinnie and William inside the jail was the closest thing I'd had to a true male bond since I'd left Chicago.

As I neared the car, April looked up. I could see her lips move as she said something to the girls, and a second later two little heads leaned in toward the middle of the back seat. I could see all of them at once, framed by the windshield, and I could feel them staring at me, waiting for me to arrive, waiting for me to take my place in the car and ride away with them. As I walked across that parking lot, surrounded by mountains and snow and the jail I had just been released from, I felt like I was moving toward something, but also moving away. Everything I thought I knew had flipped, like a snow globe turned upside down.

T W E L V E

"It's easy to see the beginnings of things," Joan Didion wrote, "and harder to see the ends."

Seventeen years after I moved to Colorado, I discovered Didion's essay "Goodbye to All That." The second I read her famous first line, I thought of my story with April, of how I can always remember exactly where Colorado started for me, and how I'm not sure about where, or if, it ended.

I do know, though, that when it came to April and me, it was a small thing that finally finished us, a disagreement really, the same one we'd had on countless occasions in countless locations, about not having enough money or respect or manners or plans, about me still working at Denny's, about me not caring enough, but our disagreement was also different this time too; it was distinctive, and I know that we both felt it that night—the true ending of our relationship.

And perhaps that's why neither of us fought it with any sort of conviction. Perhaps we were simply too exhausted by the monotony of it all. The night it ended, while the girls slept upstairs and, outside, stars poked through a black sky that was just beginning to cloud, it seemed that one moment April and I were talking, and the next moment we were arguing, and it had all the markings of another monstrous fight, an April and Tim special, a blowout like one we'd had hundreds of times before. But just as it reached that volcanic point—the moment when every other fight would have erupted out of control—this fight stayed right where it was, idling. I folded my arms across my chest where I was standing, took a deep breath, and lowered my voice to what I hoped was an even tone. "I can't do this anymore, April. We can't do this anymore."

I thought of myself as wise in that moment, as a person who had learned from his mistakes and was finally exerting the self-control that had eluded him for so long, but at some level I knew that simply wasn't true. I was merely tired and scared. Tired from constantly fighting. Scared of going back to jail.

I walked near the door, looked to the ground where my shoes were lined up against the wall next to a pair of Winnie the Pooh sandals. I bent over and grabbed them, pulled them on.

"I'm going to get a few things and then I'm going to go." I waited for April to explode, for our fight to manifest in the way it always did, but she just sat there, eyeing me, probably waiting for me to explode. She leaned over to the side table and grabbed her cigarettes. Lit one. Finally landed on words that must have seemed right.

"If you leave tonight, you're never coming back here." It wasn't a question, but she didn't seem angry, either. It was as if she were testing out an idea, letting her sentence hang in the air, so we could both get a feel for it.

I nodded, then turned and walked upstairs to the bedroom I'd shared with her since we'd moved to the new apartment. I flipped on the light and walked to the closet where the large, red duffel bag that I'd moved to Colorado with was jammed into a corner, the baggage tag from my departure flight from Chicago still attached to the handle. I grabbed the duffel, threw it on the bed, and then stuffed a few pairs of jeans and boxers, some T-shirts, a couple of sweatshirts inside. I walked to the bathroom and grabbed my toothbrush, looked under the sink and found a half-used tube of toothpaste, and then I slung the bag over my shoulder and walked into the hallway, stood at the top of the stairs. The girls' doors were both closed. I thought about stopping, going in, and kissing them each on the cheek, waking them and trying to somehow explain that I wasn't leaving them. "It's just that things with your mom aren't working," I might say. "I love you two so much. Someday it will make sense." But would it ever make sense, even to me?

When I got back downstairs, April was still sitting on the couch. "You're really leaving?"

I nodded, grabbed my jacket from the hook by the door. Put it on.

April got up, looked like she was going to say something, maybe ask me to stay, maybe yell at me to go, but she just stood there. I moved toward the door.

"Where are you going?" she asked.

I adjusted the bag on my shoulder. "I don't know. I'll figure it out." I grabbed the doorknob. "I'll call you at some point and let you know where I end up." She started to say something, but I was already pulling the door shut behind me, both sad and relieved, watching the ground as the light that had spilled onto the concrete gave way to the dark.

* * *

By one o'clock in the morning, the traffic on Highway 9 in Silverthorne had thinned out and almost disappeared completely. The wind had died down considerably, but the occasional gust still found its way inside my jacket. The sky had clouded over completely now, and it looked to be holding snow. I figured the air temperature was hovering somewhere in the teens.

As I walked, I replayed what had just happened with April. It was two weeks before Christmas 1998. April and I had been together, more or less, for two years. Had it really been that long? I looked across the street, let my eyes trace the foothills, where single-family homes lined the mountainside, lit windows flickering like lightning bugs, smoke from fireplaces saturating the air with the smells of burning conifer and pine.

It was just over a mile to the factory store outlets and Denny's.

Maybe I could stop in and see who was working, try to wrangle a place to stay for the night. I knew I could probably call Travis, but I didn't want to yet. He'd been on the receiving end of so many of those phone calls that I just wanted to postpone it. There was an ironic sense of peace in the fact that no one knew where I was or what I was doing or how things were going.

Behind me, I heard a rumble and looked up as a semitruck drove by, its Peterbilt badge flashing in the streetlight. It had chrome exhaust pipes, smoke-blackened at the ends, stabbing at the sky. The truck was pulling an empty flatbed, and its diesel engine knocked through the quiet night, the hollow, metallic sounds of the vibrating fifth wheel momentarily shattering the stillness. I shifted the duffel bag to my other shoulder, stopped just long enough to look at everything around me, to sweep my head from side to side, so the whole landscape looked like a panoramic picture, and it occurred to me that I'd traded Lake Michigan for Lake Dillon, skyscrapers for mountains, a family that loved me for a failing relationship with a girl whose problems mirrored mine. I felt foolish. The escape I had tried to make had been futile, like I'd robbed a bank and tried to flee on a treadmill.

I kicked a piece of ice free from the sidewalk and watched as it slid to a stop just before the driveway to the Grease Monkey. I thought back to when I'd hid behind it after hitting April, and then walked back to her apartment with that crushing feeling of shame for what I'd done. Even though she'd taken me back after that, it still felt unforgivable.

Above me, a sign hanging over one of the shop's glass garage doors advertised a $9.95 oil change. I fingered the few bucks in my pocket—fifteen, maybe twenty. I needed to pick up a shift at Denny's as soon as I could. I had called Debra the day after I'd gotten out of jail, and she'd given me my job back as soon as I asked. She'd always had so much compassion for me, even when I was constantly screwing up. I couldn't wait to talk to her.

The breeze quickened, and I jammed my hands deeper into the

pockets of my jacket. I pulled out a pack of Marlboros and lit one, tilted my head back and blew the smoke toward the sky, watching as the stream disappeared into the night, into the air around me, and thought about how everything seemed to disappear just like that smoke, how my mother and stepfather were over a thousand miles away, how my daughter was upstairs in her crib at April's, sleeping in the apartment I was now walking away from. I thought about Maddie, about when, or if, I'd see her again, about the way her little arms wrapped around my neck when we hugged, how the first time she'd sat on my lap and rocked with me I'd felt so much love for her. I still held onto hope that it would all work out one day, that it was possible not to be with their mother, but still somehow be there for those girls.

I took one last drag of my cigarette and used my thumb and middle finger to flick it into the street where it landed and burst into a tiny fire flower before rolling into the curb. The light up ahead turned from red to green, the snow at my feet sparking like jade illuminated by the sun. Jade. Sparkling like Haley Jade. The image nearly dropped me.

A block ahead, just past the light, was Denny's. Just past Denny's was the entrance to I-70. I-70 East would take me to Interstate 80. I-80 would take me to I-88. I-88 would take me to I-290. I-290 would take me home, to Chicago. Eleven hundred miles between Summit County and Cook County. I could feel the distance. I could literally *feel* the distance. Because I knew that even if I kept walking from that moment, never stopping, I still wouldn't be home for a month.

Up ahead, a pair of headlights drew closer. The car reached the entrance ramp to I-70 and turned, its taillights fading as it drove up the incline toward the Continental Divide. Snow began falling, and the air smelled of winter, of dried leaves and evergreen trees, of wood smoke.

I passed the stoplight and crossed the street by a liquor store that was closed for the night. By the time I walked by Denny's and saw that its parking lot was empty except for two cars, which I assumed belonged to the graveyard server and the cook, I was absolutely freezing. I pulled the hood of my jacket up and walked past Denny's, keeping my head down, not wanting to be seen by the server on duty or anyone else who might recognize me.

I crossed the street that wound through the Factory Store Outlets and headed toward Mikasa, a home goods store with windows filled with dinner plates and carafes and water glasses and high-balls and champagne flutes and all the things it occurred to me I'd never actually owned. Just behind the window was a large, wooden dining room table set for an elaborate dinner, and it reminded me of the suppers I'd had at home as a child. We had always eaten at five o'clock, which was earlier than most of my friends. My stepfather would get off work at 4:30 and walk home, his light blue shirt stained with tar and sweat, smelling like the streets he'd spent the day paving. He'd leave his work boots on the stairs and walk into the kitchen in his socks, the house shaking under his weight, and take his seat at the head of the table. He would tell us kids to quiet down and bow his head, and then he would pray, thanking God for his job and the casserole and his family, forever grateful for the blessings we had, no matter how small.

I had always complained about those family dinners, about how they were too early and lasted too long, but now, as I cut through the parking lot and turned down the alley behind the store, walking past a dumpster filled with corrugated cardboard while snow fell softly around me, I realized I'd give anything to be back there, to be home, to be picking at my tuna casserole and watching the endless current of traffic streaming down Central Avenue.

Halfway down the alley I came to a pile of boxes lying beside another dumpster. I slipped the bag off my shoulder and let it fall to the pavement, feathery snowflakes billowing out in all directions as it landed. I grabbed one of the larger boxes and began breaking it down, just as I'd done for years in restaurants, ripping the tape that held it together and unfolding it. I laid it flat on the ground and grabbed another box. Did it two more times until I'd covered a section of the ground that was big enough to lie on. I unzipped my duffel bag and pulled out a T-shirt and folded it into a makeshift pillow, and with the brick wall on one side, the duffel bag on the other, and my head near the dumpster, I lay down onto my back and stared into the blue-black darkness above.

It had to be after 2 a.m. by now, which meant it was 3 in Chicago. The house on Central Avenue would be dark. The traffic would have slowed. The red light from the radio tower two blocks away would be blinking in the night sky, high above the sleeping neighborhood.

I rolled over and pulled my knees to my chest, the brick wall inches away from my face, and closed my eyes. For the briefest of moments, right before I fell asleep, I was back in Chicago. It was before Colorado, before Haley, before I'd smoked my first joint, snorted my first line, took my first drink. The table was set for dinner, and the sounds of traffic wandered in through the open kitchen window and mixed in with the voices of my family. I stood there in the doorway to the kitchen, a younger version of myself, watching them, yearning to be like them, yearning to be with them. And for just a second right before I fell asleep, I felt like maybe all the things I had run away from I could actually run back to, and my stepfather and I could have a real conversation, and the process could begin, of closing the distance between us, of starting to make amends.

* * *

When I awoke a few hours later, it was still dark, the snow was still slowly falling, and I was colder than I'd ever been in my life. I stood up, dusted myself off, grabbed my bag, and walked to Denny's. When I arrived, the graveyard server, a guy named Logan whom I'd only met once or twice before, was sitting at a booth reading the paper.

I walked up to him. "Hey, you remember me?"

He looked up from his newspaper. Glanced at the large bag I had just set on the floor. "Yeah, of course. Tim, right?"

"Yeah." I glanced out the window, watched as a car pulled into a parking spot. "Man, I don't really know how to even say this, but I need a place to crash tonight. I'm going to head to that five-top in the back of nonsmoking and try to sleep for a couple of hours until the morning crew gets here." I tried to gauge his reaction, but he really didn't have one. He'd probably seen and heard it all by working the graveyard shift. "You good with that?"

He shrugged. "Works for me."

I picked my bag off the ground, said thanks, and turned to walk away.

"Hey, Tim."

I turned. "Yeah?"

"You sure you're okay?"

I thought about falling asleep in the alley, about what I was going to do now that I had no place to live. I probably wasn't okay. Maybe I hadn't actually been okay for a while now.

I forced a smile. "Yeah," I said, taking another step back. "Everything's fine."

* * *

There are days and nights, even now, more than a decade into sobriety, when I miss the feeling that overwhelmed me each time I snorted a line of crystal meth, that mixture of emotions and chemicals, that concoction of joy and love and dopamine and danger and adrenaline and peace. Addicts often refer to the endorphin dump as a rush or a flood or a surge or a charge, and there is indeed energy and movement inside drugs, there is indeed an incontestable force. But that doesn't quite capture it, though, doesn't quite get to the heart of it, because it always felt to me more like a sustained emotion, a deep and abiding tenderness that finally gave me permission to love myself. It was short lived of course, this love, and that permission never lasted long enough, but it was the closest I came in those years to accepting myself, and those moments felt better than anything else I had ever experienced.

But once I'd walked out the door of April's house for the final time, drugs were much harder to come by—the only people I knew who had access to crystal meth, my coworkers Darren and Sarah, had moved away. But that didn't stop me from drinking as much and as often as I could, a near-endless effort to stay drunk. I spent my nights almost always hammered, either sleeping in the Silverthorne hostel or a cheap hotel room, or in the back booth of Denny's, where I could prop the old thirteen-inch television I'd found on the table and lose myself in the mindlessness of late-night programming. But on nights when I didn't feel like doing any of that, when money was low or I was just sick of trying to figure it all out, tired of not having a place to call home, I would simply schedule myself for the graveyard shift. I'd learned that sometimes the easiest way to negotiate the night was to simply not give in to it.

One night while I was working the graveyard shift, a girl who looked to be a little older than me came in. She was alone, and she ordered coffee, and she had short blonde hair and tanned skin and was pretty in a plain way that didn't require much makeup or too much fuss in front of the mirror. There was no one else in the restaurant, and not long after I'd brought her coffee, I was sitting in the booth across from her, talking. She was from Denver and she was visiting friends in Summit County. They'd gone out to a bar earlier, but she hadn't felt like going back to their place, and so she didn't. She didn't appear drunk to me, but every so often when she laughed, I would catch the faint scent of alcohol on her breath. After some time had passed, she asked me if I partied. I said I did. She asked if I did meth. I said I did. And then she said she knew a place in Denver where she could get some. "You up for it?" she asked.

I was, and when I got off work at 6 a.m., I climbed in her rust-covered pickup, its back bumper held in place with electrical wire, and we started the hour-long trek to the city. "Sorry about the mess," she said, as I brushed a cold french fry off the seat.

During the ride, I looked at the passing mountainside, hyperaware of the fact that I was riding to Denver with a girl I didn't know, in a truck that seemed as if it could break down at any second, to buy crystal meth from a dealer who may or may not even exist. I had forty or fifty dollars on me, enough to get a little of something but not much of anything, and by the time we reached the city limits, I wished I had never come. The exhaustion from not sleeping the night before, and from not really sleeping all the nights before that, was catching up with me, and she looked over at me, this girl I hardly knew, and said that we needed to make a stop before we met with her dealer. My heart pivoted, began beating in a way I could feel on the underside of my chest, and I wondered whether I was about to get jumped and robbed. I asked her where and she said not to worry. "It won't take that long," she said. Her eyes widened. "Shit, now that I think about, you should do it, too."

Do what? I thought, too tired to even ask, too nervous to even truly want to know.

We pulled into the parking lot of a strip mall off Sixth Street in Denver. "What is this place?" I asked. "It's a plasma donation center," she said. We pulled into a parking spot, and she turned the car off.

"What are we doing here?" I asked.

She put her hand on the door handle. "We're getting some more money."

"By donating plasma?"

"Yeah," she said, opening the door. "Now let's go. It takes a while."

* * *

It seems almost impossible to comprehend now—that day, that girl, that trip to Denver. I followed her into the facility, filled out the paperwork, succumbed to the medical exam, and then sat in a chair while my protein-rich blood was drawn through a needle in my arm. I watched as my blood traveled through a thin plastic tube and into a machine that separated out the plasma. I watched as the plasma was collected in a jar. And then I watched as my nutrient-depleted blood was mixed with saline solution and circulated back into my body through another tube.

The process took somewhere around ninety minutes, which was far too long, and gave me far too much time to think about what I was doing; and I was far too tired to be there that day. Like so often then, I seemed to be accidentally becoming something I didn't want to be. The words "junkie" and "meth head" and "tweaker" bounced around inside my skull, and as I sat in that chair with my blood rushing through a tube, giving plasma for money I would use to buy drugs, I wondered what April would think of me, what Maddie and Haley would think of me when they were older and could articulate how they felt.

When we were finished and had each collected a check for forty dollars, we drove to a currency exchange to cash them. I gave the girl I didn't know the money I received for donating, and we drove to an apartment complex where we parked in a back lot. She asked me to wait in the car. "I'll just be gone for a minute," she said, her eyes already wild with anticipation. "And then we can head back." She slammed the door and scurried across the parking lot, disappeared inside a door, but she was gone for too long, and I tried not to fall asleep, tried to keep my eyes on the building, so I could see something, so I could see anything, but I couldn't fight it and when she came back, my eyes snapping open as soon as she pulled on the door handle, she said that she couldn't get any meth, that her dealer was out. I knew she was lying—I knew it because her eyes were red and dilated to the size of the buttons—and she knew I knew, but it didn't matter, because all I wanted to do was get back to Summit County and never see that girl again, to fall asleep and not wake up until I could somehow forget just how far I had fallen.

THIRTEEN

Christmas Eve 1998 I sat alone in a booth at Denny's. I wasn't working, but I had nowhere to go, no place to be, no one waiting for me to carve a Christmas turkey or exchange presents. I wasn't sad—at least I didn't think I was, but I wouldn't let myself think about it. I wouldn't let myself think about April or Maddie or Haley, what they were doing or the presents I hadn't given them. Instead, I drank coffee and tried to do the crossword puzzle and thought about how badly things needed to change. I looked up from newspaper just as the double doors to the restaurant swung wide. Travis walked through the door and stomped the snow off his boots. He saw me and came over. "Get your shit," he said, grinning. "It's Christmas, man. You're coming with me."

* * *

It would be years before I would have enough perspective to fully appreciate what it meant for Travis to find me that Christmas, to pick me up and drive me to his house, so I could be with people who cared about me. He had watched my relationship with April unravel time and time again, always shaking his head in frustration, but always stretching a sheet across his couch and letting me sleep there anyway.

I stayed with Travis through Christmas and the New Year, joining the rest of America in resolving to change my life in 1999. I backed off on drugs completely around that time—partly because I was worried I might have to take a drug test as part of my sentencing, partly because I couldn't find any—but I still drank as much as I could, grateful that Travis was old enough to buy liquor for me.

I understand now that by age twenty my alcoholism was fully formed, as much a part of me as athletics and skating were in my youth. I looked forward to drinking in the same way that people look forward to holidays and pay raises. There was no occasion too happy or too sad to drink, and the idea of not drinking, if even for a short time, was as difficult to comprehend for me as physics.

* * *

There were six days between Haley's first birthday and the day I was sentenced for assaulting April and kicking her door down, but I managed to make it to only one of those two events—my sentencing. If I had to posit a guess as to what I was doing when April helped Haley blow out the candle on her first birthday cake, I would say that I was probably drinking until I couldn't feel my body, telling myself lies like "I'll call her in a few minutes," or "she'll never even miss me," or "she's better off without me." But the thing about telling lies to oneself is that it's easier to tell them than to believe them. Regardless of how I tried to justify not being there when my daughter turned one, the guilt burned in my stomach like an ulcer.

* * *

When I got to the courthouse on the day of my sentencing, the district attorney presented me with a plea bargain. If I pled guilty to third-degree assault and harassment, they would drop the trespassing, criminal mischief, and felony burglary charges. I would have to serve a total of sixty days in jail, a figure that seemed enormous at the time, but they would give me credit for the twenty-eight days I had already served. I would also be on probation for two years, subject to random drug tests, and put on the prescription medication Antabuse, a medicine designed to dissuade alcohol abusers from drinking by causing extremely uncomfortable side effects when combined with alcohol.

My public defender urged me to accept the deal, and taking the case to trial seemed too risky—I had admitted to the entire episode in the police station the night of the incident—so even with my glazed-over eyes and alcohol-infused vision, I could see that no jury in the world was going to acquit me.

* * *

Sometime in February, Travis dropped me back off at the Summit County Jail, and I began serving the remainder of my sentence. April had quit working at Denny's, so it wasn't as if I would see her there, but she was now serving tables at the Village Inn restaurant a few blocks away. The courts didn't like the idea of me working so close to her, so in order to be eligible for the jail's work release program, I'd been told at my sentencing that I had to secure a temporary job.

I got myself hired by a local plumber named Charlie, who had lived behind April and me at the Sierra Madre apartment complex. Charlie needed an assistant, and so he would pick me up outside the jail every morning during the week, lend me some work gloves and his old pair of Carhartt winter-lined overalls, and drive me to a construction site where I would spend my days trudging a path through the snow to his truck to get tools, sweeping up the jobsite, and arranging pieces of copper piping, so he could sweat them together with his blowtorch. When the work was complete for the day, I would either walk or take the bus, or Charlie would drop me back off at the jail. "See you tomorrow, kid," he'd always say. "Hang in there."

"Thanks for the ride, Charlie," I'd say while getting out of the truck, sad to be going back to jail, but happy that I now had one less day to serve.

* * *

By the time I had finished the remainder of my sentence—twenty days total due to the twelve days of Good Time I had been awarded—it was nearing March. Travis picked me up from the jail in the new truck he had just bought, with a fresh pack of cigarettes and a hug, and together we drove through Breckenridge and Frisco, chain-smoking as I stared out the window at the huge profile of Buffalo Mountain. It was completely covered in snow, and for a moment I wished I could climb it, wished I could strap on my snowboard and carve long lines through the fresh white powder. Wasn't that what I had come here for in the first place? To snowboard, to ride? It seemed like so long ago, that dream—and it had faded so much that I wondered if I'd ever actually had it at all.

I turned my head and looked over at Travis, his chin-length brown hair tucked behind his ears. He was wearing his Oakley sunglasses, their lenses oscillating between orange and blue.

"Do you ever think about moving back to Chicago?" I asked.

He seemed surprised at the question. "Moving back? Hell no. Why, do you?"

I turned and looked out the window again as evergreen trees flew by, endless shades of green. "Sometimes. It just seems like nothing is really working for me out here."

Travis kept his eyes on the road. "I'm not going to argue with you there." He took a drag of his cigarette, downshifted his truck as we neared the traffic light that signaled we had entered Frisco. "You just need to be done with April. Like really done. As in never-getting-back-together-with-her done."

I stayed silent as we stopped at the red light. Stared at the side of the road and realized there wasn't a single piece of trash or litter that I could see. I wasn't sure I had ever seen that back home. Chicago was clean, but there was always something that needed to be picked up, some piece of garbage that managed to avoid a trashcan.

The light changed, and our heads jerked back as Travis shifted through the first three gears. I rolled the window down a little farther.

Used my thumb and forefinger to twist my cigarette filter until the cherry fell out. I reached over and put the butt in the ashtray.

"I know, man. You're right about me and April. We need to stay done."

Travis grinned and reached his hand over. Made a fist and gently hit my thigh. "Dude, let's not talk about this right now. You just got out of jail, right? Let's grab a bottle and celebrate that shit."

I leaned back in the seat and reached in my pocket, pulled out a small prescription bottle and held it up.

"What's that?" Travis asked.

"Antabuse."

"What the hell is Antabuse?"

"A pill that's supposed to keep me from drinking. They say it will give me some sort of violent reaction if I drink while I'm on it. They've been making me take it the whole time I was locked up. They monitored me taking it too. Checked my mouth to make sure I swallowed."

"Shit. So no booze?

"Fuck that," I said, suddenly pissed at the world. At the law. At myself. "Let's get a bottle anyway."

Travis looked over at me and shook his head, smiled. "Man, you're crazy."

I looked back out the window, took in everything around me—the mountains, the nature, the bigness of it all. I wished I could disappear inside of it. Shrink right into the shadow of Buffalo Mountain.

"No, man—I'm not crazy. I just don't give a fuck anymore."

I turned and looked back out the window, thought about Haley. I wished I could simply take her from April and leave. Start a new life with just the two of us, one where I could be the type of dad who made smiley-face pancakes on Saturday mornings and read to her at night. I closed my eyes, took a deep breath, and then let it out slowly. No matter what I told myself, I knew that starting over with Haley would never happen. My life was a disaster. I was literally on my way home from jail. Take care of child? I couldn't even find a consistent place to sleep. I wanted to forget about all of it. About my entire life. About Haley and April and Maddie and my parents and jail and snowboarding and high school and Colorado. I wanted to be annihilated, to be wiped out, to completely erase myself and forget that any of this had ever happened, and that I ever felt anything at all.

* * *

That night Travis and I sat at his kitchen table, a bottle of vodka and two shot glasses between us.

"What's supposed to happen when you drink?" he asked.

"I'm supposed to get nauseous and throw up and pretty much want to die. When they started to administer the dosage in jail, they told me I had to be careful if I wore cologne or used certain types of shampoo because they can contain alcohol."

Travis's face looked legitimately worried. "What am I supposed to do if you get really sick?"

I laughed. "I don't know. Hold my hair back?"

Travis shook his head. "Jesus, Tim. This might be a really bad idea."

I grabbed the bottle and filled the shot glass. "Maybe." I picked it up. "But there's only one way to find out." I smiled and threw the shot back, and then grimaced as the liquor burned its way to my stomach.

For a small percentage of people who take Antabuse, the drug is ineffective. When I drank on it, my face would turn a dark shade of red and sweat would bead on my forehead and upper lip. My heart would begin beating faster. Not pounding, but it would quicken, and I would momentarily feel nauseous. It was mildly uncomfortable at first, like the onset of the flu, but six or seven drinks in, it would barely register. It was really nothing more than a mild nuisance, a small price to pay for the peace that came with being blotto.

* * *

At some point while I had been finishing my sentence in the Summit County Jail, April had also made a trip to the Justice Center, though this time it wasn't to visit me. She must have come to the conclusion that the possibility of us reconciling was unlikely, so she filed for child support, and by the time I was released, the support mandate was issued and ruled upon, back pay was ordered, and new charges were accruing.

April had correctly deduced that I would likely go back to Travis's after I was released, and while nursing a hangover the day after I returned, I read the paperwork he'd left lying on the table.

It's embarrassing now to admit that when I read through the order that day I was furious. It felt so wrong to me at the time, that a judge could order me to be financially responsible for a child when my relationship with that child's mother was damaged beyond repair. But I also now wonder if that's precisely what my father had felt, and if it's part of the reason he stayed away. Was he so angry with my mother that he believed that anger, or what he felt was unfair about the situation, should negate his responsibility to pay? Or visit? It was so easy to blame him before I'd had Haley.

My anger at April clouded all my thinking, and I hadn't yet sorted out how much of that anger was really shame at the catastrophe I had made of our lives. My responsibility to support my child, too, was confused in my scrambled brain with April's decision that I shouldn't be allowed to see Haley until I'd paid what I owed and showed that I could be a responsible adult. I reasoned that I shouldn't have to pay child support when I wasn't able to see my child.

So instead of coming up with a plan to satisfy my arrears and pay my monthly child support obligation, instead of figuring out a way to make it work with April, so I could spend some time with my daughter, I ripped up the paperwork, threw it in the garbage, and took a nap on Travis's couch.

* * *

In mid-March, I turned twenty-one. I still didn't have a driver's license because of the mess in Illinois, but I was able to visit the Colorado Department of Motor Vehicles with a copy of my birth certificate and get a state identification card. I was then able to use that card to enter bars, and buy beer and vodka, and the way I consumed alcohol for most of 1999 was quick and hard and intentional. No matter the day or time or occasion, I drank until I destroyed any feeling of any type. If it was vodka I was drinking, I would tip the bottle back and swig, allowing my taste buds to adjust and my gag reflex to disengage. I would swallow a few times first, preparing my throat, knowing that my body would ultimately try to reject the amount of alcohol I was about to force into it, and so I would try to lull it into a state of relaxation. I might take a quick drink of Kool-Aid or Gatorade or beer or orange juice, whatever happened to be around, and then I would tip the bottle back again and drain as much of it down my throat as I could. I would do it over and over until the bottle was gone, and then I would sit back and drink beer and wait for the numbness to engulf me.

I didn't remember much from the nights I drank like that, but Travis did, and some mornings I would wake up on the floor, a dark stain in my pants and in the carpeting, smelling of urine and vomit and sweat. My eyes would be red and swollen and difficult to open, their corners sticky with mucus and dried tears from throwing up. Many times my hands would be bruised and sore, my knuckles scabbed, and Travis would tell me that it took two or three people to hold me down, to restrain me so I didn't destroy the apartment, or myself. I would have raged until the rage either left me or I was too exhausted to feel it anymore, and then my eyes had closed and my body shut down to sleep.

The next morning, as I scrubbed my own urine out of the carpeting and wiped my own vomit off the side of the toilet, pale and nauseous, I would feel nothing but a deep and cavernous sadness that stemmed from humiliation and remorse. Often, on those mornings when it hurt even to breathe, to move my arms, I would think about Haley's soft skin and how I hadn't changed her diaper in a long time and how her hand had always felt so small in mine and how I still hadn't paid very much child support and how the money that should have gone to her had gone down my throat instead. I would think about April and how I was so angry with her, so furious at how screwed up things had gotten between us, and then I would think about how much I missed her, how much I still loved her, how I still felt like maybe we could figure it all out. And then I would hear a voice in my head that would tell me I was kidding myself, that all the problems I had were my fault, and it was never going to get better, it was never going to be fixed, and I would hate myself with an intensity that burned like a blowtorch. And by the time I was done scrubbing the toilet and apologizing to Travis and anyone else I had wronged during my drunken episode, promising to be more careful and not to do it again, I would already be thinking about the next time, about how quickly I could once again drink until I arrived at the place where nothing in the world could hurt me.

* * *

On some nights, before alcohol had completely taken away my ability to reason, I would call April. She would almost always answer the phone, and I would almost always think that it was a good idea to call, and sometimes we would talk and things would seem easy, and for a second or two I think both of us would entertain the idea that maybe, with enough hard work and fortitude, we could actually be together. Haley would have her father at home and Maddie would be happy to see me, and April and I could finally fall into a normal routine together and have the relationship we wanted. Maybe I would work two jobs—construction during the day and Denny's a few nights a week—and April would stay home and take care of the kids. "We could go to counseling," she might say, and I would nod to myself on the other end of the phone. "Yeah, and we'll finally be able to figure things out. Maybe that's all we need—just a little counseling to get us back on track." It would all seem so hopeful.

But other times when I called, we would argue quickly. "When are you going to pay your child support, Tim? I'm already doing it all by myself and now you won't even man up and pay for your own kid?" I would take a swig of the alcohol I was almost always drinking, maybe take a quick, hard drag of my cigarette and say, "Why the fuck should I pay more child support when you won't even let me see my kid?" And then the volley would be hers and she would say, "I'll let you see your kid when you pay your child support," and around we would go, back and forth, until one of us let out a profanity-laced tirade and hung up.

Many of the conversations April and I had on the phone happened in Travis's house, and many times he heard nearly everything I said. If we were happy and optimistic things might work out, he would shake his head and ask me what the hell I was thinking. If he heard us fighting, heard all the vile things that came out of my mouth, he would ask me what the point was. "Dude," he would say. "Why do you even talk to her?"

Looking back, it was inevitable that Travis would ask me to leave, but he waited as long as he possibly could. After three months of watching absolutely nothing change, he sat down on the couch next to me.

"You're my friend, Tim," he said, trying to smile but succeeding only in looking sad and uncomfortable. "I care about you. I really do. But man, I can't watch you do this anymore. I need you to find another place to stay."

I looked at him, not angry, not upset, not disappointed. "Okay," I said. "Thanks for letting me stay here as long as you did."

He smiled and nodded, and there was a part of me that was

relieved he was asking me to go. Because without Travis watching, without anyone I knew watching me, I could drink and use as much and as often as I wanted.

* * *

Months had gone by since I had last spoken to my parents. It was hard to face them, even on the phone, and so for long periods of time I would simply not call.

But part of me missed them dearly, and one day after I'd worked a swing shift, a few days after Travis and I parted ways, I bought a phone card and called home from the pay phone at Denny's.

"Hey, Ma," I said when she answered. I leaned against the wall, the metal cord attached to the receiver stretching all the way out. "How are you?"

"Hey, sweetheart." Her voice was soft and loving, and in that moment I missed her more than I had in the entire time I had been gone. "You doing okay out there? We haven't talked to you in a while. Call a little more often? We worry about you, Tim."

I wanted to say okay, to tell her that I *would* call more often, and that the next time I called I would have so many good things to tell her she'd have a hard time remembering them all. I wanted to be able to give her an update on Haley, to say I had just dropped some new pictures of her in the mail and they'd be there any day now. Instead, I stared at a small dab of ketchup that had splattered on the top of the black rubber-soled dress shoes I wore to work.

"You don't have to worry about me, Ma. Things are fine."

I could hear in my voice how unconvincing I was. I could hear in my mother's how unconvinced I'd made her.

"Where are you staying now?" she asked.

"Here and there."

"Are you still with April?"

I used the heel of my other shoe to smear the ketchup on my toe. "No," I thought for a second. "I think we're done for good this time."

I didn't want to tell her that after I left Travis's house I'd been back to staying in hostels and hotels and any couches I could find. Debra had even let me stay at her townhouse for two weeks while she was on vacation. I'd spent almost the entire time drinking and staring at her television, wondering if I'd ever make enough money to afford a home that nice.

"I talked to one of the cooks here at Denny's, and he said I could stay with him for a while if I gave him a few bucks. We work most of the same shifts, so I think it will work out pretty well."

Through the receiver, I could hear the bells from the railroad crossing a block down from our house on Central Avenue begin to ring, signaling that a train was coming. I thought of all the times I'd heard that sound in my life. Thousands, I guessed.

My mother's voice: "Tim?"

"Yeah?"

"Why don't you just come home? Just come home."

I felt in my apron pocket for my cigarettes, realized I had left them in the break room.

"Ma, I can't leave Haley. You know that."

"If you and April aren't together, then are you even seeing Haley right now?"

I'd seen her briefly, when I ran into April in Walmart a month ago. Haley had grown bigger in my absence—she was just over a year old now—and when I saw her in the toy aisle she was standing with a pacifier in her mouth, holding onto a handful of April's jeans for balance. I'd felt scared when I saw her, because I could see how real she was, or more precisely, how real my absence was, and how my absence from her life wasn't stopping her. She was growing up without me, and she'd continue to grow up without me unless something changed. Had I expected something different? I remembered that one moment I'd wanted to pick her up and run out the door with her. The next moment I found myself wondering if she'd even recognized me or if she'd just start crying the second I scooped her up. Instead of finding out, I turned down another aisle and avoided them altogether. One night shortly after, I'd stopped by April's house and written her a check for a thousand dollars. It had felt good to write it, to contribute an amount that felt substantial, but I knew it wasn't enough. It would never be enough. Money couldn't fix what was wrong with me.

I took a deep breath and smelled onions grilling in the kitchen. "I haven't seen her in a little while, but it's just because April and I haven't been seeing eye to eye."

"And you think things are going to change?" she asked.

I sighed. "Eventually. Listen, Mom, I don't want to get into all of this. It is what it is right now, and there's nothing I can do about it. I just wanted to call and see how you were."

When my mother spoke next, I could tell she had started crying. I could picture her face, full of love, as if she were standing right in front of me. My eyes welled up.

"Okay, sweetheart." I imagined her wiping her nose, her mascara running the way it always did when she cried. "Okay. Just know that I love you. That *we* love you—and that you can always come home."

I wiped my eyes. Squeezed the handle of the phone until my hand ached from the pressure.

"All right, Ma. I know. I love you too."

* * *

By the end of summer, I had moved in with Jason, the Denny's cook. He lived in a small, worn-down house in Kremmling, a tiny town roughly forty miles northwest of Silverthorne on Highway 9. With two bedrooms, a small mildew-laced bathroom, and a living room adorned with Grateful Dead posters and overflowing ashtrays that were almost never emptied, it was exactly what I thought a frat house would look like, though there wasn't a university anywhere near it, and no one who lived there had any plans of going to college.

Jason was right around my age, and he lived there with his

roommate, a short Hawaiian kid—deeply tanned with jet-black hair—named Kaleo. They'd met a couple of years before while working construction together, and when Jason had saved up enough money, paid the down payment, and bought the house, Kaleo moved in to help out with the mortgage.

Jason's mother lived a half block down the street, in a similarly sized house with a better-kept lawn, and she would stop in from time to time, always with a mix of amusement and disgust on her face as she walked inside. "Jason," she would say, pausing just inside the door with her hands on her hips, looking around. "This place is a damn pigsty. You guys are a bunch of animals." Much of the time we'd be sitting on Jason's couch, drinking beers or smoking, maybe playing his old Nintendo 64, and Jason would look at her, his eyes lighting up every time she walked into the room. "Well, why don't you help out your poor son and clean it up for him?"

She would laugh and shake her head, say, "fat chance," or "nice try," or "you wish." I would watch the interaction from my spot on the stained couch, smiling during their exchange, relishing it. I knew almost nothing about them except for what I saw in those moments, but it was enough, and it made me miss my mother in a way I could physically feel.

In Kremmling, there was no one watching me, which meant I could drink unapologetically, draining beer and alcohol in amounts that would eventually render my body useless. My tolerance was high, but there was only so much alcohol one's liver could metabolize.

One morning as Jason and I sat on the couch, hungover and digging through ashtrays looking for cigarettes to smoke, he handed me one that had a good amount of tobacco left.

"Dude, when you passed out last night, Kaleo and I sat here watching you. You were snoring so loud it was damn near unbelievable."

I lit the cigarette, swallowed my nausea. Blew the smoke out. "Yeah, so?"

He lit the already-smoked cigarette he'd found and took a drag.

Grimaced and examined it closely to see what brand it was. He got up and walked over to the front door. Opened it and spit outside. He turned back to me.

"So every few minutes you would stop snoring completely, and then we noticed that when you stopped snoring, it actually looked like you had stopped breathing. Your chest would stop moving. You'd be as still as a corpse. Just when Kaleo and me were about to start shaking you, you would gasp and start breathing again. It must have happened twenty or twenty-five times. We finally turned you over onto your side."

I felt a flash of aggravation. "Well what the fuck do you want me to do about it?"

He walked back across the living room and sat down next to me. "Nothing, man. Relax. I'm just telling you that maybe you should take it easy for a little while. I'm all for getting fucked up, but the last thing I need is for you to choke on your vomit or quit breathing while you're sleeping or some shit."

I put my cigarette down and watched it burn. Cleared my throat and swallowed the phlegm. Maybe Jason was right. Maybe taking some time off drinking wasn't a bad idea.

I picked my cigarette back up. "Maybe I'll take a few days off. Dry out for a bit."

Jason nodded and opened the door again, walked outside. I looked around the room through the cigarette smoke, saw the disarray, the empty cans and bottles, the stained carpeting. I looked over toward the window and fixed my eyes on the red Marlboro bag that sat beneath it, everything I owned in the world packed inside, ready to leave with me as soon I slung it over my shoulder.

FOURTEEN

On October 13, 1999, at eight o'clock in the evening, I was arrested again. The records show it was a Class 3 misdemeanor offense for harassment, and the bail amount was a set at one hundred dollars.

It's strange to think that, all these years later, I have no memory of the incident, no memory of what really transpired. There's just a dusty memory of the court proceedings that played out after. It feels logical to assume, though, that my arrest had something to do with April. A phone call perhaps. Maybe a drunken drive-by of her apartment to hang out the window and yell. It occurs to me now that there are endless ways to harass.

* * *

Not long after that, on December 15, I stood in a courtroom I'd been in before, in front of a judge I'd been in front of before, on a charge I'd been accused of before.

"To the charge of harassment, from October 13, a Class 3 misdemeanor, how do you plead, Mr. Hillegonds?"

I took a deep breath. "Not guilty, Your Honor."

"Very well. We'll set the matter for trial. Mr. Hillegonds, do you want a trial by judge or jury?

"Jury, Your Honor."

"Okay." He nodded. Glanced down at the paperwork in front of him. "Trial is set for February 10 of next year."

* * *

The cycle that occurs with addicts and alcoholics is as old and predictable as the alcohol and drugs themselves. We drink. We use. We feel regret and remorse. And then we make promises to change, to become better, to become different.

In the moments we make those promises, we believe them truly possible to keep. We can be different people, we think. Better fathers. Better mothers. Better daughters. Better sons. We believe that change is just a few good nights of sleep away. That all we need to do is try harder this time, to truly try, to try with the same assiduity we chased our substances with. And perhaps we even make good on that promise for a while. Maybe we show a slight change in behavior and give someone a glimmer of hope. Maybe a good thing replaces a bad thing. Maybe someone sees a flash of the person buried behind the substance.

The problem, however, is that it's almost always temporary. Inevitably, we break our promises and settle back into those familiar behaviors, those ruinous habits that somehow feel so natural, so right, so normal, as we do it all over again. The irony that's often lost on the world is that we are, in fact, being our truest selves: addicts and alcoholics know only how to act like addicts and alcoholics.

And an addict and alcoholic is what I was and still am, and it's why certain things played out the way they did in my Colorado years. When my relationship with April was at its best, it often felt like we were a real family. Our lives were chaotic and dysfunctional and rarely made sense, but we had each other, and that made it seem like we were somehow insulated from the rest of the world. There had been times—certainly at the beginning of our relationship, but also in between our biggest fights—when no problem seemed insurmountable, like all we had to do was stick together and we could power through anything. It was as if the pressure from the outside world—financial, vocational, familial—gave us a common enemy to fight, a reason to link up. For a time at least, we forgot we were fighting ourselves.

Perhaps that's what I was thinking about when I called her from the pay phone at Denny's a few days after court.

"What do you want?" April said.

"Another chance. To see the girls. To change."

She paused. "People like you don't change."

I wondered if she was right. Could people like me change? Could they change if they stayed standing in the same place, with the same person, doing the same things over and over? Could they change when the only thing they knew how to do was to keep doing the things they'd always done?

I turned to look out the window, but it was dark and all I could see was myself staring back—tired eyes drooping, white shirt that needed to be washed, a stained Denny's apron. My hair was shorter, and my eyebrow piercing was gone—the hole had closed up while I was in jail. In my white shirt and tie I almost looked presentable. I wanted to be presentable. I wanted to change.

"Let's spend New Year's Eve together. You know, all of us. Like a family."

She laughed. "You're kidding, right?"

I sighed. "No, I'm serious. Let's just be together, all of us, for one night. For the new millennium." It sounded so important—the new millennium. Y2K. A once-in-a-lifetime experience that demanded to be shared with someone else. With someone you loved.

"After all the shit that's happened lately? After all your bullshit? Not paying child support regularly, living wherever the hell you want, doing whatever the hell you want?"

I felt tears behind my eyelids. Blinked. Blinked again. I was so tired of the game. The runaround. The effort it was taking to be alive.

I steadied my voice, and it came out gently—no anger, ripe with remorse and loneliness. "Yeah, April, even after all of that." I paused. "Please? Let's spend it together."

"I've already got plans. I'm going out."

"Then let me go with you."

She was quiet, and so was I. Above me, the radio pumped music into the dining room. I leaned against the pay phone. Felt a cold breeze from the entrance drifting around the corner and shivered.

"I'm probably going to regret this at some point," she said, "but okay. I'm dropping the girls off at my friend's before we head out that night. Meet me at the apartment around nine."

It sounded like I wouldn't be able to see the girls, but I could still see April, and maybe that was okay, maybe that would be the start of everything changing between us.

"Okay, April," I said. "I will."

"Don't make me regret this."

"I won't. I promise. I'll see you then."

* * *

It was New Year's Eve, and I was standing in the living room of April's apartment, and we were both already a few shades past buzzed. She looked so good to me, and it felt so normal, so like it used to be, and the curls in her hair were styled so they fell in specific places on her shoulders, her blonde hair on that black shirt, blonde on black. Her jeans were tight and her top was, too, and she held out her hand in front of her, like she was presenting me with an actual silver platter. "Here," she said. "Eat this."

I picked up the small piece of paper from the palm of her hand and said, "I've never done acid before," and she said, "then you're in for a treat because it's New Year's Eve right before the new millennium, and the whole world is about to change."

I smiled and laughed because I wanted my world to change, maybe more than I wanted anything else in my life. I said, "That sounds perfect, April," and I placed the acid on my tongue and waited while it dissolved. She smiled back at me and did a little spin and then she said, "How do I look?" and I said, "You look so beautiful April, so good," but I couldn't stop thinking about the acid on my tongue and how my world was going to change. It didn't taste like anything, didn't taste bitter like I thought it would, and so I started to wonder if maybe I got a dud hit or something, that maybe there was a drug dealer somewhere who was slacking on the job the night he made my hit, and I was about to ask April about it, but she was pulling me out the door because, "The cab is here, and it's time to fucking gooooo."

And then we were in the back of a moving cab as it got on the highway to Frisco, so we could go to the bar. But we weren't paying attention to the time, and I thought we were cutting it close, and I wasn't ready for the new millennium just yet. I was about to say something again, but it was hard to talk and my mouth felt like it was chewing on a rubber toy, and the lights, holy shit the lights looked so fucking amazing. "April," I said, "Do you see these lights? *Do you see these fucking lights?* Oh my God, these lights are amazing." She looked at me and smiled and her teeth were perfect and white and happy, and I wanted to tell her that, too, but then she was pulling me out of the taxi because we'd made it to the bar, and she'd already given the cabbie a twenty-dollar bill and told him to keep the change. We made it to the line of people waiting in the freezing cold and then we were standing in it and the lights were back and I was looking at them again, wishing I could put them in my pocket, wondering how I never noticed them before. And then the sidewalk was moving, or maybe it was just me, and I heard voices counting down, counting backwards from ten. I looked around at the line full of people and I didn't know any of them, and I didn't really want to, and I was starting to feel nervous about it, but then April's hand was on my shoulder and her face was right in front of me and her voice was saying, "You're okay, you're okay, just breathe, just breathe." And she was right, I was okay, and I was just breathing, and then it was "three, two, one," and then we we're kissing, but it was just a quick one, and we hadn't done it in so long that even the quick one felt strange, and then the line was moving and April pulled me through the door and there were people everywhere and it was the new millennium and how the fuck did I even get here, to Colorado, to April, and where is my fucking daughter? Because I have one, right? A daughter? A beautiful, small, perfect little thing that I used to hold all the time but now I never do and I miss her so badly and I think she might miss me too. But then we were on the dance floor, and I was drinking a beer and it tasted so good in my throat, those bubbles, scratching away, and I thought when I was done swallowing I might start purring like a kitten because the bubbles felt so good, and maybe that would too, but then April was pulling me out the door again because the bar was closing, and it was time to go home. April had our jackets and I pulled mine on and we started walking down the street and the ice was crunching below us and it was so cold out and the lights weren't quite as amazing, and we couldn't get a cab, so we started walking with our thumbs out, hitchhiking. A car pulled over and April said, "Can you get us to Silverthorne?" and the guy was wearing a plastic party hat and he said, "Hell yeah, it's too cold to be walking, so get in," and he drove us all the way back to April's. He dropped us off and we said thank you, or maybe just April did because I'd been having a hard time talking all night, and I thought I would really just rather be listening this time anyway, but when April opened the door I realized that I would really rather be sitting on the ground, warm, watching TV. So that's what we did, April on the couch, me on the floor, with our jackets on in the dark that comes right before dawn. On the television was a replay of the ball dropping in New York, and I still couldn't believe it was the new millennium, and I was about to say that to April when I heard a noise. I turned to her and I saw that she was crying, sobbing actually, her eyes glassy and wet. "What's wrong, April?" I said. "What's wrong?" But now *she* couldn't say anything, and so she just cried, streams of tears running down her face. And so I started crying, too, because I didn't know what else to do and maybe this was what the whole night had been leading to anyway, a whole bunch of weeping, the sparkling ball in New York dropping slowly on the television, the two of our faces flashing in the dark, heavy and wet with tears.

* * *

For all of January 2000, it felt as if I were waiting for something. I drove with Jason from Kremmling to Silverthorne and back again almost every day, waiting while we rode to Denny's, waiting while I smoked cigarettes, waiting for the lights to change from red to green and back again. When I arrived at Denny's for my shift, I waited to get off. When I got off my shift, I waited to get back to Kremmling. When I got back to Kremmling, I waited to get annihilated, to pass out and wake up and do it all over again. I waited to become a better man and a better father and then I had simply waited too long.

I had missed Haley's second birthday.

* * *

During a break in my shift at Denny's one morning in the beginning of February, about two weeks after Haley's birthday, I called April and tried to make it right. She must have checked the caller ID because she picked up almost as soon as the phone began ringing.

"You're a real piece of shit, you know that?"

"I know. I'm sorry. I meant to call. It's just that—I don't know. I didn't know what to do."

"You missed your daughter's birthday, Tim."

I looked at the floor. "I don't know what to say."

"Then don't say anything," she said, and the phone disconnected.

I hung up the receiver and walked to the window. It was midmorning and the sun was still low in the sky, still climbing, bouncing rays off the snow so brilliantly I couldn't look directly at it. I turned around. Dug in my pocket for a quarter. Dropped it in the slot and dialed April's number again.

"Can't you take a fucking hint?"

"April, I just want to know how the birthday went. That's all. Was

Haley happy? What did she get? Did she get that doll we used to see at Walmart? The one she would always reach for?"

A beat or two passed. Then another. And then, "I'm going to make this real clear for you, Tim. Never call us again."

The line went dead for the second time, and I hung up the receiver, fighting the urge to slam it. I picked it back up again, gritted my teeth and dug for another quarter. Dropped it in the slot and dialed the number.

"Stop. Fucking. Calling."

"Come on, April." I wanted to punch something. "All I want to know is how Haley's birthday party went and when I can see her next."

"Do you even know what an asshole you are, Tim? I mean, seriously. Do you?" She paused and I stayed silent. "Here, I'll help you with the answer. You're the kind of asshole who gets to go to jail."

What was she even talking about? I shook my head. "Last time I checked I had to do something wrong to go jail."

"We'll see," she said, and hung up the phone.

* * *

The suv had "Silverthorne Police" decals layered across the doors. Two officers got out and walked toward the entrance to Denny's. I recognized both of them, had been arrested by both of them before. One had short, dark hair parted to the side. The other one had brown hair that was slicked back, fifties greaser style.

I walked around the cash register and grabbed two menus. Leaned back against the counter and waited until the door opened.

"Two for nonsmoking?" I asked as they walked in.

The one with greaser hair spoke. "Put your hands behind your back, Tim."

"For what?"

"I said put your hands behind your back."

I did as I was told and he approached me.

"Did you just make a phone call to April Murphy?"

"Yeah, I called to talk about my daughter's birthday party."

The officer with the parted hair walked over to the pay phone and pulled his notepad out of his shirt pocket. He leaned forward, wrote the number to the pay phone down in it.

The officer standing in front of me took his handcuffs off his belt. "Turn around."

I complied, and he fastened the cuffs and spun me around. "You're being charged with harassment, Tim. April said you called her repeatedly and that you threatened her."

"That's bullshit."

"Says you."

"Yeah, says me." I glared at him, wanted to head butt him across the bridge of his nose. "So you're just going to take her word for it? That's it?"

"No," he took a step back, "we're going to drive over to April's house and check her caller ID. If that pay phone number is on there, then we're taking you in."

I shook my head. "I just told you that I called her. I'm not denying that. What good is that going to do?"

The officer grabbed my shoulder and started pushing me toward the door. "Just keep walking, Hillegonds."

I was placed in the back of the squad car, and we made the short drive to April's house, where we parked on the street. The officer with the greaser hair got out. I could see the door to April's apartment open and then close again while she let him inside.

In the front seat, the officer's radio jumped to life, and he responded with some sort of police code, then turned the volume down. He looked in the rearview mirror at me.

"Tim, you remember me, right? From the night that you kicked the door down?"

I turned my head in the opposite direction of April's apartment, stared into the distance. "Yeah."

"Then you can probably figure out why we're not just arbitrarily taking your word that you didn't harass and threaten April."

A car drove by, and I did my best to shrink into the seat. I didn't want anyone to see me in the back of a police car again. I was so tired of police cars. Of cops. Of making the drive over to the Summit County Jail.

"Here's the reality of your situation, Tim. You've got a record, and that means you're always going to be looked at a little harder. You're always going to have to try a little more than the average guy to convince us that you're not doing anything wrong."

I turned my head, looked into the rearview so I could see his face, but he was looking toward April's apartment. "The other officer that went in there—he knows the situation too. He knows about the history of you and April. He's going to look at that number on the caller ID and it's going to be the same as the one on the pay phone and we're going to have to take you in on a harassment/domestic violence charge."

"But I didn't *do* anything."

"It doesn't matter, because she said you did, and the number you called from is on her caller ID." He turned his head and looked at me. "Don't you get it, Tim? She's better than you at this game. You're always going to lose."

The door to April's house opened, and we both looked in that direction. The other officer emerged and started walking toward the car.

"Think about it, Tim. That's all I'm saying."

* * *

I spent that night back at the Summit County Jail, where I called Debra collect and apologized for getting arrested at work. "Are things ever going to change, Tim?" she'd asked me, but what I heard was "things are never going to change, Tim." I didn't know how to respond. Maybe things would never change. Maybe this life, this crazy, cyclical existence was all there was for me.

To my surprise, I was released the next day when the judge failed to find enough probable cause to charge me. At first I thought I'd caught a break and that the charges would simply be dropped, but not finding probable cause wasn't the same as not being charged in the first place, and I still had to appear in court.

In the days after that arrest, I worked as much as I could at the restaurant, trying to cobble together enough money for court fines and fees, and one night after I'd worked a double, after I was tired and lonely and exhausted and feeling sorry for myself, I struck up a conversation with one of the new servers, a girl named Heather, who had wide eyes and perfectly shaped eyebrows and chestnut-colored hair that fell to just past her shoulders. Her skin was smooth and she had a sway in her walk, a confidence that made me think that she'd probably spent time on a stage at one point or another—maybe acting or modeling or singing. I knew she had a boyfriend, a guy I'd met a few times when he'd come into the restaurant, and I knew I should respect that boundary, that I should watch how I acted, but I didn't care because it felt so good to talk to a woman who wasn't April, a woman who wasn't mad at me, and so I said, "Do you want to grab drinks at Old Chicago tonight?" and she said, "Sure, but I can't be out too late," and I smiled and said, "Of course not, we'll just have one."

But it was never just one with me, and that meant it wouldn't be just one for her, and so by the time the first pitcher of Fat Tire was nearly empty, we were laughing and telling stories and arriving at that place where alcohol and desire and laughter intersect. And soon there was another pitcher and more stories and even more laughter and suddenly April and Haley and Maddie were a distant memory, and so was Heather's boyfriend, and we were lost in the moment, oblivious to anything else, to the danger or the risk or the conse-quences. But there's gravity in lust, and also in loneliness, and we must have felt both of those things, because as we finished the last drops of the second pitcher of beer, that gravity pulled us toward the front desk of the hotel Old Chicago was attached to, and then toward the room, and then through the door and onto the bed and into the fluid anarchy of skin and breath, of two strangers being intimate.

Maybe neither one of us thought about what we were doing, or maybe we both did and didn't care, but when we had finished and we lay there in the darkness of that room, wondering where the comfort we had felt only a moment ago had gone, Heather said "I should go," and I nodded and said, "I understand." And once she was gone and I lay there on that hotel bed alone, replaying what had just happened in my mind, I could clearly understand another truth about myself: there was nothing I wouldn't do to feel better. And feeling better never lasted.

* * *

On February 10, 2000, when I arrived at the courthouse for my harassment charge, I checked the docket to see what courtroom I was in, wondering how things were going to play out. Once I knew where I was going, I walked slowly down the hallway and sat on a bench just outside the courtroom. All around me, lawyers and clerks and administrative assistants busied themselves with files and conversations, and it struck me as odd that there was such a palpable difference between all of us, such a huge divide between those building careers and those losing them. We'd all made such different choices, which is the way it always is, although perhaps nowhere more evident than inside a courthouse.

I was a little over an hour early. Jason was to work the early shift that morning anyway, so I'd caught a ride with him to Denny's, and then took the bus from Silverthorne to Breckenridge.

I heard footsteps that sounded like they were walking toward me and looked up just as a middle-aged man in a dark suit with a chevron mustache walked up.

"Tim Hillegonds?"

"Yeah?"

He smoothed out his suit coat. "I'm District Attorney Brett Winters. I'd like you to come with me, so we can sit down and talk about your case."

I stood up. "Okay, lead the way."

I followed him down the hallway and through a large wooden doorway, and I was grateful that I'd decided against wearing jeans. I was wearing my work uniform—black dress slacks and a white button down—but at least it was clean and somewhat professional. We entered into a small conference room that held a long cherry-wood table. He pulled out one of the large, faux leather desk chairs and motioned toward it with his hand. "Have a seat."

Mr. Winters walked to the front of the table and sat down. I did as I was told, and a minute later, a door on the other side of the room opened and a young woman walked through it. She was blonde and attractive in a fitted pantsuit, and looked like she may have been only a few years older than me. She handed him a three-inch accordion file and he thanked her. She took the seat immediately to his right.

Mr. Winters cleared his throat. "So here's the deal: We're willing to drop your most recent harassment charge in exchange for a guilty plea to the harassment charge from last October," he said, shuffling through papers in the file until he found what he was looking for.

"What about jail time?" I said. "If I'm going to have to do more time, I might as well just take my chances with the jury trial. The charges are bullshit anyway."

Mr. Winters glanced at his clerk. "We're not interested in jail time." He looked back at me. Leaned back in his chair. "We'll ask the judge for sixty days, but suspend fifty-nine of them and give you credit for the one day you served. One year of probation and $220 in fines, going to the usual places for DV cases—Victim Assistance Fund, Cost of Care, Victim Compensation Fund."

I thought about what he was saying. If I wasn't going to do jail time, then what did it matter if I pled guilty? My record was such that one more conviction, especially for a misdemeanor, wasn't going to make much of a difference.

I leaned forward in my chair until I could feel my chest touching the side of the conference table. "You sure I won't do any more jail time?"

"We won't ask for it, however, to be clear, it's always possible the judge could impose it on his own. But I have history with this judge, and he's never gone against a deal I've offered." He paused, grabbed his file folder and pulled a few pieces of paper out of it. "There's one more thing you'll need to agree to."

Mr. Winters tapped the two sheets of paper he'd pulled out of the file on the table to even them out, and then laid them down in front of him. He studied the top sheet, and then switched it for the bottom sheet. Spun it around with his fingers and slid it toward me.

"Additionally," he used his finger to point to a paragraph near the bottom of the page, "there's this."

I scooted my chair closer to the table and pulled the papers toward me. Read the paragraph he indicated.

"Come on, Mr. Winters." I gripped the edges of the table with both of my hands. Squeezed. "I have a daughter here. You can't do that to me."

"We *can* do that, Mr. Hillegonds, and we have. Frankly, my office and the court are tired of the dance we've been doing with you for the last couple of years." He pulled another set of papers from his file and began reading from one of the pages. "Burglary. Criminal mischief. Assault. Underage drinking. Harassment. Trespassing. Damage to property. Resisting arrest. Eluding the police. Domestic violence." His eyes met mine. "It's time to face the facts, Tim. This place just isn't working out for you."

I looked back down at the paperwork and reread it again. "Further established in this Plea Agreement, the Defendant will vacate the State of Colorado within thirty days of executing this Agreement.

Until further notice is issued by the Court in which this Plea Agreement is entered, Defendant shall hold residence outside of the State of Colorado."

Mr. Winters pushed a pen toward me.

"Isn't there anything else you can offer me?"

"I'm afraid not. You also need to understand that if you don't take this deal, if you try to roll the dice in court, we're going to ask for the maximum sentence in both of your cases."

"Which is what?"

"Six months and a $750 fine for each one."

I put my elbows on the table, dropped my head into my hands. It felt like the floor was dropping away from me, like everything I'd ever held onto was slipping from my grip.

I lifted my head. Tried one last time. "There's no other way?"

"I'm afraid not, Tim." He leaned back in his chair again.

I looked at the pen he'd laid on the table. It felt like I didn't have a choice. I picked up the pen and signed my name.

Mr. Winters leaned forward and grabbed the papers. "Good. I'll see you in court in an hour, and the judge will approve the deal officially. Good luck to you."

* * *

In the month that passed in between signing the plea agreement and the day I was to have left the state, I made exactly zero changes to my life. I didn't pack. I didn't see Haley. I didn't buy a bus ticket. I simply entertained the same tired fantasy where I woke up one morning and my life had been miraculously fixed. Even though it was nearly impossible, it was still so easy for me to believe that I was always one day away from turning thing around.

On deadline day, I sat in the break room at Denny's, talking to Jason, who was slouched in one of the metal folding chairs across from me.

"Today's the day, right?" he said. "So what are you going to do?"

I had picked up a bottle of vodka earlier, and I poured part of it into a glass filled with pink lemonade from the soda machine out front. I took a drink. Swallowed.

"Yeah, today's the day. But I don't know what I'm going to do yet."

He took his hat off and ran his hand through his hair. Put it back on backwards, and then crossed his arms on his chest. "Do you even have a way to get back to Chicago if you wanted to?"

"No."

"Then it sounds like you've already made your decision, man." He grabbed a smoke from the pack on the counter. Lit it. Watched me.

"Give me one of those," I said. Jason held the pack out, and I grabbed one. He held out his lighter. "Thanks." I lit the cigarette, threw the lighter on the counter and it slid to a stop near his ashtray. "Is it cool if I keep staying with you?"

"It's fine with me, but you know they're going to issue a warrant as soon as they find out you didn't leave."

I took a drag. Shrugged. "So?"

"So? What do you mean, 'so'? So it's not a good plan."

"Yeah, but how am I supposed to leave Haley?"

"It's not up to you anymore, man. She's here. You can't be." He brushed off an ash that had landed on his knee. "You don't have a choice."

It was the opposite of what my stepfather had always said. *You always have a choice, son. No matter what.*

I took a drag from my cigarette and blew it out.

"Fuck them," I said. He was right, but I hated that he was. And no matter what anyone told me to do, it was my choice. I'd sooner get arrested before I left Haley the same way my father had left me. "I'll leave when I damn well want to."

Jason shook his head and stood up. "Okay, man. Whatever you say." He reached over and ashed his cigarette, and then disappeared around the corner.

* * *

I couldn't leave Haley. I couldn't physically be in a different state. Even though I wasn't seeing her or holding her or spending time with her, even though I may as well have been in another state already, even though the gulf between us felt wider than the Rockies, wider than the sky, wider than the distance between Chicago and Colorado, I still felt like crossing back over the Continental Divide would be unforgivable, the ultimate betrayal.

I can see the absurdity of it now—how staying in the state of Colorado in the condition I was in was no different than leaving— but back then it made perfect sense to me, or maybe it just made less sense than leaving did. I was so determined not to become my father, not to do the same thing to Haley that he had done to me, that I convinced myself my physical proximity to my daughter made up for my lack of interaction with her. Which is crazy, given that my own father lived four miles away from me and never came to visit. I had become a shadow of the man who left me, a shadow my daughter couldn't even see.

* * *

I came into Denny's late one afternoon in March, roughly a month after I was supposed to have left. The sun was just beginning to set, just getting ready to drop below the Rocky Mountains for the night. As soon as I walked in, Heather came up to me with a worried look on her face, both arms outstretched. Her palms landed on my chest. "Tim, you can't be here." There was urgency in her voice, and she pulled me over toward the pay phone where I was somewhat out of view. "The police were just here looking for you."

I felt my body temperature jump a few degrees. "How long ago?"

"I don't know, maybe an hour?"

I glanced toward the front of the restaurant as the door opened. It was an elderly couple. The man held the door for his wife who was using a walker.

"So what did they say?"

Heather reached down and adjusted her apron. Looked up at me with genuine concern in her eyes.

"They said we should call them if we saw you. Tim, what's going on?"

"It's the deal I made with the district attorney. I was supposed to have left the state a while ago." My breath caught as it hit me. "They must know I'm still here."

Summit County was such a small place that I was sure someone— one of April's friends likely—had seen me and told her I hadn't left. I couldn't be sure but I'd bet money on the fact that April had told the police I was still around. I leaned against the wall, squeezed my eyes shut. Began rubbing my temples. "Fuck."

The drawer of the cash register crashed open, and we both looked over as a server totaled out a man with a toddler clinging to his leg. My stare lingered on the child. Was Haley really that little? Was I really going to leave her?

I looked back at Heather. We were standing close enough for me to smell the vanilla from her perfume, and I thought about the night we'd shared. How it had felt so good and then so bad. She tucked a long strand of brown hair behind her ear.

"Tim, I think you better go." She reached in her apron pocket and pulled out a roll of cash—what looked to be all the tip money she'd made on her shift. "Here, take this. Just go."

"What? I can't take that."

She pushed the money into my hand. "Just take it, Tim. Please."

I didn't want to take her money. I wanted to decline her offer and bury my face in her neck and smell her vanilla perfume. I wanted to forget about what was happening.

I stared at the folded bills in my hand and figured there was probably about eighty dollars there. A wave of emotion crashed down on me, and I tried to fight it as best I could.

I looked up at her, tried to smile. "I don't even know what to say. Thank you."

She waved away the gratitude with a flick of her hand. "So what are you going to do?"

I shrugged. Felt like I was out of options. "Leave, I guess."

Heather nodded and reached out to hug me. I hesitated at first, but then I pulled her close to me, thanking her again as we embraced. I felt so grateful for what she was doing for me—for the money, but also for her compassion, and as we stood there hugging in the restaurant I had worked in for almost three years, hearing forks scraping plates, knives clinking, I breathed her scent deeply, the vanilla and lavender, thankful for someone to hold on to.

* * *

The sun had nearly set and when I walked out into the cold Colorado winter—the third one I had experienced since I'd moved here—I looked around, wondering if I was truly going to leave. In such a short amount of time, I'd turned into a wanderer who settled for whatever life gave him. Even after I had left high school for the last time, when I knew that my path forward was permanently changing, I never imagined a future where I ended up this aimless, this unhappy. I had no career, no place to live, no outlook that extended further than my next scheduled shift at Denny's, and now not even that. I was a criminal with a felony, a man who hit a woman, a binge drinker and hard-drug user, a father who was about to leave his child.

As I walked across the parking lot, I saw Buffalo Mountain and the Factory Store Outlets and the alley where I'd slept the night I last left April. In the distance I could almost see the first apartment we'd shared, the bank where William had been arrested, the hostel where I'd stayed for a few nights when I had no place else to go. All around me were things that were in some ways familiar, but they all felt foreign to me too. No matter how many times I had told myself I belonged, I knew in my heart that I didn't.

Jason was working, and when he got off, he was going to drive me back to Kremmling for the night. While I waited for him to finish his shift, I walked to the City Market grocery store to call my parents. The store had moved from its previous location near April's first apartment and was a few blocks up the hill now, but I needed the walk, needed the space to breathe and think about what was happening. I stayed off the sidewalk as much as I could, scared the police might see me, walking behind Wendy's and the gas station and thinking about what I would say to my parents. More than anything, I just hoped they would answer.

The pay phone was located in the small entryway at the front of the store where they kept the carts. Shoppers walked in and out of the automatic doors, and I picked up the receiver and dialed the number I'd dialed so many times as a child. My mother answered, and before I could even say a word, the tears were flowing down my cheeks and all the things I felt, all the pain and remorse and guilt and resentment and sadness, came spilling from my eyes.

My mother's voice came through the phone clearly, and I wanted to be there with her so badly, just to see her face, just to see that look that used to make me feel like things, whatever they were, would be okay.

"Tim," she said. "Tim, what's wrong?"

I was sobbing now, trying to catch my breath and make the tears stop, trying not to make a scene, trying to hide my face from the shoppers walking by. "Mom."

"Tim, what is it?"

"*Mom—.*" Even then, at that moment, the words were so hard to say.

"Tim, talk to me."

"Mom, please. Mom, I need to come home. *Please*, I just need to come home."

"Oh, Tim." In the background, I could hear her say something to my stepfather. I heard him pick up one of the other phones in the house, and then they were both on the line. My stepfather's voice was full of compassion.

"Son? Are you okay?"

"Dad, no, I'm not okay. I'm so sorry." My voice was cracking and my nose was running. "I need to come home. Will you let me come home? Will you?" I used my sleeve to wipe the tears from my eyes. "Please?"

"Yes, Tim," my stepfather said. "Of course you can come home. When?"

"Tomorrow. There's a Greyhound bus leaving in the morning. I have like eighty bucks, but it's not enough for the ticket."

"Where are you right now?" my stepfather asked.

"At the grocery store."

"I'm sure there's a Western Union there. I'll wire you the rest of the money."

My mother spoke, and I could tell she'd started crying too. "I want you home, Tim. We all do."

In that moment, her words felt so good, perhaps better than any drug I had ever ingested or smoked or snorted. I told my mother I was coming home, and she said she could hardly wait, and everyone seemed so happy about it, so relieved, and before we hung up the tears were abundant and even my stepfather was crying. Yet even though there was so much relief in knowing I was finally giving up and going home to a place I knew and loved and missed with every good and decent piece of me, there was still an enormous part of me that felt fractured and ashamed. Because the denial I had been actively pursuing was no longer possible. It was real now, and the certainty was crystal clear: In fewer than twenty-four hours I was going to leave my daughter behind.

FIFTEEN

In memory, it's the smallest details I see the clearest. The cool night air coming in from the doors every time they opened. The tinny crash of the grocery carts. The tone in my mother's voice that made me think that if love could manifest itself as a sound, that would be it.

When I called my parents that night, I felt an enormous sense of relief, as if the referee in a boxing match I was losing badly had just waved off the fight. I wanted to stay in the ring, to keep throwing punches and turn things around, but there was nothing left to do but call it before I got permanently hurt.

I had always been scared of being hurt. Beneath the never-ending stream of curse words I hurled at anyone who said something I didn't like, or was perhaps too close to the truth, I was terrified. Terrified of continuing the insane dance I was doing with April. Terrified of leaving Haley to grow up without me. Terrified of being arrested again. Terrified of not being arrested and living in fear of the police. Terrified I had turned into my father. But more than all of that I was terrified that if I left, I would never come back, that I would never have a relationship with Haley, that when I got back to Chicago and started my life over again, Haley wouldn't be in it. How could I live with myself then?

At the same time, I knew on some deep level that in order for me to have any chance at being a father to Haley, I had to leave Colorado. I needed to heal, to fix what was broken inside me, to deal with the colossal addictions and anger I couldn't stop feeding.

As I slowly walked back down the hill toward Denny's to catch a ride with Jason back to Kremmling for what would likely be my last night in Colorado, it was the word "failure" that kept popping into my mind. By the time I was riding in Jason's car back to his house, the headlights carving triangles through the dark, the word had wrapped around me like a vine, adding weight to my depression, threatening to pull me down completely.

* * *

The following morning, Jason drove me to the bus depot in Frisco. Our goodbye was short and awkward. He said to call him and stay in touch. I said I would. I thanked him, and then he was gone.

I walked into the depot through an aluminum door with a glass window and adjusted the giant duffel bag on my shoulder. Inside, the small room had four rows of chairs, all connected to each other and bolted to the ground. A drinking fountain was mounted to the wall in the back, next to a vending machine, a *Summit Daily News* newspaper rack, and a pair of doors that led to bathrooms. I found a spot against the far wall, dropped my bag, and sat on top of it.

I was wearing a pair of baggy Tommy Hilfiger carpenter jeans and new pair of white Adidas shell-toe shoes. The long hair I moved to Colorado with was gone, and the eyebrow piercing was gone, and my earrings were gone. My shirts weren't quite as baggy. I imagine I looked both different and the same as when I arrived.

Across the room a man was reading a newspaper, and another man stood by a pile of luggage and looked out the window. Near him, a woman sat filing her nails. I swallowed the saliva pooling in my mouth and realized my whole body was buzzing from fear and adrenaline. I dropped my head and stared at the ground, tried to will myself to calm down. The bus was scheduled to arrive any minute. All I needed to do was get on the bus. All I needed to do was not get arrested right before I did.

The door swung open, and I glanced over at a man with a

Breckenridge Ski Resort ball cap who was pulling a black roll-aboard suitcase. I let my eyes drop to the floor again. Put my head in my hands. I thought about Haley, wondered what she was doing at this exact moment. She had no idea I was leaving, no idea that I was making a decision that would affect her for the rest of her life. I felt nauseous and blinked back tears. There was no right choice now—I had squandered my right choices. I looked across the room at the pay phone and wondered whether I should call April and ask her to forgive me for all the things I had done. But I knew she wouldn't forgive me, and she probably shouldn't, and even if she did, it would likely all go bad and I'd end up in jail again, which wouldn't help anybody.

Through the window I saw the bus pull to a stop and its doors open. I stood up and swung my bag over my shoulder. Walked through the door and climbed on the bus.

Soon after, the driver boarded the Greyhound and the doors folded inward and then the depot was gone, and we were headed east on I-70, past the Silverthorne exit, past the Factory Store Outlets and the Old Dillon Inn and the City Market grocery store, past the first apartment I moved into with Travis. It all seemed so long ago too—the plane ride, the night I met April inside Denny's—and it momentarily felt fabricated, like a story someone told me once, or maybe a story I once told someone, but then I heard the bus downshifting, and the feeling left me, and I felt the weight of my betrayal as we began the climb toward the Continental Divide.

I stared out the window. I'd seen it all before, but I wanted to remember it now, wanted to close my eyes and think of it whenever I needed to. Rocky slabs of granite. White mountain peaks. An impossibly blue sky that outlined everything my eyes could see.

The bus rocked and swayed, and I rested my head against the window. The vibration from the road reverberated through my seat and up through my spine. I thought of my father. Is this how he felt? I thought of Haley, of Maddie, of April. Would any of them ever forgive me? Would I ever forgive myself?

I couldn't have imagined it then, but five years later, when Haley was seven, after I'd gotten a job that wasn't waiting tables and spent twenty-eight days in a rehabilitation facility in Minnesota, after I'd paid the back child support I owed and hired an attorney to help me deal with the warrant I left behind in Colorado, after I'd called April and apologized for all that had happened and all that I'd done and asked her for forgiveness, I would return to Colorado and to my daughter's life, to the shadow of the mountains where so much had happened, and Haley and I would sit across from one another in a restaurant. She'd be coloring on the kids' menu, her lips pursed in concentration as I watched her, studied her, memorized her, and she would suddenly put down her crayon, walk around the table, and climb up onto my lap. It would be the first time I'd held her since she was one, and I would know with certainty in that moment, as I leaned forward to color over Haley's shoulder, catching the faint smell of apples in her hair, that I would never stop trying to be the father she deserved, that I would refuse to spend even one more second acting like my own father, and that no matter how great the distance between where I lived and where she lived, between her home and mine, I would never stop traversing it. I would never stop journeying west. And while fulfilling the promise I made that day was harder than I could have ever imagined, I never have.

None of this seemed possible on that bus out of Colorado, though, when I only knew what I felt in that moment, which was not like a father but like a failure. And perhaps what disturbs me most as I look back on those days is the way it was all so pathetically textbook, so easy to recognize. The telltale signs of the addict are everywhere: over and over, the attempt to assuage the wound on the inside with what's found on the outside.

As we neared Denver, I began to think about home, about Chicago, about the fact that I was actually going home. I still had to deal with warrants there, still had so many things to make right with my family, so many relationships to mend, but maybe, I thought, there would be time for all that. Maybe, I thought, this was the beginning of a change, or a reckoning.

I rested my head against the seat and let it fall toward the window. Outside the Greyhound, the ground rushed past.

After

Years after Colorado, after I'd finally found my way into the rooms of
AA and gotten sober, I learned about the "geographical solution"—
when a person, usually an addict, tries to change their situation
by changing their geography. Change the place, the thinking goes,
and it will surely change the person. The problem is that it almost
never works, because wherever you go, there you are. By which I
mean to say, it's not that fucking simple.

In the first years after I returned to Chicago, change came very
slowly. So much had happened in Colorado, so much that I needed
to unpack and figure out and be accountable for, and I had neither
the clarity nor the sobriety to manage that. Instead, I returned to
my job at Baker's Square, and it was almost as if I'd never left at all.
I was the same part-time waiter with no driver's license, no GED,
and absolutely no quit in the way I drank and drugged.

And yet I wasn't the same person. I was now a father and a felon,
and both of those labels meant something, something that would
change the trajectory of my life.

I called April occasionally in those early years, propelled by guilt,
often when I was so drunk I could hardly speak. "How's Haley?"
I would ask in the early hours of the morning, slurring the S and
struggling to keep the phone to my ear. "I miss her so much."

April would sometimes tell me and sometimes hang up on me
and sometimes scream at me, and I was okay with all of those
responses because what could I really expect? I had left my daughter

in Colorado, and for that I felt that I didn't deserve forgiveness or updates or even happiness. So I did what I always did: drank and drugged myself into a place where—at least for a while—I didn't remember all the things I couldn't forget. I strained to erase the history I'd created—the violence, the abandonment—but no matter how much alcohol or ecstasy or cocaine I put in my system, erasure was elusive and, ultimately, not possible.

* * *

I've often looked at geography as the solution to my problems. When Chicago wasn't working for me I moved to Colorado. When Colorado wasn't working for me I moved back to Chicago. The answers to my questions and my troubles were always just off in the distance, just past the horizon, just beyond what I could see.

What I see now, though, is difficult to look at. It's been more than twenty years since I moved to Summit County, and I still wish I could revise my narrative and amend who I was. I wish I could change the way I treated April, the way I hurt her, the ways in which I participated, during those three years, in the long history of violence men have brought to the lives of the women they say they love. When I think back to that night at her friend Lauren's, and that night in her apartment, the two times that I physically assaulted her, and also to all the times I used cruel, sharp words to hurt her emotionally, I want to rewrite my story into something less offensive and harmful. But if I've learned anything in recovery, it's that true change, real change, happens only after a complete and honest appraisal of oneself.

I can't pretend to understand exactly how my actions affected April, and how they may have shaped her future, but I am deeply sorry for the man that I was and the hurt that I caused. What I do understand, though, is that apologies don't always accomplish a whole lot, and that leaves me unsure of what to do with my history. I don't want to be defined by my worst mistakes, and writing a book that explores many of them, in a way, sets me up for that, but as a writer, as a man trying to inhabit a healthier, less harmful definition of masculinity, I know no other path to confronting the past than to write about my experience of becoming the man I never intended to become. This book is an attempt, however flawed, to understand my mistakes, to keep on nodding terms with the person I used to be, so as to never again be the man I was.

* * *

In January 2005, eight days after Haley's seventh birthday, I once again boarded a plane and flew to a new geography, this time to Minnesota, where I entered a twenty-eight-day rehabilitation program. I was unexpectedly given a chance at recovery that I didn't earn or deserve and one that, in the beginning, I didn't understand.

A week after arriving, I woke up in a twin-size bed, clean and sober for the longest stretch of days since I was eighteen. I had spent the previous week in an emotional sequence of AA meetings and therapy sessions and finally felt the weight of all that I had been running from, and it leveled me. I called April from a phone booth lined in knotty pine paneling, my voice shaking, my forehead wet, and told her that I was sorry and that I was going to change and that I was going to be in Haley's life from that point forward. "It's going to be different," I said. "I promise it will."

She didn't believe me, of course, and I understood why, but I knew that I meant what I said and I would change. I had no idea yet how hard it would be, or how much sobriety would demand, but that day, that call from that rehab in Minnesota, was a true beginning. It was the first step forward in the long journey back to my daughter, the long journey I continue on every day, toward becoming a decent father and a decent man.

A Certain Loneliness: A Memoir
by Sandra Gail Lambert

Bigger than Life: A Murder, a Memoir
by Dinah Lenney

What Becomes You
by Aaron Raz Link and Hilda Raz

*Queen of the Fall: A Memoir
of Girls and Goddesses*
by Sonja Livingston

*The Virgin of Prince Street:
Expeditions into Devotion*
by Sonja Livingston

Such a Life
by Lee Martin

Turning Bones
by Lee Martin

In Rooms of Memory: Essays
by Hilary Masters

Island in the City: A Memoir
by Micah McCrary

Between Panic and Desire
by Dinty W. Moore

*Meander Belt: Family, Loss,
and Coming of Age in the
Working-Class South*
by M. Randal O'Wain

Sleep in Me
by Jon Pineda

*The Solace of Stones: Finding
a Way through Wilderness*
by Julie Riddle

*Works Cited: An Alphabetical
Odyssey of Mayhem and Misbehavior*
by Brandon R. Schrand

Thoughts from a Queen-Sized Bed
by Mimi Schwartz

*My Ruby Slippers: The
Road Back to Kansas*
by Tracy Seeley

The Fortune Teller's Kiss
by Brenda Serotte

*Gang of One: Memoirs
of a Red Guard*
by Fan Shen

Just Breathe Normally
by Peggy Shumaker

*The Pat Boone Fan Club: My Life
as a White Anglo-Saxon Jew*
by Sue William Silverman

Scraping By in the Big Eighties
by Natalia Rachel Singer

In the Shadow of Memory
by Floyd Skloot

*Secret Frequencies: A
New York Education*
by John Skoyles

The Days Are Gods
by Liz Stephens

Phantom Limb
by Janet Sternburg

*When We Were Ghouls:
A Memoir of Ghost Stories*
by Amy E. Wallen

Yellowstone Autumn: A Season of
Discovery in a Wondrous Land
by W. D. Wetherell

This Fish Is Fowl: Essays of Being
by Xu Xi

To order or obtain more information on these or other University
of Nebraska Press titles, visit nebraskapress.unl.edu.